Stratagem of the Corpse

Stratagem of the Corpse

Dying with Baudrillard, a Study of Sickness and Simulacra

Gary J. Shipley

ANTHEM PRESS

Anthem Press
An imprint of Wimbledon Publishing Company
www.anthempress.com

This edition first published in UK and USA 2021
by ANTHEM PRESS
75–76 Blackfriars Road, London SE1 8HA, UK
or PO Box 9779, London SW19 7ZG, UK
and
244 Madison Ave #116, New York, NY 10016, USA

First published in the UK and USA by Anthem Press in 2020

British Library Cataloguing-in-Publication Data
A catalogue record for this book is available from the British Library.

Library of Congress Control Number: 2021936499

ISBN-13: 978-1-83998-071-8 (Pbk)
ISBN-10: 1-83998-071-0 (Pbk)

This title is also available as an e-book.

Death is an event that has always already taken place.

– Jean Baudrillard

Philosophy ought really to be written only as poetry.

– Ludwig Wittgenstein

CONTENTS

ACKNOWLEDGEMENTS

I would like to thank the indefatigable Edia Connole for her continued support and advice. It is no exaggeration to say that were it not for her this book might never have left my hard drive. I would also like to thank William Pawlett for his generous foreword, and for choosing this as the inaugural work in Anthem's *Radical Theory* series. I must also express my sincerest gratitude to Nick Land, Dominic Pettman, Richard G. Smith and Jason Mohaghegh for their kind endorsements.

Earlier versions of parts of this book were published in the anthologies *Dark Glamor: Accelerationism and the Occult* (Punctum), *Phono-Fictions and Other Felt Thoughts – Catalyst: Eldritch Priest* (Noxious Sector) and *Mors Mystica* (Schism); and in the following journals: *Bright Lights Film Journal* and *Fanzine*.

FOREWORD BY WILLIAM PAWLET

Did you ever get the feeling that critical and expositional works on Jean Baudrillard were missing something? Something important, but hard to pin down? That they were missing something of what might, loosely, be called the radicalism of Baudrillard's ideas? Shipley's work is one of the rare exceptions. Some of Baudrillard's best-known, but least understood, ideas are here unleashed, freed of the disciplinary apparatus of academic convention – and rightly so. When higher education has abandoned all pretence that ideas matter, why should ideas be pressed into the service of this 'spiralling cadaver', this 'zone of surveillance'?

Baudrillard's notions of simulacra and simulation have indeed suffered a fate worse than death; they have been reduced to a pulp and then reconstituted as supplements to the inventory of banal notions – globalization, mediation, performativity – that constitute media, cultural and communications studies in the twenty-first century. Shipley, in contrast, finds in Baudrillard what was always there, and reanimates what was killed off: the corrosive, pataphysical effects, the diabolical ambivalence and the deathly irony. Shipley also reminds us of something we had almost forgotten: Baudrillard was serious, and he often takes us just a little further than we want to go.

The author examines the many guises of death in Baudrillard's thought: the medical and technological processing of death; the production of cadaver as 'stuffed simulacra' and the commodification of death; virtuality and the expulsion of death at the core of the social; the denigration of the dying and the dead, but also death in its symbolic and fatal forms: disappearance, suicide, the uncanny appearance of the double that foretells death as inescapable destiny, the radical otherness of our own death. Yet death is also examined here in ways that are far from familiar, that are not pursued by Baudrillard but are not absent from his work either: death without end, immunology and virology; death than resists both meaning and non-meaning; death which refutes the comforts of nihilism and atheism – which are today the very strategies of the system of control.

Shipley's work is rare in reading Baudrillard's post–*Symbolic Exchange and Death* work against the earlier work; *Seduction*, *Fatal Strategies* and *The Perfect Crime* are central to this new reading. In the last 20 years or so Baudrillard's notion of symbolic exchange has been the focal point for new interpretations, challenging the earlier and erroneous views of Baudrillard as disillusioned Marxist or irresponsible and detached postmodernist. Shipley sets out from Baudrillard's position in *The Ecstasy of Communication*, later reinforced in *Carnival and Cannibal*, that symbolic exchange cannot be located in opposition to integral reality without itself falling into simulation, and that simulation is itself dual and reversive.

While this is certainly not *Baudrillard for Beginners*, paradoxically the student of Baudrillard will find much of value here. There are acute and incisive discussions of many of Baudrillard's most suggestive themes and ideas: hyperreality, implosion, terrorism, seduction, suicide, fatal strategies and poetic reversal, doubling and duality, failing, desertification, integral reality, the perfect crime. This study takes us further into the simulacrum than we have been before. It is an uncomfortable journey, but one that should be made.

William Pawlett, 2017

INTRODUCTION

But there is perhaps another, more joyous way of seeing things, and of finally substituting for eternally critical theory an ironic theory.[1]

The function of theory is [...] to seduce, to wrest things from their condition, to force them into an over-existence which is incompatible with that of the real.[2]

If Georges Bataille had us laughing with the dead, sharing risible chuckles at the expense of our faecalized cadavers, then Jean Baudrillard shows how it is that such laughter has become increasingly nervous, nervous to the point of no longer being laughter, tremulous at a death whose voice we can scarcely hear and with which we cannot commune. To cease laughing with death we must first cease weeping with life, and to achieve both we flush ourselves out to drown in the world, a being-in about which Martin Heidegger could only fantasize,[3] and while drowning grab hold of whatever's left from 'Integral Reality's' rapacious appetite, that is, variant forms of nothing and unknowns. Morbidity is the reclamation yard of our identity, and this book attempts a posthumous itinerary of that yawning network of scrap and decommissioned utilities.

In order to ingratiate myself as much as possible with this particular Baudrillardian sickness unto death, I chose not to forgo the necessary immersion, in all its excesses and sacrificial demands. This is, after all, not a *dying from* or a *dying for* but a *dying with*. This book is a world of death, of death becoming Baudrillardian, and if it does not, in part at least, seduce as this death must seduce, it has then failed in its worldliness, which is of course an otherworldliness – an otherworldliness without another world, an end extending beyond its own end with no possibility of beyond. If from its terrain and bad air no giddiness or palpitations are evident, then this dying world will have perished as one that exists through dying perishes: from the asphyxiating insinuation of the real, whereby a world of dying just collapses into the world (the world of living), or else from its own self-destructive principles mimicking too closely those of death's own (propensity for) integral vanishing.

Most likely, in the end, this book is less a making sense of death and more a transcript of what occurred when death made sense of us, a reverse thanatology in which death delineates the variant forms of our encroachment. It is an eschatology of humanness from the perspective of the end that expires and inspires that humanness. It is not so much death as seen by Baudrillard, but Baudrillard as seen by death.

Bataille had his 'I' and Baudrillard, like Yevgeny Zamyatin's D-503 (himself an uneasy manufacturer of the INTEGRAL),[4] his 'we'. Bataille had the human body, bestiality, and resolutions of violence; and Baudrillard the increased transparency of that human body, the fading relevance of the beast (now evacuated), and the necessity of ironic distance from a violence made theoretic, made paradox. But as with Friedrich Nietzsche, his other forebear, there is still the want to destroy, the need for violence to count, even if that destruction, that calling to ferocity, has been neutered and stripped of moral substance, so that ultimately Baudrillardian violence is the violence of freedom, for freedom in its antagonism against systemization is always violent, even if only conceptually so (which for Bataille was the purest violence). And it is with death, with this communal 'we' of death, that we find violence and freedom merge most convincingly, merging to form a combined and self-multiplying stench of the perpetual disinterment, the hypertelic ruptures of a human corpse in the process of freeing itself from itself. For horror of the real is a sickness to which life provides not panacea but embodiment. All of this being human is the work of the human corpse, and what we will become has already made us what we are. We are already what we will be, and this is our version of immortality. Only this way can our contemplations of death resonate with a joy commensurate to and in conflict with our vanished state, for as Bataille writes: ' "Joy before death" belongs only to the person for whom there is no beyond; it is the only intellectually honest route in the search for ecstasy.'[5]

Unlike Arthur Schopenhauer who, while it may be considered a thin gruel, endeavoured to imbue our disappearance with meaning, Baudrillard offers no such consolation and no such good death: there is only an empty transparency, and the systematized eternity of the virtual and the hyperreal. And yet in this terminal sickness there is something to be said for death, a redemptive fervour in there being no redemption, some germ of some enigma there in redemption's atrophied waste, because Baudrillard's concern was Nietzsche's before it was his, and it amounts to a distaste for those distortions of death that while intended to facilitate an inhumanly human edification, achieve what they achieve only to our detriment:

> The certain prospect of death could sweeten every life with a precious
> and fragrant drop of levity – and now you strange apothecary souls have

turned it into an ill-tasting drop of poison that makes the whole of life repulsive.[6]

And what Baudrillard realized, that few others realize, is how this fatuous wanting is redeemable in the very theory of its fatuity. What Baudrillard learns and so teaches is how the failings of theory are also the possibilities of theory, and how those failings are not sources of despair but potential reservoirs of emancipatory giddiness, Nietzsche's lost levity sequestered in the decay of our explanatory apparatus.

Obscenity and death are intimates, and both run through the work of Baudrillard like the intermingled rivulets of some insidious and corrosive effluent. Like Bataille before him, he details and exploits all the various definitions of 'obscene' in order to better dissect our circuitous relations with these particularly human remainders, the origins of which are to be found in the late-sixteenth-century French word *obscène*, or the Latin *obscaenus*, meaning inauspicious or abominable; and in which there is also the notion of being literally positioned above waste, slime, or uncleanness: *ob* (on) *caenum* (scum/filth). For Baudrillard, to be obscene is to be visible without reason, visible to no end, irredeemable and obvious, like the ape's shamefully public anus, so frequently correlated with obscenity in the work of Bataille, who himself found the obscene in all that was low – in the unhidden anus, in blood, in sexuality (echoing St Augustine), in the formlessness of spit and spiders, in excreta, in decay, in the cadaver – and what's more saw man *rooted* in it all, recrudescent in 'the least rupture of equilibrium [each of which] suffices for the liberation of the indecencies of nature'.[7] Obscenity, like the death we're looking for, is grounded in nothing but our disapprobation of it: a malleable source of revulsion whose flavour we might yet come to complicate and so to relish. Even Baudrillard's elliptical engagement with the impossible is prefigured by Bataille in connection with obscenity, when he advocates treating the impossible as some final compensation, some apogean achievement, as opposed to the resting post of the idle and the weary: 'the impossible attained indolently through the neglect of the possible is an impossible eluded in advance: confronted without strength, it is only an obscene gesture.'[8] For both Bataille and Baudrillard, obscenity, in its intricacies, has the requisite properties to prove redemptive, to offer up the possibility of a limit-experience, a cleansing and communicative trauma that no longer enervates but invigorates:

> Obscenity is a zone of nothingness we have to cross without which beauty lacks the suspended, risked aspect that brings about our damnation. [...] If I contemplate the nothingness of obscenity independently of desire and so to speak on its own behalf, I only note the sensible,

graspable sign of a limit at which being is confronted with lack. But in temptation, the outer nothingness appears as a reply to a yearning for communication. [...] Crude obscenity gnaws away at my existence, its excremental nature rubbing off on me – this nothingness carried by filth, this nothingness I should have expelled, this nothingness I should have distanced myself from – and I'm left defenseless and vulnerable, opening myself to it in an exhausting wound.[9]

If I appear, then, to be taking Gilles Deleuze's lead, and so similarly engaged in fucking my chosen philosopher up the arse, I hope I am at least recipro-cating in some small measure, not only with this mutated offspring, whose very mutational[10] character is very much in keeping with its subject's own shift in scrutiny ('I used to analyse things in critical terms, of revolution; now I do it in terms of mutation'),[11] but in equal measure with a soft-handed reach around in the shape of my own shrinking edifice, of what my death might become, if it isn't already behind me. And if I am dead already, then let this book be my putrefactive odour bidding to encapsulate some hard-won and pensive comicality.

Notes

1   Jean Baudrillard, *Fatal Strategies* (Los Angeles: Semiotext(e), 2008), 120.
2   Jean Baudrillard, *The Ecstasy of Communication* (Los Angeles: Semiotext(e), 1998), 98.
3   Heidegger's *Being and Time* (Oxford: Blackwell, 1962) is a premonition of the comfort-able Hell of the virtual world and of our virtuality within it. And while Baudrillard's forebears were undoubtedly Friedrich Nietzsche and Bataille, we should not ignore this correlation with Heidegger, with his project in *Being and Time* of establishing *Dasein* as us and *Dasein* as worldly, as being-in.
4   See Yevgeny Zamyatin, *We* (London: Penguin Books, 1993).
5   Georges Bataille, 'The Practice of Joy Before Death', in *Visions of Excess: Selected Writings, 1927–1939* (Minneapolis: University of Minnesota Press, 1985), 236.
6   Friedrich Nietzsche, 'The Wanderer and His Shadow', in *On the Genealogy of Morals and Ecce Homo* (New York: Vintage Books, 1969), 185.
7   Bataille, 'The Jesuve', in *Visons of Excess*, 76.
8   Georges Bataille, *The Unfinished System of Nonknowledge* (Minneapolis: University of Minnesota Press, 2001), 24.
9   Georges Bataille, *On Nietzsche* (New York: Continuum, 2004), 23–24.
10   'This means a crucial mutation from a critical state to a catastrophic one. The real and historical world, with its mass of tensions and contradictions, has always been in crisis. But the state of catastrophe is another thing. It does not mean apocalypse, or anni-hilation; it means the irruption of something anomalic, which functions according to rules and forms we do not and may never understand. The situation is not simply contradictory or irrational – it is paradoxical. Beyond the end, beyond all finality, we enter a paradoxical state – the state of too much reality, too much positivity, too much

information. In this state of paradox, faced with extreme phenomena, we do not know exactly what is taking place' (Jean Baudrillard, *The Vital Illusion* (New York: Columbia University Press, 2000), 67).

11   Jean Baudrillard in *Baudrillard Live: Selected Interviews*, ed. Mike Gane (London: Routledge, 1993), 43.

Chapter 1

ON DECAY AND OTHER SYNTHETICS

To realize that simulation is variegated is to outline a diagrammatic order of decay that is no less real for exercising its effects on bodies and materials that are not. It is pointless at this stage to talk of truth, only of decay. For veridicality is not to be found in the blown and liquid remains of some once living creature, or the shards and shreds of buildings or machinery, but in the transformative process through which an illusion can be seen to grasp at mortification: 'Imagine the true that has absorbed all the energy of the false: there you have simulation.'[1] And if decay is thought to correlate with or addend either malfunction or death, it is only because we've failed to realize how decay was there first, always there, at the beginning of things. If there's anything still claiming itself as a model of the real, it's the hyena in bed with its throat cut.

When I woke in the desert, I saw only haze. And the sand was integrated there only allegorically, by implication of where someone else might observe me, or where my hands might orientate their relative stillness. There was nothing to ground a sense of the abstract existing on the periphery of everything else: 'the charm of abstraction'[2] coincided with the lifelessness of sand, unable to separate itself, no longer charm, no longer abstraction. I felt my feet sink into the mad lie of *this*-place-as-opposed-to-*that*, its resistance to thought dispersing, accommodating the superstition of territories outside of itself. If any hope of sense remained it was that of disappearance, disappearance in an instant, or rather in no time at all – rot like a soundless, heatless explosion undoing 'this imaginary of representation',[3] this simultaneous occupation of the nucleated, of the thinged zero.

When we hear about some new case of someone's face rotting off, can we do anything but groan? As if it is needed where we're going. It is no longer credible to attribute synthesis to facial expressions. For you to see me, I'd have to plunge my face into a liquidizer. At that moment we could both forget to breathe, as if the air no longer needed us. And to think we'd ever imagined ourselves engaged in acts of imagination, that our synthetic operations could exist outside these operations, that decay was a process that somehow inaugurated a stratum. What the parodic implies, even what signs imply, is the misdirection in what is directionless. The face is a geometric anomaly: it has no inside surface. The face is not a solid sphere, it's a flat earth with no underside, made from 'a material' not only 'more malleable than meaning',[4] but more malleable than the possibilities incurred by the death of all meaning.

The philosopher has nothing to say if he isn't drowning as he says it. If everything has not become water around him, he asks only that we bear witness to a feat of magic that he cannot explain, because it is this that explains him. If he only imagines himself as something, it is no weaker than if he were shown some area of the brain in which he was scientifically proven to reside: in both cases there is only 'the simulated generation of differences'.[5] Imagination can only process what we're fed and what we feed ourselves, and it's only language that separates these modes of entry. Abstraction is just another representative model that has nothing to represent and so does not abstract but, rather, creates instead. To retain the possibility of abstraction is to retain the possibility that something can be fixed as real and be manipulated by some transformative agency, some deadly serious (or seriously deadly, or terminally preposterous) yet recreational amphibology, that does not merely consume it as more of itself.

1.1 The Enigma of the Carcass

In the eyes of the world, I am 'a machine for making emptiness',[6] a machine for making myself. But then the world does not have eyes, and so what emptiness I create gets translated as essential – as an additional ingredient, as meaning – with me as collaborator, as executor. The Pompidou Centre is a self-portrait of the human, in the realist tradition. And that the skeleton can be seen and the digestive process witnessed is no inversion, for this is how I consume myself, how I consume my simulated versions, in the world, in words, in pictures, in tumefied offerings that have absorbed the sensate to achieve transparency. That this metastasized clotting should reinforce nothingness and so enable excavations of space (space for the sake of space) is to be expected: emptiness only gleans shape through that which surrounds it, achieving a contradictory vitality by absorbing materials into its perimeter without disclosure of such a surface, and without that surface even belonging to it, which amounts to repulsion. The materials are repelled and, having been so repelled, bear the mark of a force, but a force that has no concrete manifestation, only the verbalized and diagrammatic indictment as of having been arranged.

The intention is always to make fuller, to provide ever more examples, to serialize, to make routines, to approach completism for its own sake. But the accumulation will ultimately cleanse, and all these many directions of meaning will become no meaning at all, and this is desirable, for our inability to keep up will reveal humanity in this failure to process its own dimensions, even as we have created them, and created them in order to see ourselves, and falling back on what is left, what was left out, the calmness of the void will envelop what had never left it in the first place. This is the religious frame of mind. This is the accelerationism of our humanization of materials, at the conclusion of which we may sleep in our never having existed. And to this end the machines are here to help us, to show the way, for machines advance a distinctly stoic religiosity:

> Nor do machines manifest that ironical surplus or excess functioning which contributes the pleasure, or suffering, thanks to which human beings transcend their determinations – and thus come closer to their *raison d 'être*. Alas for the machine, it can never transcend its own operation – which, perhaps, explains the profound melancholy of the computer. All machines are celibate.[7]

That our solitude has been made 'artificial' provides a clue as to the increased artificiality of our deaths. And a global swell of atheism far from decreasing this artificiality is directly responsible for its amplification. Death as absolute zero is both the most plausible outcome of having existed and the most incredible, the most distant – a simple mathematical sum that, while true, is never other than abstract. Death is always the end of something else. And this zero is always out of reach: our successful adherence to the truth of our own subtractions makes death less real and more mysterious than when we believed any number of miraculous narratives that were destined to follow it. This zeroing, then, is in many ways a dishonest tactic, placing far too much emphasis on the thing removed, and so ultimately 'still too romantic and destructive'.[8] The unimaginability of nothing is every bit the bubble that heaven was, more so in fact. When even the state of solitude has turned abstract, and the notion of removing ourselves from the human world a cryptic anathema of existence itself, how are we ever to be expected to remove ourselves entirely from the fabric of the universe? Or maybe complete eradication is our only means of access to what it might be to be alone again. That to be alone is simply to cease to be anything, and we can make sense of this, but crucially we cannot embody the necessary disembodiment.

It is worth remembering those vitrified bodies that await reanimation as if it will be more than reanimation, as if what surrounds them will reward them for never accepting death, reward them not with mere resurrection but with an entirely new birth. But ultimately it is a false reward, because stasis was not the void, and there was never the illogical solitude of death, not even the protective carapace of its artificialized mystification. The vitrified body is not the temporarily stilled yet lasting monument of the person still to return, but instead a signposting of personhood as fragility, as something forever caught in transit, a thing pushed into the future so that it might fulfil its destiny: to be eternally recycled and never settle.

The vitrified body still retains something of life, something of its '[p]anic in slow motion'[9] – a panic in stasis. Even at rest there's a sedated panic, and the corpse defies us because it has relinquished this essential unease. It's not so much that the person has gone, but that the balancing act of life is no longer being played out. The vitrified body though, still and quiet as the dead, nonetheless manifests its panic in the shape of its cryoprotectant paraphernalia. The panic is dispersed into chemical solutions and containers, into valves and dials and various other instruments for measuring and sustaining temperature. We see a corpse enmeshed in the technologized panic of life, and death's former finality is thereby diluted, infiltrated by this all too demonstrable anxiety-toward-death that keeps the body intact as the final rejection of its own necessary demise. And in place of our usual panic, when confronted with these unsanctified remains, is instead the sensation of plummeting, having first been emptied out: 'After the living man the dead body is nothing at all; similarly nothing tangible or objective brings on our feeling of nausea; what we experience is a kind of void, a sinking sensation.'[10]

The zeroing of death amounts to the death of death. It is for this reason that the atheist can come to sound so very celebratory and evangelical, as they become joyous in their mourning of an end that had for so long successfully eluded truth. With the truth of zero in place there is no more culture of death, only death itself and death as nothing, but this is no effortful disaster but instead a far more excessive peculiarization of death, providing all the formerly absent truth with no possibility of consequence, [11] because to describe something (a future self) in purely negative terms, and more specifically to engage in the apophasis of death, is to relinquish care not for the thing itself but more importantly for the circumstantial detail of that thing, and thereby escape in life what can no longer be congruous to it. The death of death is the release of an end without ever having to confront it. Death is killed, embalmed and so neutralized. And what remains is a neutered curiosity, enough to sustain our proclivity for seeking goals, and yet sufficiently (i.e. absolutely) empty to never have to assimilate what it might mean. Nothing turns the world into more of a dreamland than this secularized apophatic terminus. It is the negation of our aporia regarding death, an anti-aporia, that by making death conform to the rigorousness of truth and certainty creates in its wake a far more resilient aporia, an unspoken aporia, that though not stated cannot be unfelt.

Zero is not the end or the beginning of numbers but the middle (between the natural and the negative), establishing itself as that between two infinite

series, one of which (the negative numbers) did not exist before its conception. Zero is responsible for mathematics becoming something purely conceptual, and also for the expansion of that abstract space. Hence it is important
to acknowledge how the introduction of zero is a creative step, and that the
resultant negatives are not only negatives but positives, allowing for the for-
mation of entirely new formulations (negative numbers, integers, decimal
fractions, etc.). The introduction of this nothing-as-nucleus both places and
displaces us in the eventuality of death, the carcass of death flayed and twisted
into a Möbius strip. The dead body is a maze.[12] We get lost there. We codify
death and then kill death. We get lost in the death of death. We feel safe there,
in our already being dead: 'This is the secret of security, like a steak under cel-
lophane: *to surround you with a sarcophagus in order to prevent you from dying.*'[13] In the
middle, raised up with the outside in sight, destined only to descend back into
the maze, to mistranslate the route, to once again get lost.

All the religious men and women that ever existed could not between them
realize the mysterious death that was given to us by philosophers, scientists and
non-believers, such that what we end up with is a 'monumental black hole'[14]
of death that, while now worthy of God, exists exclusively in his postulated
absence. And while it is because of this new otherness of death that the dead
are remembered in more exhaustive detail, as a last line of defence, as a means
of shoring up existence against its removal, this remembering has lost its
memory, because mass accumulation is just a covert route to forgetting: lives
filed away like so many billions of phalangeal bodies in compact mausoleums
that nobody need ever visit. All of our corpses are filled up, and yet never in
the history of human life have they been so empty: empty because life has
been abandoned there like some pickled organ in a jar, like some violation
of departure, the unrest of a ghost in a maze retracing its footsteps forever,
over but denied the incompleteness of that conclusion, full of information but
empty of the legacy of that former finality that recognized a life's end without
thereby censoring growth. The corpse like death consumes everything and yet
contains nothing. All that's left is a labyrinth without walls: the idea of a labyrinth. No, not even that and more than that: the possibility of misplacement.

The conventional destruction of cadavers in the crematorium is rooted not
only in a scientifically informed view of death as the ultimate and irretrievable
end, but also in the, not necessarily rationally acknowledged, notion of the
body as a vessel and the dead body as one such spent example – the idea that
if indeed there ever was any such thing as you that it has either run its course
in a no-longer-functioning brain, or else is in no way integrally linked to the
human body it once animated. This violence, this reduction to ash, is fully in
keeping with death as liberation, as a being done with this world, as a recognition of a former oversaturation of existence, and that if any hope remains

it skulks away in anything but this – as if the one recourse left to us was some apogean act of subversion, whereby the life that is done with us is also one that we are done with in return. Having absorbed energy to the point where we can no longer realize its potential externally in the world around us, we lose it and ourselves in an involute darkness, in the warm and indiscriminate breezes of death.

The notion of death as a return, as a regressive step, as a retreat back to an exhaustive inertia, carries with it all the sentiments of a corrective, of life as an aberration to which no one is forced to bear witness forever. Yet death is still incalculable, because nothing is never the edge but always the middle, always looking both ways, directions in which it can be less than itself as well as more, and where those negatives are no mere mirror of their positive counterparts.

1.2 Forgetting Life as a Solution to Death

When we talk about death, we are talking about what it would be like to talk about death, how such monologues or discussions might be formulated if we were able to articulate them. In talking of death, we talk only of life. Death is a mute, death eludes, and it does so because it is the middle – and the middle is always lost. If death has a language, it is memory. (But then memory is not a language so much as the reflux of the bad meal of being human.) Without memory it is not even possible to die, and not because you've died already (which is much of what we see) but because without what's gone there is no to-come. What's so sad about these fade-outs is not that death eventually arrives before they can return to face it, but that death never arrives. All that happens is that the return is made impossible, and something that was once forever forgets to die, so that what we are left with is the most superficial of solutions to dying: the erasure of life without which there is no prospect of death. But while this may be thin and artificial in its construction, it does isolate the crucial misconception: nobody wants or needs or would benefit from a solution to death; what's required, what's always been required, is a solution to life – which is something only the enigmatized nothingness of death can provide.

The ability of the advance of technology to inspire fear is frequently thought to emanate from concerns that our creations will one day supersede and oppress us, that we will find ourselves helpless victims of our own ingenuity. An altogether homely notion, this scenario is adapted from a narrative we know to make sense – and so one which we can also easily reroute, for the true source of this fear is something else entirely. And this something else is the fear of sameness, the fear of the possibility of perfect replication, that everything each of us is might be laid down as the code for some future identity – the fear being not that we will one day be killed this way, but that such a future will never allow us to die. Inseparability, rather than alienation, is the new concern: 'The new technologies, with their new machines, new images and interactive screens, do not alienate me. Rather, they form an integrated circuit with me. [...] Man or machine? Impossible to tell.'[15] These fears are not as disparate as they may at first appear. For is there not a death that rids us of death? An obliteration by excess? An eternity that rids us of eternity and a God that rids us of God?[16]

Death is the ultimate commodity. Nothing outsells it. Everyone's a customer. Its variations are equal to its ubiquity: nobody gets someone else's death. It happens every second of every day and yet its allure remains undiminished. The sum of its parts is only a mist, the chicanery of an advertising method that never reveals what it is that's for sale, or the how or where of any direct points of purchase. After all, the selling of death is the selling of a dream, and if the dream is to remain a dream it can never be reduced to its allusions, however great their number. And that the dream sold is also the end of a dream – the dream of waking from something or even of sleeping ever deeper, of escaping the sleep of life by either an increase or a decrease in that sleep's intensity – is still to say virtually nothing of it that is not merely the reiteration of a habit. We readily relinquish the world and ourselves many thousands of times throughout the course of our lives, ending up everywhere and nowhere, encountering horrors or pleasures that are either forgotten or disowned, and yet there is nowhere near the level of alienation felt towards death. 'But that's because we come back every time', is the line we quite reasonably seem compelled to take. Nevertheless, does the inexplicable weirdness of, for instance, our nocturnal excursions really escape us so completely? (And do we actually return to ourselves when we wake, or rather to our non-existence? For it isn't 'true that we need to believe in our own existence to live. It is not necessary. [...] We are only indistinguishable from ourselves in sleep, unconsciousness and death.')[17] The medium of sleep is the message of sleep, and that message is 'Normalize me or else!' It is this normalization that consecrates the state of waking, that lets us remember sleep as sleep, as a mere supplicant of our wakefulness, that has us from the very start remembering only the rememberings of where it was sleep took us. For these reasons, death is sold and sleep given away – or sold so cheaply that we do not acknowledge its price at the point of purchase. However, sleep is never far from the marketing archetype, as we believe only in the packaging and not the contents – a belief that is integral to our modern societal existence. Sleep's insides are absorbed into the chatter of make-believe, so that we never have to question just how essential its outskirts are to the business of living.

'Disaffected, but saturated. Desensitized, but ready to crack':[18] this is the point at which death's value as an idea is fully consummated. This is the point at which you realize that death is not sold as the curtailment of and negative backdrop to all our innumerable lifestyles, but is itself a lifestyle, or rather *the* lifestyle. Death is what is lived when life is no longer liveable – but lived as one lives a lifestyle, which is not living as a dream of its history, but living as the hyperreal mirror of itself. Truth is, there was only ever one lifestyle (the lifestyle of death), only we weren't able to see it. The exhaustion of lifestyles is necessary for the inescapable imposition of the one inexhaustible lifestyle to become visible. In other words, when life is transparent it is death that shows through.[19] And when death does show through, it is only as the nothingness of life as a lifestyle; though, not as a continuation of that nothingness, but rather as the possibility of possibilities, the figment of a surplus, the abreaction of an escape tunnel leading from nowhere to nowhere else. The revelation – if it can be called that at this stage – when all such shocks and becomings have rotted out, is that life was always just advertising-space for death, its myriad lifestyles acting as billboards for a yet-to-be-accepted transparency, behind which was always the observable nothing, the only lifestyle left, no longer a concatenation of subtractions but the addition of a zero – a return to the middle that life had made unavailable. Unsurprisingly, Georges Bataille too isolates this surplus in death:

> Death does not come down to the bitter annihilation of being – of all that I am, which expects to be once more, the very meaning of which, rather than to be, is to expect to be (as if we never received being authen-tically, but only the anticipation of being, which will be and is not, as if we were not the presence that we are, but the future that will be and are not); it is also that shipwreck in the nauseous.[20]

The aesthetic of this lifestyle of death is negatively transcendent, the beyond that removes itself, the escape that allows you to stay. This stylized living of death absorbs all former lifestyles lived under the guise of life, making art of its artifice, turning everything – both desperate and calm, anguished and silly, from a toothpaste commercial to the finest Greek tragedy, each with their own particular brand of denticulation – into variously honed muscle around bones that cannot be moved because they have always been missing. Death, then, is the apogee of commodities in virtue of all other commodities leading us to it, as if they had only existed as some subtle sales technique for this one true commodity that when seen is only seen as its own disappearing.

Isn't it obscene, this paying for death, for what is inevitably ours as just a consequence of being alive? And what is the currency used to purchase it? First, the charge of obscenity misconstrues the dynamics of filth and the requisite offence initiated in response to it. For it is not that death has always had a price that should result in consternation, but that anyone ever believed that rent was due on abandonment all the time that deliverance remained free.[21] To imagine that death has always been yours to do with what you will is to imagine freedoms that go beyond you. Recall those dinner-party guests in Luis Buñuel's *The Exterminating Angel*, the guests that do not leave because they cannot leave, even though there is nothing stopping them – except whatever it is that does in fact stop them. No matter how tired they are, some imperceptible threshold is evidenced beyond which they cannot venture. And yet despite the absurd irregularity of this invisible snare, nobody makes mention of the predicament, and it is ruefully accepted by the guests who set about making the best of the facilities on offer. The following statement appears at the beginning of the movie: 'The best explanation of this film is that, from the standpoint of pure reason, there is no explanation.'[22] That you remain without question requires and receives no logical justification, only what may then transpire once the circumstance of your incarceration has been recognized is susceptible to such ruminations. All of which brings us to the question of currency, to the expenditure that necessitates the commodification of death, and that currency is hope, minus the investment of which there would be nothing. And death is the purchase that cleans you out; but it is not only at the end that death is turned into a commodity, for every transaction of hope up to that juncture has incorporated a percentage set aside for death.

To die with a remainder of hope not yet expended on your death is not so much dying as it is becoming corpse – it is going to the crematorium with change in your pockets.

1.3 My Corpse the Double

My double not only 'signifies imminent death',[23] it becomes my corpse in place of me, for its becoming and signifying my own death is also the prelude to its death. This materialization of the double, of the clone, is just my corpse becoming itself, my dream of my other me extinguished by the reality that can no longer accommodate the possibility of oneiric detachment. The confusion between the original and the clone, between the cadaver and the living, takes place at the precipice of the illusion of identity and of meaning's inhering in matter:

> That which is no longer illusion is dead and inspires terror. This is what the cadaver does, as does the clone, and more generally, anything that can be so confused with itself that it is no longer even capable of playing its own appearance. This limit of disillusion is that of death.[24]

But if the double shows up for my death, it is this double, this clone, that made and makes my life the something of a something, a process unimpeded by death, a perpetual motion machine replicating its own non-existent sameness: the intimacy of my continual autocloning, my subject reiterating its limbo of (extra-limbic) sameness like a bad dream dreaming it is a good dream, the only dream – worse, a necessary dream.

I'm the miracle of me: the perpetual immaculate conception of myself, a procreative masturbation of a phantasm by a phantasm. But because this is not a closed circuit, I always become a version of myself. The importance of the other should not be forgotten, however, for as Ludwig Wittgenstein showed with his private language argument, regulation comes from outside. I cannot successfully self-police my own continuity without having some external means of determining the occurrence of distortion, without being able to validate the concept of success itself.

The circuit of the double cannot be thought of as either simply closed or open, but only as immanently ruptured. My double becomes me in death, embodied in my corpse, so that my autocloning practices may continue, even if what's cloned into eternity is nothing, is zero. It is not that my double is not me, he must be and yet cannot be (How else can he embody this paradox that is being me?), or that I somehow do not die when my double dies, when my double substantiates the material proof of that event, but rather that my double's arrival, his manifesting, is like the breaking of a spell (through the incarnation of a dream) that frees me to die without my body, whatever it is that death, that divorcement from materiality, might involve. In other words, the abstraction of my death is imposed on reality in such a way that death can remain materially ambiguous at the same time as my categorical ceasing to exist. The limit of death is, after all, the disillusion of limits.

My double and I were always a death sentence. There never was any other conclusion. We were always two, always the same without being the same, combining to form the *place* and the *placing* of death. Unlike autocloning, there was never the facility of adding to myself here, only of replacement, or of multiple occupation of the same – someone to be my corpse, so that even if I am nothing I am not that, some string-less marionette rotting in the earth. Regeneration on this model is also prohibited, as each of my double's parts are my parts, the restoration of one part implying a possible restoration of all parts, and what is conceived and born in the concept and the eventuality of death cannot then realize itself in rejuvenations in the reversal of itself.

Double life entails the notion of double death. / In one of these two lives you may already be dead, doubtless without knowing it. Sometimes it is the dead element that pulls the living along. In faces even, often one part is alive and the other already dead. / A double life entitles you to two deaths – and why not two amorous passions at the same time? So long as they remain parallel, all is well. It is when their paths cross that the danger arises. You may from time to time desert your life – one of the two – and take refuge in the other. The one in which you exist, the other in which you don't. / Where this living death doesn't exist, life takes its place. Just as the person who loses his shadow becomes the shadow of himself.[25]

My ostensive uniting with my double in death, in the corpse, the corpse that escapes me and that I in turn escape through its dying as me, but without me, is not a copulation made of parts, each degrading and fucking the other, but of two wholes sharing a death – sharing it to death.

Although autocloning adds to me, through those versions that follow me and that thereby constitute my continuity, it also removes any need for speaking of essences, of the continuance of any one thing aside from the very operations of that continuance. My far-future autoclones are no further from me now than my present autoclone is from some autoclone of last week, for not only has the original gone, but the theoretical apparatus of there ever having been one has been stretched into a vanishing point of endless replications of an increasingly ephemeral sameness.

Autocloning is a cancer and the tumour is us – stretched out through time, some malignant growth in a panic to exist. Without reparation, utility or death to impede us, our temporal expansion goes unchecked. No faults are corrected in the autocloning process, because the faults are integral to what is being reproduced: *Here I am, faults and all.* Temporal growth is the only criteria for success, and that growth's redundancy is an irrelevance:

One is dead in one's lifetime itself; multiple deaths accompany us, ghosts that are not necessarily hostile, and yet others, not dead enough, not dead long enough to make a corpse. [...] At any rate, we have all already been dead before living, and we came out of it alive. We were dead before and we shall be dead again after. [...] Death and life can reverse themselves from this standpoint. And this implies another presence of death to life, because it – not simply an indeterminate nothingness, but a determinate, personal death – was there before and it does not cease to exist and to make itself felt with birth. [...] This connects up with the genetic process of apoptosis, in which the two opposing processes of life and death begin at the same time. In which death is not the gradual exhaustion of life: they are autonomous processes – complicit in a way, parallel and indissociable. / Hence the absurdity of wishing, as all our current technologies do, to eradicate death in favour of life alone.[26]

Ultimately, what is apoptosis but the body 'dreaming of abolishing death',[27] and what is the end of death but the end of life as well, the autophagy of a dream.

Notes

1 Baudrillard, *Fatal Strategies*, 27.
2 Jean Baudrillard, *Simulacra and Simulation* (Kalamazoo: University of Michigan Press, 1994), 2.
3 Baudrillard, *Simulacra and Simulation*, 2.
4 Ibid., 2.
5 Ibid., 3.
6 Ibid., 61.
7 Jean Baudrillard, *The Transparency of Evil: Essays on Extreme Phenomena* (New York: Verso, 1993), 53.
8 Baudrillard, *Simulacra and Simulation*, 64.
9 Ibid., 70.
10 Georges Bataille, *Death and Sensuality: A Study of Eroticism and the Taboo* (New York: Walker, 1962), 58.
11 A cleansing of God, even: 'There are two atheisms of which one is a purification of the notion of God' (Simone Weil, *The New Christianity*, ed. William Robert Miller (New York: Delacorte Press, 1967), 267).
12 A maze that never stops growing, for 'infinity, once an ideal abstraction, is materialized as well in infinite growth […] and we are now prisoners of this irreversible dimension – unable to reinvent a finite universe' (Jean Baudrillard, *The Agony of Power* (Los Angeles: Semiotext(e), 2010), 83).
13 Jean Baudrillard, *Symbolic Exchange and Death* (New York: Sage, 1993), 177, (emphasis in the original).
14 Baudrillard, *Simulacra and Simulation*, 66.
15 Baudrillard, *The Transparency of Evil*, 58.
16 The curse of Palmer Eldritch. See Philip K. Dick, *The Three Stigmata of Palmer Eldritch* (New York: Doubleday, 1965).
17 Jean Baudrillard, *The Conspiracy of Art*, (Los Angeles: Semiotext(e), 2015), 162.
18 Baudrillard, *Simulacra and Simulation*, 91.
19 Transposing 'life' and 'death' for the 'good' and 'evil' found in Jean Baudrillard, *The Intelligence of Evil, Or the Lucidity Pact* (London: Bloomsbury, 2013), 109.
20 Georges Bataille, *The Bataille Reader*, ed. Fred Botting and Scott Wilson (Oxford: Blackwell, 1997), 243.
21 'The nothingness of obscenity can't be subjected to anything. The fact that it's not a cancellation of existence but only a notion, and one resulting from contact, far from alleviates, and actually increases the disapproval generally felt. It is unrelated to value. It is not as if the erotic summit is something heroic attained *at the cost of* harsh sufferings. Clearly, the results bear no relation to the efforts' (Bataille, *On Nietzsche*, 28).
22 Luis Buñuel, *The Exterminating Angel* (Gustavo Alatriste, 1962).

23 Baudrillard, *Simulacra and Simulation*, 95.
24 Baudrillard, *Fatal Strategies*, 74–5.
25 Baudrillard, *The Intelligence of Evil*, 156.
26 Baudrillard, *The Intelligence of Evil*, 157.
27 Jean Baudrillard, *Why Hasn't Everything Already Disappeared?* (Calcutta: Seagull Books, 2009), 19.

Chapter 2

STRATAGEM OF THE CORPSE

The fake death, the simulated corpse, the staging of human remains, evokes more of the human end than the real thing. Jeremy Millar's *Self Portrait of a Drowned Man* represents Millar's own fictionalized death by drowning, its depicted removal from himself becoming a spectacle of its own disingenuousness, his absence an intentioned presence (both as object and creator); and yet its conflation of hyperrealism and obvious fakery is more a manifestation of what isn't, and wasn't, than that managed by any real drowned man. With both, I imagine lives that might have led to this: with the sculpture I know I'm playing along with an object, giving it its due, paying it the courtesy of engaging in the way that is asked of me; and in this respect I do nothing different with the actual corpse, as I engage my empathetic strategies in order that the object in front of me can justify itself. But where they differ is in the threat that is posed, because it is only the ersatz death that has already happened to me, is at this and that time happening, is constant and irremovable, whereas the real death is always elsewhere, realized in someone other than me, buried in all its *unrecoverable* counterpart deaths. I can pass the latter death off in opposition to my present state, and like this reaffirm life and death as not so much diachronic as synchronic. In other words, my conscious existence embraces the simulated and rejects the real. The reality of the dead man on the quayside is therefore made less real in virtue of its representing a reality to which I have no access, and it is for this reason that while the staged corpse is more of a threat, the real corpse is more viscerally impactful – at least for those of us not in the habit of seeing them. The loss of this impact in those who have for whatever reason become desensitized to seeing dead human beings, those for whom 'the human body [exists] as an object, an anonymous thing belonging to no one, which one could dispose of in an arbitrary manner', an aggregation of 'indifferent brute matter'[1] even, allows them to acknowledge the real corpse's threat and so defend against it, as if it were its faked counterpart. The systematic dehumanization of our dead (which is often in evidence long before death has occurred) is a protective device, a simulation of anonymous substances, of the antihuman as proof of the human, but ultimately a line of defence that instantiates the very thing it must defend against. The impact of seeing what was once alive and human is the very thing that distances you from it; and if we attempt to reduce this impact – by removing all past similarities – we thereby increase our contiguity with death, for the very act of extracting the threat, of a presentful non-presence that must be extricated from what it means to be human, enacts an inhuman death, a copy of death, a death less *event* than it is *thing*. 'Simulation is infinitely more dangerous because it always leaves open to supposition that, above and beyond its object, […] [*life and death*] *themselves might be nothing but simulation*.'[2] I contradict the real human corpse and become more recognizably human through the contradictory state of the corpse's humanness and lack of humanness. But as soon as that impactful contradiction is removed, the representation of the dead human body maintains a propinquity to my conscious states through its never having been human, while at the same time mimicking convincingly what it is to be a dead one. And this is also the art of the funeral home:

> A faked death, idealised in the colours of life: the secret idea is that life is natural and death is against nature. Death must therefore be naturalised in a stuffed simulacrum of life. In all of this there is on the one hand a refusal to let death signify, take on the force of a sign, and, behind this sentimental nature-fetishism on the other, a great ferocity as regards the dead himself: rotting and change are forbidden, and instead of being carried over to death and thus the symbolic recognition of the living, he is maintained as a puppet within the orbit of the living in order to serve as an alibi and a simulacrum of their own lives.[3]

The absence of decay is essential to the threat: the body freeze-framed, its processes halted, the parody of decomposition scarcely attempted at all. And that death has no smell here just serves to accentuate the hazard, as death is depicted visually while the only aromas available are your own and maybe those of the living humans around you. All osmic data relate to the still alive, and the only decay on offer is the animated kind we recognize as humanly purposeful. Purged of the stench of death and death's inevitable telos – its advanced putrefaction and eventual substructural reveal – the pretence of death is substantiated *as* pretence, its ability to convince the senses deliberately flawed in such a way that the reality of the simulation of death is what's on offer, as I am asked to confront death as a known unreality and to confront also the point at which the confrontation itself becomes assimilation, and it is this awareness of unknowing that has more to reveal about death than the projected (the thrown) unknowing that is acted out with real corpses. This antianimatism of the corpse amounts to a conscious refusal to assign the remains of consciousness to some thing, as if to suggest that that thing had colluded in the trick of escaping itself and we, the spectators, are distrustful of the results, its durability, its sameness:

> The counterfeit still only works on substance and form, not yet on relations and structures, [...] cast in a synthetic substance which evades death, an indestructible artifact that will guarantee eternal power. Isn't it a miracle that with plastics, man has invented an undegradable matter, thus interrupting the cycle which through corruption and death reverses each and every substance on the earth into another?[4]

The 'useless violence'[5] of treating human corpses as raw materials for the manufacture of insulation, swamp fill and gravel, differs from the useless violence (this very uselessness being an oft-used and apt definition of art itself) of the faked human cadaver, in that respectively the one performs an act of irreverence while the other, reverence. And though it might seem counterintuitive, it is this reverence that poses a threat to us here.[6] For the difference between the real and the simulation has been cancelled out, shown not to exist, in one very important way, in a way that permits the signposted unreality to cause harm (and by harm I mean a beneficial, honest harm, harm done to a deserving recipient of it: the exorcising of self from the other and, following that, from itself). I am talking here of a reverence that is felt unjustifiably: an emotive response that is undermined by its own attendant principles of appropriate application. To abuse the dead is to still acknowledge the threat of the dead, as if death had not removed everything, as if death had only compounded what it was about the living body that had made death necessary. Hence this irreverence is always a failure, is always a symbolic gesture of a powerlessness to remove, or to remake, or to control. Death is found not to have done the work demanded of it, because it does not redeem its cause. Irreverence post death is quite obviously an admission that death is not enough, that death always leaves behind incompleteness. Such irreverence translates as reverence for the irreversibility of life, for some life having existed at all, and the impossibility of removing history. The faked corpse, however, has already had its history removed, so that death itself can appropriate the space it left. Almost as a curative measure to those who would abuse corpses, death is not only enough but too much – it is everything, and so can redeem the existence of the corpse-thing you see before you, as only a surplus can redeem itself. The reverence here, though, cannot be for a life departed but instead a full presence of death, exhausted by death because there has been no life – or even exhausted *to* death, which is seemingly the desire of marathon runners, who 'are all seeking death, that death by exhaustion that was the fate of the first Marathon man some two thousand years ago'.[7] And so the viewer reveres the end, not of something else, but the end in itself, the absoluteness and integrity of death, of death that is no longer just some qualification of something else, but its own reality of permanent absence. This perceived lack of grounding in the real (unfulfilled) business of dying endorses death, gives it a momentum all of its own, a conceptual realization whereby it shrugs off the constraints we've created for it, its human colours, so that death instead is remade as something beyond our understanding of it, as something not only arbitrary, which after all was only our distaste at its human untimeliness, but as manifestly alien and monstrous. This is how death is produced when its reality is in jeopardy, as an independent source of nothing but itself. Deadness too 'floats like money, like language, like theory'.[8]

The referent in the case of *Self Portrait of a Drowned Man* is a living man, an artist imagining his death by drowning as the most accurate portrayal of his being alive; but with Ron Mueck's *Dead Dad*, there is a real death referenced: Mueck's own father. The pale, obsessively detailed and scaled-down body lies on its back, elevated off the floor only by the thickness of a white marble slab, and we look down, crouch to see the lines and the crinkles, the insane meticulousness of death as diminishment, as if we, so remote from it, are giants in this life of ours. The realism here, as with *Self Portrait of a Drowned Man*, is the simulation of death via a real death, but a real death that does not recognize itself. Thus the alteration in scale makes this lack of recognition explicit, so that our relative enormity comes to feel not like power or overcoming or imperviousness, but a fundamental untruth, a disclosing of an immaterial distance, inside which life is grasped only in terms of the pervasiveness of its removal – which is itself only the removal of an hallucinated distance.[9] And although the positioning of the body more than suggests death – it's the visual reeking of its state – there is nothing to the face that is more or less absent than sleep. That something so archetypal in its end still retains this perceived aptitude for waking is yet another reason for us to recognize death beyond that of some conclusive predicament, and as instead the created organ of some larger body of temporized unfinishing. If death were not inconclusive in this way, we would not recognize it as death at all: what we would see in its place is the demolition of a building no one ever entered. (How else would death become its own negation: 'One must pay dearly for immortality; one has to die several times while one is still alive.')[10] That there are attempts at such seeing – that remain attempts for the effort expended is never fully effectuated – is spurred on both by the deepest disgust at the unknowing we've made of our real, and by a longing for some resolvable stratagem to exist for being less than human and yet so much more for having conceived the need to contrive an escape.

What, we ask, is the strategy by which we can mourn ourselves forever? And shouldn't every instant of our lives bear the marks of this mourning, thereby establishing death as both beyond us and precarious? This mythopoeia of death is what it means to enfold and comprise the reality of simulation, to at once accept that life and death have become equivalences, each lacking autonomous reality, but also to establish death outside of ourselves as a mock-up resurrection of some agent of destruction that has nothing whatsoever to do with us. In other words, death is revived as an embodiment of nothing, just as being is nothing, but a nothing around which we trace a line for fear of never being able to tell the difference.

On this account, murder is no longer the facilitator of death but rather our attempt at sacrifices in its honour. Death is the simulacrum of death, because to fall back on its supposed reality would be to nullify our necessitated allegiance to its potentiality, and it is only from this death of death that anything resembling (but only resembling) life can emerge.

The real corpse is presented to us only to help obscure the fact that there are no more corpses. The only deaths that happen are the deaths we see every day, those representations of real death, the dead that may or may not actually be dead. For now we have less stake in death, dying well is just equivalent to not dying at all, and where dying itself has become synonymous with attendant excesses of pain we just replace it with sleep.

2.1 The Art of Death

Because art is definitely not the world, we can see it in focus. Even when art contrives to be indistinguishable from the world, its unblurred resolutions establish its artful success and so its ineptitude at worldliness. If philosophy is the art of dying well, it is because it is the art of never dying at all, or rather of dying artfully, which amounts to the same thing. If we consider the imagery of death, we discover not our dead selves but the murder of an image, for 'human beings are no longer victims of images, but rather transform themselves into images'.[11] All there is is the image disclosing its human habitation, and thereby disclosing its death at the hands of the human it signifies, so that if we see our death as an image, we see also the death of that image – by seeing only ourselves, only ourselves dead, and not the image we became or the image that put us there. But then to say that encased in this imagery we do not die is to some extent to forget what death has become, and to imagine we ever saw it unencumbered by affect. If, as Baudrillard claims, 'there is no longer even time for the image to become image',[12] that it is murdered in each instance by that which it signifies, then when we die inside the image we die both without the shield of appearance and without being afforded some rare glimpse of a human reality stripped of human securities, whatever that might look like, if it looks like anything. 'The obscene is everything that is uselessly, needlessly visible, without desire and without effect',[13] and so this (artfully artless) death is just such an obscenity: a death voided of the real and of the art of the real, an inconsequential finality, a faking of what we'd mistook for death.

How detrimental to dying well it is to have our death as images mean something, to have meaning come between us and the negation of us? The art of death should be left to the becoming of the image, thus moving away from the memento mori of skulls and rotting corpses towards the *Ars moriendi* of the death that lives in the perpetuation of its means of capture. This art of human death would mean no more than the living prerequisite to it means: it would be hidden in all its glory in nothing but the divorcement of the image from its content. After all, just as art must remain useless so too must death: it must not educate us as much as offend and pleasure us with its emptiness. As art 'denies its own death',[14] so our corpses freed from having lived deny theirs. And so what art there is to life must be 'an art of simulation, an ironic quality that resuscitates the appearances of the world each time to destroy them. Otherwise art would do nothing more, as it often does today, than work over its own corpse.'[15] For this reason, any art worth the name must be in the mode of this immersive puppetry of the dead, this reanimation of decaying bodies, so that they can be made to die again, die better, more convincingly.

To die well is to embody only a miniscule fragment of death, to leave its wholeness to the endless white sleep, to the borrowed translucence of its failing signifiers, and become instead mysterious again, an elliptical component of the greater death that would swallow you whole. This of course amounts to repudiating your death's realization, to a reclamation of death's abstractness; but not to the extent that the art should abstract, but to the juncture where abstraction is completely beside the point.

Nevertheless, our desire to physicalize has not withered as it should with this move into abstraction, and this physicalizing becomes itself an imaginary and excessive form of realization, an ad hoc manoeuvre to concretize the escape from the concrete. Baudrillard remarks on this enigmatic move:

The paradox of abstraction is that, by 'liberating' the object from the constraints of the figural to yield it up to the pure play of form, it shackled it to an idea of a hidden structure, of an objectivity more rigorous and radical than that of resemblance. It sought to set aside the mask of resemblance and of the figure in order to accede to the analytic truth of the object. Under the banner of abstraction, we moved para-doxically towards more reality, towards an unveiling of the 'elementary structures' of objectality, that is to say, towards something more real than the real.[16]

By abandoning a representational depiction of death we do not get further from reality, but rather further that reality. Our fragmental, abstract death eludes one kind of realization only to inaugurate another. The mystery we sought to reclaim from death, some dreamlike ephemerality of the non-existence of the real, is unable it seems to transcend its worldly image, serving instead to only deepen its barbs, to reveal a real behind, or hidden in, the real, and a death hidden in death. Yet it is here in this hiddenness that we continue to pursue death, in a manifested abstract, in a fragment turned into a universe, in a paradox of deathless dying that does not escape reality as intended, but rather exposes its inescapable and endlessly curious salvational fathoms, in an abstract that explodes the real of death in order to better see it, in order to better find humanness there.

An issue with any art of death is that art is only ever concerned with itself as art, and so any art of death will first and foremost be the art of an art of death, and so a displacement of that death. But is this not the point? Is this not a reason for us to become image in order to die? If a painter only 'paints the fact that he paints',[17] the concept of art is not only bolstered from within, but is also made impervious to the harmful infiltration of all possible subject matter. The art of death is therefore the death of art, but like our own deaths this inverse relation is just the realization of a new direction, as it was with the death of the novel (to the few who took note), a transmogrification of rotted viscera into healthy tissue. Our blindness when it comes to what can be seen, again becomes so many different ways to see the dark, becomes in fact the only type of seeing still meriting the designation.

The ready-made-ness of death is not an affront to our artistic reimaginings, but an invitation to establish an inscrutable filter between us and it, a way of seeing that transforms the object from an object of thought into a thought object. For with 'the ready-made it is no longer the object that's there, but the idea of the object, and we no longer find pleasure here in art, but in the idea of art. We are wholly in ideology'.[18]

This is an area discussed at length by Arthur C. Danto,[19] who argues that Andy Warhol is responsible for turning art into philosophy; for unlike Marcel Duchamp's ready-mades, Warhol's *Brillo Boxes*, the focus of Danto's case, were made (sculpted) by Warhol, and so it was them and not Duchamp's found objects that expanded art's invisible umbrella to include not only any object but any potential copy of any object, and so anything at all. Is this art of death (and death of art), then, more correctly considered a ready-made death or the *counterpart* of a real death? Death considered as a Warholian counterpart would not only rely on the re-evaluation of what already exists, but would itself be a creation born from such a re-evaluation, the manifestation of the pure thought of the ready-made, both the augmentation (via the additional layer of objectification) and the deconstruction (via the haptic intimacy with the idea of art itself) of the distance found there, and it is here in this squirrelling corporeality of death's idea that we learn to see ourselves dying, in the complex gestation and birth of new progeny to the art of death's gluey corpse.

Art in all its uselessness and emptiness and farcicality is the perfect conduit of death, as it is of the life that precedes it. And with post-Warholian extrapolations of his project, this state only intensifies:

> I have great admiration for Andy Warhol, but none at all for the current New York artists who simply reiterate and reproduce familiar modes of simulation. To assert that 'We're in a state of simulation' becomes meaningless, because at that point one enters a death-like state.[20]

The event is gone, and the simulation is over. Whereas with Warhol, art's significance is its insignificance, its meaning its lack of meaning. But this is not to claim it is nothing but a mirror held up to human life and death; for its purpose, though it self-identifies as purposeless, is to become the spectacle of this predicament, and through being a spectacle indulge in 'exorcizing [the decay of our absurdity] as spectacle',[21] and so provide palliative care to the necessity of its own existence, an existence already diseased beyond cure, diseased beyond death – flourishing in its own decay.[22] This is art's force of evil, its taunt to life and the living, its ridiculing of death as a solution to the human non-event. However, to explicate this approach to death we must first be clear by what we mean by non-event. Baudrillard explains it in the following way:

> The non-event is not when nothing happens. It is, rather, the realm of perpetual change, of a ceaseless updating, of an incessant succession in real time, which produces this general equivalence, this indifference, this banality that characterizes the zero degree of the event.[23]

The non-event so described is no mere non-occurrence, but rather busyness to a fault, an exponential increase in activity for the sake only of being active, of not pausing for breath, of never stopping. The non-event has no nerve for self-assessment. It must repeat and change without cessation, or else implode into the vacuum at its core. Art's task is to be the pause that nevertheless mimics this empty perpetuation of human industry: it is the pause that never sleeps. And what it is that art does to remove the vanity of death as a resolution to such a life is show how our death has already been co-opted into this non-eventfulness. It shows that the non-event cannot cure itself and that the only semi-curative measure is to bear witness to the damage wreaked on death, through its inclusion in life, by embracing the inherent violence of art's position. Any art of death, on this account, must restore violence to our human dying, the violence of seeing in unfiltered detail, and from outside of life, the sickness of our continuing to survive, our dissolution of finality.

2.2 Models of the Models of the Real

If prisons are a model of the country outside them, theme parks and movies vehicles to enhance the reality of the reality they temporarily displace, then how is it the model comes to exist at all without there being a model prior to it that has already united itself with the real in such a way as to appear indistinguishable? In these instances I am thinking primarily of *crime* and *acting*. Without these models of circumstance and validation there are no prisons and there are no movies, there are only the less than imaginary orchestrations of circumstance. We had to have first hyperrealized our crime and acted as models distinguishable and removable from living. And if the problematical reality of these models' subject matter is not obvious, we must remember that the criminal is a darling and the actor a murderer, both supposedly encapsulating some tangent of reality that is readily recognizable, while remaining essentially hidden in the fact that nothing out of the ordinary has happened, until, that is, a model is made of what it is they have done. That one can 'commit' some other thing and the other 'pretend' something else is already dependent on those things being cognizable as real. No one can commit crime or act something other than the real without having established that possibilities exist for things that happen that are beyond those things just happening. The prison therefore is a model of a model of the real: a model not directly of a country but of its reconstruction, in which commercial interests have been exhaustively integrated into the land mass, a model in which even objects break the law – in turn requiring no great leap for the objectification of its inhabitants, its prisoners. The movie is a model of a reconstruction of the real in which acting and the simulated reality have already been acknowledged and established as a narratorial corrective of that for which it is a model. And while conflating the two in some simulacrum of the real may serve to inoculate the horror of the world without us (the horror of anything just happening), it cannot make sense of why it is this third layer has become so naturalized.

If our make-believes feed reality into the hyperreality of what we rely on taking for real, it is only to further remove us from the horror of a real to which we have no access. Our inherent childishness is not only indulged in these make-believes but in the commerce on which they rest. The very act of paying 'real' currency for these admissions to 'pretence' confirms not only the reality of the subsequent transportation, and so the place from which we've come, but also the omnipresence of our dreams, which otherwise might suffer from proximity to someplace that exists only in virtue of them holding no sway there. The buffer zone is deep, and it needs to be deep and to become progressively deeper, lest there should exist a Real that should somehow become visible, despite all our efforts to co-opt it into non-existence.

Hyperreal civilizations do not have waste products. And this is not to say that those products are instead used to that civilization's advantage, for that does not preclude them starting off as waste. The point is that you cannot call waste what is so obviously devised as (core) end product. To label these products waste is to imagine dreams as an offshoot of the real, rather than the real as an offshoot of dreams. How would we have even singled it out as a something separable from itself had we not first sought to distance ourselves from it? The bare concept of the real is first and foremost the mark of our initial retreat, of our looking away.

Walking cannot draw enough attention to itself, and running being either indistinguishable from sport, from training, or else evoking fleeing and criminality, is likewise assimilated by a larger context that undermines its isolation. Only the middle way, jogging, shouts out what it is, becomes the template of exercise that is chosen for itself, for being exercise and nothing else. The attraction is its purity of purpose. There is only the fitness/health aspired to, and no race to win, and no place or person to escape from or escape to. But what is the purpose of this stripping back of purpose? What is the perceived function of establishing realms of functionality that deliberately exclude the functionality external to them, to establish modes of freedom that look like concentrated instances of self-imposed subjugation? (Why must everything, even one's own deliberateness, become so painfully deliberate?) And so the answer is revealed: it is not the touching, the plain foods, or the jogging we are after, but the possibility for servitude, for servitude to ourselves. If we can do what we've set out to do with no reason outside our doing it, then not only is a sense of control established, but more importantly there is something (that is me) over which control can be exerted. When the world controls you, you disappear, but if you can control yourself then the opposite happens, or at least appears to happen, which is enough. All techniques of self-improvement eschew outside motivations because that is to let the world back in, and the world must be kept out if the control scenario is to remain unadulterated. The subterfuge here is glaring: you must believe you are something, that your being this something is important; you must control yourself for the sake of controlling yourself, and dream only of how hideous it would be to only exist.

Notes

1   Primo Levi, *The Drowned and the Saved* (London: Abacus, 1989), 99.
2   Baudrillard, *Simulacra and Simulation*, 20.
3   Baudrillard, *Symbolic Exchange and Death*, 181.
4   Ibid., 53.
5   See Levi, *The Drowned and the Saved*, ch. 5.
6   Which is not to claim that irreverence cannot itself be a threat, for the difference here is one of contextual immediacy: the instantaneous conceptual menace on the one hand and the indefinitely postponed physical menace on the other.
7   Jean Baudrillard, *America* (New York: Verso, 1988), 19–20.
8   Baudrillard, *Simulacra and Simulation*, 24.
9   'That is why *today this 'material' production is that of the hyperreal itself.* It retains all the features, the whole discourse of traditional production, but it is no longer anything but its scaled-down refraction (thus hyperrealists fix a real from which all meaning and charm, all depth and energy of representation have vanished in a hallucinatory resemblance). Thus everywhere the hyperrealism of simulation is translated by the hallucinatory resemblance of the real to itself' (Baudrillard, *Simulacra and Simulation*, 23).
10 Nietzsche, *On the Genealogy of Morals and Ecce Homo*, 303.
11 Baudrillard, *The Intelligence of Evil*, 74.
12 Ibid., 78.
13 Ibid., 73.
14 Ibid., 88.
15 Baudrillard, *The Conspiracy of Art*, 118.
16 Baudrillard, *The Intelligence of Evil*, 84.
17 Ibid.
18 Ibid., 86.
19 See *After the End of Art: Contemporary Art and the Pale of History* (Princeton, NJ: Princeton University Press, 1998) and *Andy Warhol* (New Haven, CT: Yale University Press, 2009).
20 Baudrillard, *Baudrillard Live: Selected Interviews*, 166.
21 Baudrillard, *The Intelligence of Evil*, 89.
22 See Baudrillard, *The Conspiracy of Art*, 96–97.
23 Ibid., 95.

Chapter 3

A BLEAK NON-HISTORY OF HISTORY

History is the future.

In keeping with Baudrillard's proclamation concerning our retro-aestheticization of fascism, we will proceed to retro-aestheticize fundamentalist terror. And even now it's easy to see that the work is already underway, for the theme is and will be the same – for like everything else it will be a remake – and that theme will not be the one displayed on the surface (people really believed such things and were prepared to act on them), but instead an undercurrent, there in all retro indulgences (there really were people who had convictions, that believed things – *anything at all* – to the point that life itself took a supplementary role): 'The death of a terrorist is not a suicide: it is an effigy of the virtual death that the system inflicts on itself.'[1]

If the cinema 'only resurrects ghosts',[2] its descendant (the video game) only resurrects us. And remember that the possibility for genuine newness being zero is not just *a* platitude, it is *the* platitude. The preciseness, even of what remains vague and seemingly indeterminate, is what marks the claustrophobia of birth onwards. There is no room for error, beyond the mistake that there is anything at all.

All talk of resurrection is misleading, for it implies that the first birth was not itself a resurrection, that originality arrived as if out of nothing, out of nowhere. Everything is living again, even when it is living for the first time, or else I'm to imagine that existence can escape its own mythopoeia. It is quicksand all the way down, and all the way up as well. The only stability is moving in order not to move. All action, all impetus to act, is inescapably nostalgic. If the autochthonic were ever to occur it would be an act of terrorism unlike any seen or envisaged. 'Terrorism is always that of the real',[3] because humanity is nothing if it is not an obfuscator of what is. The pessimist tries to make us see the extent of the terror, how our whole lives are intricately played out variations on an essential cringe, and its attendant analgesic utilities. And here we have the reason for God: a placeholder for the violence of the possibility of any genuine source. The tiniest unit of unprecedentedness would destroy us, murder the world in its sleep, cast the blood of our thoughts into the first instance of fire. It's for this reason that the way out is always nothing, always negative, always elusive and void: God, reality, death, ourselves.

We do not even resemble ourselves. There would need to have been access to an original referent to make such a resemblance possible, and there was never such a thing. Via our senses, resemblance takes care of itself, and even contiguity of data follows this model; but where access itself is the issue, there is only resemblance looking back at itself: a 'hyperresemblance' working like a patch that is itself patched or reapplied and so a constant point of weakness – but a weakness that we have come to depend on, resembling so closely as it does a possible means of abscondence. Because the human map of the world, of the universe, moves without moving, it's hard to distinguish ourselves from the dead, as real as we are conscious, as breathing as we are rotting, perfectly incomplete and inextricable. That we remain fascinated, however much we submit to being anaesthetized and accept the bland cruelty of our predicament, is something that cannot be unlearnt, that no one can teach us to overcome, for even the most depressed of depressed men are held by the fascination of what it is to be depressed. This our progress:

> Our atrocity is exactly the reverse of that of earlier centuries. It consists in eradicating the blood and cruelty by use of objectivity. A colourless, programmatic, bloodless atrocity, like the white-noise torture of sensory deprivation cells.[4]

3.1 Filming the Apocalypse

There'll be footage of the end of everything, and we're watching it now, and its most salient feature is its patent inability to conclude. Maybe at some point there will be the footage and no one left to watch it, which is the joke, of course; but the apocalypse will always find its audience, for what else is it but our own boredom at the spectacle of this never-ending termination. If we get the end we deserve, and we must, it will not be unequivocal, but something like Samuel Beckett's defeated cruelty, that 'ghastly hallucination, such as the square root of minus one.' An apocalypse that was not suitably phantasmagoric, that did not obliterate us with our own special effects, or even reference our heightened facility for holocaust, could never be worthy of the name. We could ignore such a finality, and we do. It would be (and is) an irrelevance. Eventually even the cameras will stop working, and we will not notice when the glut of our recordings resurface themselves as perpetually new. The definitive blockbuster, the most fanatical of all extravaganzas, cannot be denied: the 'sacrificial joy' of seven or more billion souls jogging[5] on treadmills into the void (into voids displayed on screens too close to our eyes for us to ever see them as screens, or the things and events depicted as anything but ours): 'The sheep have taken over from the beasts of the Apocalypse.'[6] The apogee of collapse will film itself, documenting its own duration even before it occurs, filming the victory of having ended, the extermination of the population of the world as a testing ground for the possibilities of pure cinematic excess. But such an event cannot transcend the same retro-megalomaniacal model of aggrandizement through scale alone, and all it has is scale, and scale is not enough: seven or more billion is deficient, is so much less than that imaginary number of consequence.

When we watch our dissolution back, we do so not as 'spectators' but as 'receivers', for even the spectator has some level of active engagement in what he watches, while the passivity of the receiver is complete: the virtuality of our own corpses is absorbed without question, without censor or hope. In a similar vein to those scientists who tell us that numerous catastrophic impacts of climate change are already locked in, are irreversible, we too have passed the tipping point of our ever being able to mean anything else, anything more. It's already too late. 'There is no longer an apocalypse. [...] The apocalypse is finished, today it is the precession of the neutral, of forms of the neutral and of indifference',[7] and all we can do is soak it up, without ever soaking it up, like the excess waters of the melted ice sheets: too full now of just how empty we've become. And so with the actuality of the Apocalypse 'behind us, among us, [...] we are instead confronted with the virtual reality of the Apocalypse, with the posthumous comedy of the Apocalypse',[8] our cacodemonic laughter played out in the silent yawns of our contented uselessness. With no reason to exist anymore, the real apocalyptic incident can be forgotten, disregarded as one more mock functionary in a world without function, as one more past event consumed by our continuous now,[9] as one more state of revelation in a world made completely transparent.

An apocalypse does not terminate, it uncovers. It is an epistemic revelation, a disclosure of mysteries, of those secrets formerly hidden, a (traditionally speaking divine) correction manifested in the world. It shocks us into submission, and from here we see how the world as we've imagined it falls away. The end of the world is no more than the end of the world's conforming to our cognizance of it, becoming beyond interpretation. The apocalypse is the disclosure of reality in a world in which only its simulated form exists. The Apocalypse has released us from the suspense[10] of life and from the subterfuge of the world. What might happen, what might be concealed, where nothing is allowed to happen and there is nowhere left to hide? After all, what evidence is there 'that events are again possible, [or] that our (unreal) reality is not an absolutely terminal state'?[11] Outside the end there is only where we are already: only this masturbatory fantasy of an end, only the promise that something might one day disappear and not come back, the hope that if a clock is ticking it is ticking towards something and not merely away from something else, something that we will never escape. In this way, for Baudrillard, the Apocalypse has already become the perfect crime.

Whether through deficit or excess, reality will inevitably continue the work of the Apocalypse – by obliterating it. The real apocalyptic event then becomes the Apocalypse's own apocalypse. Just as Kafka's Messiah arrives too late, and suicide is always similarly unpunctual, as E. M. Cioran informs us,[12] the Apocalypse is also immanently belated through its already having effected its destruction, its end. The essential paradox here is clear: in virtue of its being premature, it fails to arrive in time. Its effects have become its cause; it is a transcendental event: it must happen because all the conditions for its existence, all its prerequisites (which are also its consequences) are already in place to necessitate it, but we never get to see it. It happens without us, and all we have is this endless streaming footage of its having already happened, the film of an event which we are precluded from ever witnessing in any direct sense. And so it's like this that we become impatient for the past to reveal itself – as the future, as 'climax and anticlimax'.[13] Likewise, death too remains 'only as virtual reality, as an option or changeable setting in the living being's operating system, [...] a reprogramming that proceeds along the lines of the virtualization of sex, the "cybersex" that waits for us in the future, as a sort of ontological "attraction"'.[14]

In order to move forwards, we move backwards. When nobody can believe that the end is actually coming, it becomes seemingly incumbent upon us to mourn its absence in what has already gone. We look back and see that nothing has really perished, and through a process of revisionism seek to finalize that which is still going on, still prevalent to the point of homogeneity, whereby it can continue largely unnoticed and unchanged. We correct the indiscretions and the horrors of history like we retroactively correct our want for wit and erudition in some past conversation, remedying so that we might be done with it, so that by repeating ourselves we do not repeat ourselves. But this iterative indulgence does nothing more than perpetuate the very failings of that apocalypse, reinforcing an end that recalcitrantly and repeatedly refuses to end, undermining whatever sense of the real might still have resided there, had we left it alone. 'This revival of vanished – or vanishing – forms, this attempt to escape the apocalypse of the virtual, is a utopian desire, the last of our utopian desires',[15] and it will never succeed. There is no emancipation from the apocalypse of the virtual to the apocalypse of the real, and the more we pursue it the deeper inside the simulation we go. Ultimately, what the Apocalypse reveals is not some conciliatory solution, the satisfaction of some long-awaited denouement, but the very absence of that possibility:

Messianic hope was based on the *reality* of the Apocalypse. But this latter has no more reality than the original Big Bang. We shall never be allowed this dramatic illumination. Even the idea of putting an end to our planet by an atomic clash is futile and superfluous. If it has no meaning for anyone, God or man, then what is the point? Our Apocalypse is not real, it is *virtual*. And it is not in the future, it is *here and now*.[16]

We have seen the apocalypse so many times that we are tired of it. It comes, it goes: nothing changes. But of course it never goes, which not incidentally is also what contributes to our weariness with it. Our imaginations are not equal to the end, they are not equal to what might be exposed in order to facilitate that end, which is what constitutes the Apocalypse, after all. And it is our failings in this regard that actually provide us with the best evidence for the veracity of the Apocalypse, and for its already having happened. To imagine the end, like Lars von Trier imagined the end in *Melancholia*, is to make the eternal fleeting because it suits us better that way, and within that juxtaposition find a residue of whatever meaning has been sacrificed in order to arrive there. But when the eponymous planet hits the earth and everything is consumed by the impact, its character's frenetic suffering is over and so too is our vicarious ordeal, our empathy, for we now are the ones that must live through what is left: the promise of an oblivion that is never ours. 'No finality, either positive or negative, is ever the last word in the story. / And the Apocalypse itself is a facile solution.'[17] What possible catastrophe could engulf us in its elucidation, and of what? What possible conclusion could consolidate a creature so obviously intent only ever to exceed itself? To extend beyond our functionality, to live out catastrophe's hypertelia, to exceed our meaning in ever more extreme and nebulous ways: nothing else delineates our predicament more accurately, or makes a future Apocalypse less feasible.

Whereas there would be a shift if the promise (hitherto empty) ever became a certainty, for in this instance the apocalypse of simulation would give way to the simulation of the apocalypse – the generation of the real (apocalypse) as if from nowhere. Arriving without precedent, it would not be possible to situate it, to accommodate its inevitability within the constructs of our speculative escapisms. As Baudrillard explains with telling candour:

> If there were an absolute term of the nuclear apocalypse in the realm of the real, then at that point I would stop, I wouldn't write any more! God knows, if the metaphor really collapses into reality, I won't have any more to do. That would not even be a question of resignation – it's no longer possible to think at that point.[18]

Yet such an apocalypse is still true to itself, still true to our imagining of it, for doesn't this at once reveal to us the immediate irrelevance of all our prior understanding. Isn't this the very epistemic revelation we were promised all along: the climax and the anticlimax, the ratiocinative divulgation that undoes thought itself, the end of reflection, understanding absorbed in its own failure, the exposure as overexposure, the final unmasking that removes the face as well.

3.2 Obscenity as the Horror of Depersonalization

In Lav Diaz's film *Norte, The End of History*, we watch a man, Fabian, first struggling to disappear into some state of idealized self-indifference, and then, having got partway, struggling against his own reappearance.[19] This inverted conjuring act is contrasted with a mother and father, Joaquin and Eliza, whose lives though societally translucent are marked by a desperately futile attempt to establish presence. Each of these two approaches seeks to overturn its own version of a history (Fabian's in absence, the couple's in presence) that is itself illusory, and an end to a particular history that can have no end, having already ended, having never begun.

Demoralized ex-student of law, Fabian sits in a café holding a xeroxed copy of *Reasons and Persons*. One of his friends asks him, 'Why would you read Derek Parfit?' To which he replies: 'Nothing, I'll just read him.' He will have its intellectual rigour, its portrayal of ethics as objectively true, as impersonal, as explicable through reasoned argument alone, pass through him like a bad meal. But we can imagine Parfit's revolutionary and reductionist account of the self holding greater charm – the idea that personhood is not some extra fact about us, and that we can be fully accounted for in terms of psychological continuity and connectedness, and that identity need not be coextensive with what matters – as something Fabian might recognize as additional justification for the act he is planning. His instinct is, like Dostoevsky's Raskolnikov, loosely fortified, we might imagine, by a simplistic act-utilitarianism, and as with his earlier incarnation we see 'a soured dreamer – a perverted idealist'[20] imposing his will on the world for the edification and betterment of all, including himself – especially himself. Both godless, both anarchic, both looking for the possibility to act, to realize an event, to perform some primal truth of justice, to obliterate an obstacle (an obfuscation) beyond which they cannot see.

Raskolnikov and Fabian each kill a moneylender, Alyona and Magda respectively, and both too are forced into a further murder in order to save themselves, Alyona's sister (Elizaveta) and Magda's young daughter. The killing of the monster in each case necessitates the killing of innocence. It is as if act-utilitarianism is given an immediate riposte, a lesson in the validity of moral thresholds regardless of consequence, indeed of utilitarianism's more cautious, rule-based version, of the need for fetters on the escalation of desirable outcomes. And that Fabian's act of double-murder is (for the viewer, and we imagine for himself) a re-enactment, a second instantiation, of Raskolnikov's original crime, weights it with further implications: 'what happens a second time becomes fatal'.[21] And so we do not need to wait for the murders to happen in order to establish Fabian's supposed superiority and independence as empty hubris and isolation, and neither does he. He is already looking back on what he will do, what he will become, what he will unbecome.

Keeping to the numerous correlations, both Raskolnikov and Fabian steal from the moneylenders they kill and bury the spoils, but deviating from his Russian predecessor Fabian retrieves his stash and attempts to do good with it, to undo part of the unforeseen (yet necessary) consequences of his act. (Unforeseen consequences would mean that his plan had been a theoretical failure if it hadn't already happened before, if that removal of innocence weren't the whole point of the exercise.) However, unlike Raskolnikov, Fabian never confesses, even though in this retelling his confession would mean the release of a man (Joaquin) wrongly accused of the crime he had committed. But then his motivations were never merely consequentialist in this way, and nor were they unequivocally tied up with establishing some imagined personal superiority either,[22] for we know from its first occurrence that human weakness itself must become the real target, that emotion and the extraneous edifice of personality is what will threaten to undermine his goal. Raskolnikov ruminates:[23] 'Was it the old crone I killed? I killed myself, not the old crone!'[24] but yet his self-murder is not complete – he gives himself up, allows suffering to redeem him – as there's enough of him left to become the recipient of external justice. In order for Fabian's version to become truly 'fatal', he must disappear. This and this alone is his quest: the eradication of self, the eradication of history. And yet despite his best endeavours to achieve these states, they will never be actualized; his pursuits are futile, as futile as the very circumstances he is attempting to transcend: 'The end of the social, the end of history. It's all absurd if one simply means "There's no more": it's absurd.'[25]

Both too are fundamentally divided (the name 'Raskolnikov' directly evokes this splitting, this core division, being derived from the Russian 'raskolot' – to 'split'):[26] Raskolnikov is a man divided from his ideals, and Fabian a man divided from his own disappearance, the felt absence of himself, a presence mourning its own absence.[27] But what Fabian knows that Raskolnikov didn't is that the murders are only the beginning, and that he needs to deepen his depersonalization to evade entirely the conceptual apparatus of being someone, to rid himself of the history of his own identity (his sister, his beloved pet), and not now in the service of ethics or some other grand ideal – although the moral crusade could still be thought of as intact, though more sophisticated: a staying true to his belief in the need to bring about 'the destruction of anything inimical to morality', starting with his own personhood – but instead what appears to be a peculiarly selfish negation of self. Heeding Baudrillard's warning, the farce cannot be allowed to repeat itself and so again become history. He must disappear and that disappearance must prove tragic, just as Joaquin and Eliza's appearance can arrive completely only at their end (with her death and the consequent dissolution of their union), by a fatal seduction, their annihilation being the means by which they each appear:[28]

> Our fundamental destiny is not to exist and survive, as we think: it is to appear and disappear. [...] Nothing is less capable than chance of making something appear: for something really to appear, surging up to the reign of appearances, there must be seduction. For something to really disappear, to resolve into its appearance, there must be a ceremony of metamorphosis.[29]

Norte is both this seduction and this ceremony, showing us how, despite their incompatibilities and variant objectives, they are destined to merge in the mutually liquefying state of liberation.

Fabian's self-destructive peregrination, the ordeal he has imposed on himself through others – from the double-murder, to the rape of his sister, to the slaying of his once beloved pet dog – is an enactment of the violence of his disappearing. For there is a moment of recognition, in which you become a fading ghost hovering somewhere in the vicinity of your body, and there is the ferocious struggle to accept this state, to no longer seek a return; but instead to increase the distance, to disembody your person, allow it to atrophy to nothing, and leave the body to its own devices. This fevered resistance is akin to the affected imperfections in the story, recounted by Baudrillard, of 'the eighteenth-century magician who had invented an automaton that could imitate human actions so perfectly that he was obliged on stage to "automatize" himself, to imitate mechanical imperfection precisely in order to save the game, to preserve the infinitesimal difference that made the form of illusion possible'.[30] The fight to preserve the seduction of being someone happens even at the expense of that presence equalling nothing but its own anguish, even because of that fact, for how could it be otherwise when the two are indistinguishable: seen this way, depersonalization disorder can be characterized by the destructive desire to retrieve something you never had – to return to some imaginary idealized state to which there is no credible route, let alone a return – or else the desire to once again become delusional, or rather to not simply feel the wool over your eyes but to actually become that wool, the embodiment of your own false impression. It is ultimately only the ordeal that keeps you personalized, that prevents you from disappearing, for you were gone already and it was only this fact becoming sensate that hurt, that incited such extreme fear and dislocation, the solution to which is to cease this emotional acknowledgment and disappear again (if there is time), disappear for good, disappear like your life depended on it, because to pay service to your loss – which was in fact an addition – it does. Part of the emotional strain is the potential endlessness of this state, a state we will not be there to finalize, reality without us and beyond us continuing forever; but the price of this infinitude is indifference, complete emotional mortification, for 'what is endless is also desireless, tension-less, passionless, it is bereft of events',[31] it is death-like and life-like, and too much like both to hold appeal for anyone who is not aware of the stark necessity of the former and the unfiltered horror of the latter.

Fabian's acts, though clearly decreasing in legal severity (from murder, to rape, to animal extermination), actually, with regard to obscenity, appear if anything to escalate. And that these acts are obscene is made conspicuous through concealment, for while we see enough to know what Fabian is doing, we do not see the acts (the insertions) themselves. We are removed from the scene by walls and by foliage, so that they happen for us *as* obscene acts, *as* hidden, *as* abominations unfit for the eye, *as* taboo, and therefore *as* something else other than what they are: the eradication of a self and a history that have already gone, that was never there, an imagined something whose absence must be punished on its own terms, by a nothing – nothing via nothing and versus nothing. And for all that, can he really 'know whether anything has taken place or not'.[32] Is he looking back at the end, or has he simply imagined the end as a perspective from which to view his own disappearance? In everything Fabian does following the initiation of this obscene sequence 'we see a paradoxical logic: the idea [...] destroyed by its own realization, by its own excess. And in this way history itself comes to an end, finds itself obliterated by the instantaneity and omnipresence of the event'.[33] Fabian becomes subsumed by this sequence, as the non-person that, having witnessed itself existing and having been revolted by what it saw, is absorbed by events to which it can no longer exist as an extension, as an agent of, as a separate entity to, but instead becomes itself hidden, lost, extinguished, the self then an obscenity to be shrouded just like the acts themselves through their increased visibility: 'More generally things visible do not come to an end in obscurity and silence – instead they fade into the more visible than visible: obscenity.'[34]

We should not though suppose that *Norte* presents depersonalization (as a felt disorder) as anything other than an aberration, for while Fabian obviously resents the absence of his parents throughout his childhood, and unwittingly sets in motion the absence of Joaquin and Eliza, parents who otherwise would have been present for their children, and by the removal of this formative presence replicates his own sense of familial removal in them, a remoteness that in his case eventually turns inwards to remove what he has come to see was never there, the fact that Ading, the aunt, at the close of the film has taken Eliza's place (now dead as the result of a traffic accident), walking between the two children as the mother had done, signifies that appearances and simulacra are still the abiding order and that disappearing, for all its footing in reality, is less real, and so remains an anomaly. As Baudrillard says:

> Obesity is another of the figures of obscenity. As proliferation, as the saturation of a limitless space, obesity may stand as a general metaphor for our systems of information, communication, production, and memory.[35]

Fabian's weight gain is such that it receives comment from his friends, his distension the physical realization of a theoretical amassment whose function has become defunct (something Fabian acknowledges), relegated to flab, his former loquacity, now gone, no longer an expenditure – all this fat and nowhere to burn it: 'A fetal obesity, primal and placental: as if [he] were pregnant with [his] own bod[y] but could not be delivered of [it].'[36] Hence we have witnessed in Fabian the epitome of flabby theory, how it grows exponentially, uselessly, the end of history becoming its own history – a liberating turn: 'Thus freedom has been obliterated, liquidated by liberation; truth has been supplanted by verification; the community has been liquidated and absorbed by communication; form gives way to information and performance.'[37] But this is also the juncture at which appearance (via incarceration) and disappearance (via freedom) meet: Joaquin finds himself liberated by his lack of freedom, finding strength and compassion and control, liberated from his failure to realize the potentials with which freedom had burdened him; and Fabian, attempting to outgrow all notion of freedom and the incarceration implied by it, by attempting to not exist at all, to disappear, to relinquish himself to what is and what does, is thereby liberated from the lie of himself, liberated from the burden of being anything. The last we see of Fabian, he is sitting in a small boat in shallow water going nowhere, while the world busies itself around him.[38] He has gone, he is nothing, and yet he still exists;[39] he still lives, and there is no contradiction in this merciful conflation, in this essential paradox, for 'it is not true that in order to live one has to believe in one's own existence. There is no necessity to that'.[40]

As well as the threat of death there is also the threat of death's non-arrival, and we find ourselves having to 'struggle against the possibility that we will not die',[41] because for all our immortal desires we have done almost nothing to marry the desire with any substantive eventuality. Quite unsurprisingly, our hopes for a perpetually extended life are congenitally fuzzy, reliant on the gift of immortality, should it ever arrive, coming complete with instructions for use. And while Baudrillard often focuses his attention on the possibility of immortality via cloning – continuation through replication, through sameness, through life undifferentiated in form, through nonhumanness[42] – the *struggle* is always ours, always personal, as it is in a death that ostensibly precludes all legitimate application of the personal. Even when 'it is clear that mankind exists only at the cost of its own death [and so] becomes immortal only by paying the price of its technological disappearance, of its inscription in the digital order (the mental diaspora of the networks)',[43] a price has still been paid, and will continue to be paid. Our sexual awakening into difference cannot be reversed, not by death and not by the removal of a variegated reproduction. Even our prospects for immortality are preloaded: 'For religion, the ideal reference of the body is the animal (instincts and appetites of the 'flesh'). The corpse as a mass grave, and its reincarnation beyond death as a carnal metaphor.'[44] The damage is done. There is no finality and no solution. For while Freud's death drive 'is precisely this nostalgia for a state before the appearance of individuality and sexual differentiation, a state in which we lived before we became mortal and distinct from one another',[45] we approach it as one who might take a rest from himself, content that the abstraction of being one's self is ineradicable. And this brings us to a third struggle: not that you will die, or that you will not die, but that you were ever born – that your history was initiated in the first place. It is this that 'a retreat from the revolution of sex and death',[46] via artificial reproduction, is seen to remedy. But this is preventative not curative care, and is preventative only superficially; for though there is the liberation from death, there is no liberation from the thought of death, nor from the (retrogressive and sexless) simulation of birth. The only successful way to reimagine death is to reimagine it as life, but only after you have first reimagined life as death, life as the perfected terrorist target:

> *Its blindness is the exact replica of the system's absolute lack of differentiation.* [...] In its deadly and indiscriminate taking of hostages, terrorism strikes at precisely the most characteristic product of the whole system: the anonymous and perfectly undifferentiated individual, the term substitutable for any other. Paradoxically, it seems that the innocent pay the crime of being nothing, of being lotless, of having been dispossessed of their name by an equally anonymous system whose purest incarnation they then become. They are the end products of the social, of a now globalised abstract sociality. It is in this sense, in the sense in which they are precisely *anybody*, that they are the predestined victims of terrorism.[47]

All possibility of remedy becomes obsolete this way, when the condition to be cured mutates at every turn to save itself, to hide, to become the very state the cure is working to effect. The only problem is the recognition of the problem, that through being recognized has already changed into something else. We mustn't ever imagine the disease holds still long enough for any person or instrument to discern it as distinct from that for which it supposedly an affliction. The tripartite struggle against death, against never-ending life, against ever being born at all, is simply the struggle against struggle itself, a struggling for the sake of struggling – a curse in search of its own needfulness, a failed dream. And this is how we maintain what we are: it's the mark of us; but ultimately a fading mark, as we turn towards our future, couched 'in terms of functions and of biological equilibrium',[48] of nonindividuation and perfectly calibrated exchange values, and in so doing crawl 'underneath the human'[49] to escape ourselves in an indifferent permanence, a state of immersion in which it is possible to unlive our lives indefinitely, to redeem our individuation for the succour of collapse, of bankruptcy.

The thought that death might then become some vicarious indulgence on the part of those wishing to relive the regret of their once having been one among many, that a personal curtailment might come to be entertainment for the now depersonalized is, pace Baudrillard, largely unthinkable. Real death and *cyberdeath* will become indistinguishable, both an irrelevance, both implausible symptoms (of liberty) that have been overcome. The world (beyondless) will happen without struggle, and nobody will recall their sicknesses (their transcendent longings), because our thinking will already have been made bloodless. There will be no more middle – no more multiplicities, no more intensities (the Deleuzean BwO starved to death) – and when we look, we see 'we are already beyond the end'.[50] Nevertheless, there remains this, this call to arms for the sick:

> But perhaps we may see this as a kind of adventure, a heroic test: to take the artificialization of living beings as far as possible in order to see, finally, what part of human nature survives the great ordeal. If we discover that not everything can be cloned, simulated, programmed, genetically and neurologically managed, then whatever survives the final solution could truly be called 'human:' some inalienable and indestructible human quality could finally be identified. Of course, there is always the risk, in this experimental adventure, that nothing will pass the test – that the human will be permanently eradicated.[51]

This surplus of functional assimilation/accelerated artificialization, this human quintessence, if found will necessarily be that which we were always

looking to appease and despairing eradicate. It will be what is left of our morality, but will not be moral by its standards, quite likely the opposite. It will
be an unending source of pain. It will reach beyond itself in all directions at
once. It will be found in the middle of a forest, dreaming itself into existence
like Bottom under a tree. It will be emaciated and obscene. It will be a child of
death. All its thoughts will be self-reflexive. And perhaps most crucially of all,
it will be more artificial than the programme of artificialization that made it
visible. Its survival would not be of this world and human only by association,
but bearing the mark of humanity's inalienable core nonetheless, as the face
(or what remains of it) behind the mask explains the device that has concealed
it. And we will not know it when we see it, but feel that it is there, that this is
something that is left of us and that it was always there, and always residual.
Our instruments of measurement and isolation will destroy it and it in turn will
destroy them – insofar as they will discover only their own operational datum,
insofar as they will reveal themselves to themselves. Transparent slime of no
mass, non-humanly conscious, amorally self-conscious, existent for the sake of
a definition, the dream of a thing within a dream, a clear goo consumed with
its own suffering, its own infrangible inexplicability: it is nothing the world
will know, but only a something it will be forced to concede to not knowing,
the near unfathomable randomness of infinity artificially concentrated into a
presence of unrecognizable yet theoretically sound authenticity. Our essence
evoked as a necessary abstraction, the most virtual of virtual realities, chimera
of chimeras: chaos in a thimble. And with this a warning, a code of conduct: 'if the human being wishes to attain this kind of immortality, he must
produce himself as artefact also, expel himself from himself into an artificial
orbit in which he will circle forever'.[52]

The promise of immortality can only ever be a detour: either we must
be led back to death, or else the path itself must get lost and become our
death – because human life, life itself, human thought, thought itself (the
raw illusions), must eventually pool, abandoning all plurality of instance and
instantiation: the end of pathways, the inception of unexpurgated spread, the
collapse of time. 'Time,' which is first and foremost ours and so susceptible
to this corrosive metamorphosis (this liberty), 'is viewed from a perspective of
entropy – the exhausting of all possibilities – the perspective of a counting
down …to infinity. We no longer possess a forward-looking, historical, or provi-
dential vision, which was the vision of a world of progress or production'.[53] To
live forever is to learn to go nowhere, to allow ourselves to become so fat with
possibilities that there is no longer a call to move, or any one direction in which
to gravitate. When the orgy has not even begun, it is much too early to ask
what it is we are to do when 'the orgy no longer takes place',[54] and of course
something of an irrelevance when the orgy is infinite – the infinite detour: 'Let

us be clear about this: if the Real is disappearing, it is not because of a lack of it – on the contrary, there is too much of it. It is the excess of reality that puts an end to reality.'[55] But this too much[56] is the meagre threat of the orgy and not the orgy as it will occur if all vision of progress is to be avoided, if death is to become one of many deviant and dissolving pathways in a swamp of excess that on its way elsewhere extends only its coverage, realizing only the as yet unimagined evil to come – the evil of a beyond that the orgy when it comes will swallow up and see itself and die of fright, and so find death again: 'The real is growing and growing; one day everything will be real; and when the real is universal, that will spell death.'[57] Thus we get the virtuality of our dying.

Science will take us to the future, but it will not constitute that future. Its truths will become redundant, naïve, laughable even. The near complete obviousness of New Atheism cannot detract from its intrinsic crudity. For where we're heading requires different fundamentals and vitalities: the need 'to have things in which not to believe. Ironic objects, so to speak, dis-invested practices, ideas to believe or disbelieve as you like'[58] – to have, in other words, possibilities regardless of truth, impossible possibilities, directions that lead nowhere, veridicalities that are palpably false, and some essential sense of nonsense. The image of the future is maybe not so simply the headless man, but instead, or as well as, the man whose head is on fire.

There is still the temptation to regard life, or rather the person-lived, as redeemable, and immortality (be it organic or inorganic) as the only valid exchange – to consider immortality as if through the other (and only 'as if' because the other is ultimately only there as a vessel for you). What underlies this line of thought is the belief that when I die, whatever or whoever kills me, I will be the one that kills myself. I'll choose my corpse like a man might choose a new hat. And it always fits. (Although the places it must be worn will always be wrong.) To imagine otherwise, the thought would be, is to suppose that we, cognizant of the empirical details of death, could die without our consent. And what makes this appear fantastical, spurious even (and of course it is both and neither), is that we supposedly fail to understand what we've already consented to, and what consenting to a future that isn't there really involves. For the answer lies in our very ability to die, in our still existing as something that death can expunge, in our not having become something else, something abstract. These are omissions to which we have consented, and the thought that you are that which brought about x and not-x[59] itself is of little consequence, because for this rejoinder to prove damning, your investment would have to be exposed as a mere acting, which is to make the rejoinder damning only on a personal level, and not theoretically where it might count. (Essentially, this distinction means nothing, for all such tales of agency are lies you tell yourself merely to survive as something that will die, 'a set of useless functions', and what is death on this account but an end to the shame your very existence evokes.)[60]

In the (supposition of an) end, is not death in some respects just a return to randomness, and so the desire for death just the realization that at some fundamental level we are not built for anything else, that while order obviously becomes us it is still somehow very hard to bear?

3.3 The Implosion of Depression as Pornography

Pornography only allowed us to see what sex already was: desire consuming itself while we watched on. The pleasure had is in our not being there. Pornography is invariably less satisfying than genuinely interpersonal sexual encounters, not through any deprivation of involvement, but through those involvements being accentuated. It is the conflation of the roles of executor and spectator that creates the greatest distance: 'a frisson of vertiginous and phony exactitude, a frisson of simultaneous distancing and magnification, of distortion of scale, of an excessive transparency'.[61] But distance from what and of what? To which the answer must be 'The real' on both counts: the real of the simulations we've assimilated. As sex morphs into pornography (if it isn't there already) this distance is lost, for by replicating perversions, that by now are commonplace and hardly worthy of the term, we do not lose ourselves, but rather indulge in imagistic titillation as if we too are screened and screening.

Pornography is the performance of sensations that are not themselves performed, sensations that are beyond performance: it is a *phony exactitude*, and an excessive one. The performance needs to be excessive, because as a perspective on what is perspectiveless it shows what is not and cannot be shown, and shows it with a melodrama of sensation, as if all time spent this way was climactic, building up not to some ultimate state of release, the zenith of a prolonged disappearance to be followed by a reawakening of sorts, but quite the opposite: a display of thwarted presence, the imperious cum or money shot (the simulacrum shot), the pure pataphysics of porn[62] ('the inane protuberance' enabling the 'empty jerk-off'),[63] and then the sleep of the real, where laughter returns,[64] nervous yet exultant at the implosion of the hyperreal.

And none of this, we are reminded, is about love (although the pornographic actress must repeatedly tell us that she loves it, even when it's patent she doesn't), although it *is* all about death. Every second of it is lived as if at its end, as if the performers were in the extended process of being put to death, a death implied and perpetrated in part by the cameras, but most of all by the slow implosion that comes of embodying a state of existence that does not exist, an existence deadened through its absorption of the impossible as a means to an end.

The camerawork in pornography provides the perfect illustration of how the panoptical system deceives. We are given the eye that gives us everything, and yet as it gives, all that haunts us is what we do not see, what we hoped to see but cannot name to note its absence. The camera hides nothing from us, often giving us more than we want, and it is because this seeing is so exhaustively invasive, every angle and orifice occupied and stretched to capacity, that our involvement and so our distance becomes lost to us. This excessive form of viewing is the perspective of the world on itself, an integrative spell that puts us in the scene as only as one more pair of eyes, only then to make sight the vehicle for its own superfluity. It makes us conscious of the work of sight, all those separate instances of noticing, and that what they add up to, what they're working towards, is your no longer needing to watch, the realization of that watching in the ultimate rejection of it. The active passivity of the viewer is instantiated from the start, as the viewer incorporates themself into the causal framework of this peculiarly methodical and self-defeating brand of looking. Its effectiveness as a self-erasing cause reminds us of the comprehensive awareness of depression: seeing like this cannot continue, can exist only to end, can exist only by becoming narrowed and assimilated, by achieving distance through involvement. Like pornography, depression puts us under scrutiny, so that our looking is no longer inoculated by who we are, but instead reminds us that seeing clearly (according to its concentrated yet accumulative structure, the anamorphosis of suffering itself) with a powerful yet manifestly brief and finite purpose – that which is the cause of the seeing itself and so infinitely circular and purposeless – can sustain itself but not us, for we must be given a clear way out, an exit that pornography embodies and that depression occludes. When we are present we can pass over the world, find our distance in our own proximity, but whatever strips us of this has the world absorb our focus to the point that only the seen exists, and thought itself becomes that which is seen, and it must end and yet it cannot end, for reality cannot end, without already having ended.

While pornography's solution is to allow us to explode, depression, having no solution aside from itself (existing in perpetuity), has us implode instead. Pornography maintains outside itself, as the beyond of it, an habitually permeable force-field, 'the horizon of the real and of meaning as the vanishing point',[65] whereas depression swallows it all, forcing the horizon to the foreground, extracting all vanishing from meaning except that of its having already vanished, and before your very eyes, over and over, its emptiness consolidated in its simply having been observed to vanish – in order that it can then reappear, as that which is vanished.

Although the hyperrealism of pornography can temporarily remove 'the distance of meaning, the gap, the difference, the smallest possible gap'[66] for the sake of a viewer's short-term vicarious indulgence, its inevitable seeping into the simulacrum of our sex lives means that its integral promise of non-permanence is one that could not ultimately be made good on. Unlike with depression, the distance fails us bit by bit, and yet these incremental adjustments look to undermine locally what depression undermines whole-sale. And while this may appear a warning, which in some sense it is, it is not therefore an admonishment, for how could I reprove the partial debunking of a distance that is itself dishonest? The connection here with death is some-thing Baudrillard repeatedly acknowledges, as in the following passage:

> Everything that is imposed by its objective presence, that is, by abjec-tion, everything that no longer possesses either the secret or the lightness of absence, everything that like the rotting body, is given over solely to the material operation of its decomposition, everything which, with no illusion possible, is surrendered to the sole operation of the real, everything which, without mask, makeup or face, is given over to the pure operation of sex and death – all this can be called obscene and pornographic.[67]

Implosion in the case of depression involves a dehumanizing concentration of conscious activity that, due to a breakdown of self-identifying relations, finds itself unable to keep the world out – while pornography's inevitable det-onation in contradistinction propels us back into the world in fragments, thus restoring our distance from and at the same time our integration with the world and its myriad associative meanings. When something implodes the pressure from outside is greater than that inside, while the exact opposite is true when an explosion occurs. Relevant to our concerns, this variant dir-ection of pressure represents the respective absence and presence of desire. While there is desire there is also a foil for distance and a means of matching and exceeding the existence of the world around you; where desire is missing the sense of being anyone or anything is squeezed into an increasingly tight space, the concentration of a zero into its negative, the world's everywhere imploded, a vanishing point of meaning and of meaning's eventual airless contraction into non-meaning.

That simulation can be reborn in this implosive eventuality presupposes some internal reversing of pressure, some equalization of the outer active pressure and the internal folding. There is nothing left to uphold the diffe-rence and so the difference dissolves to leave something shrunken yet formid-ably dense. A new imperviousness and a new distance are formed, both at the cost of the failing simulations that gave rise to them. Distance is no longer a relaxed falling into the world, but a self-imposed refusal to despair at the groundless alterity, an admission of defeat but not an acceptance. Distance becomes floating, and while this suspended state implies superiority, and there is no denying that a sensation as of being elevated is present, it's the distinction of the destroyed, of the collapsed that finds it can continue, the gristle that is not swallowed but coughed back up, not into the world but into (inside) its perimeter. The resulting invulnerability is the product of having already been pulverized, but still there remains a cautiousness not to return to, not to reconstruct, what it was that proved weak. The simulation therefore born out of this annihilation is survival pure and simple, nothing more. The found conditions of continuing are thereby upheld, and while they are known to be simulative in their own way, they do not set up in replication of the real, and nor do they oppose it, rather they exist as something that is only because of all that it is not, and so a simulation of the reality of simulation's failure.

Notes

1   Baudrillard, *The Agony of Power*, 94.
2   Baudrillard, *Simulacra and Simulation*, 48.
3   Ibid., 47.
4   Jean Baudrillard, *Cool Memories* (New York: Verso, 1990), 17.
5   'Decidedly, joggers are the true Latter Day Saints and the protagonists of an easy-does-it Apocalypse. Nothing evokes the end of the world more than a man running straight ahead on a beach, swathed in the sounds of his Walkman, cocooned in the solitary sacrifice of his energy, indifferent even to catastrophes since he expects destruction to come only as the fruit of his own efforts, from exhausting the energy of a body that has in his own eyes become useless.' (Baudrillard, *America*, 36–37.)
6   Baudrillard, *Cool Memories*, 134.
7   Baudrillard, *Simulacra and Simulation*, 160.
8   Baudrillard, *The Vital Illusion*, 36.
9   Apocalypse Then becomes quite literally, if virtually, Apocalypse Now.
10 'The only suspense which remains is that of knowing how far the world can derealize itself before succumbing to its reality deficit or, conversely, how far it can hyperrealize itself before succumbing to an excess of reality (the point when, having become perfectly real, truer than true, it will fall into the clutches of total simulation)' (Baudrillard, *The Perfect Crime* (New York: Verso, 1996), 4).
11 Baudrillard, *The Intelligence of Evil*, 12.
12 See E. M. Cioran, *The Trouble with Being Born*, trans. Richard Howard (New York: Arcade, 1998), 32.
13 E. M. Cioran, *On the Heights of Despair*, trans. Ilinca Zarifopol-Johnston (Chicago, IL: University of Chicago Press, 1992), 52.
14 Baudrillard, *The Vital Illusion*, 11.
15 Jean Baudrillard, 'Hysteresis of the Millennium', in *The Illusion of the End* (Cambridge: Polity Press, 1994), 117.

16 Ibid., 119, (emphasis in the original).

17 Baudrillard, *The Intelligence of Evil*, 126.

18 Baudrillard, *Baudrillard Live: Selected Interviews*, 116.

19 As Baudrillard writes: 'the opportunity to disappear is as important as the chance to appear, anyway it is equivalent in a way to disappearance, the equivalent of the chance to appear and in fact only that which has appeared can disappear; when one can no longer disappear in any way, one no longer exists' (Paul Sutton, 'Endangered Species? An Interview with Jean Baudrillard,' *Angelaki*, 2:3 (1997), 217–24). And it is somewhere amid this penumbral state of appearance that Fabian finds himself.

20 Richard Peace, *Dostoyevsky: An Examination of the Major Novels* (Cambridge: Cambridge University Press, 1971), 19.

21 Baudrillard, *Fatal Strategies*, 226.

22 He informs us rather bluntly that any such well-trodden theoretical justifications (be they utilitarian or broadly Nietzschean) will necessarily be unable to encapsulate his motivations: 'Let's not rely on what those stupid philosophers said.'

23 Not unlike British serial killer Dennis Nilsen ('I was always killing myself, but it was always the bystander who died'), Joaquin's fellow inmate, a man who has committed numerous murders, also confesses to no longer being human.

24 Fyodor Dostoevsky, *Crime and Punishment* (New York: Vintage, 1993), 420.

25 Baudrillard, *Baudrillard Live: Selected Interviews*, 183.

26 Ibid., 34.

27 Known clinically as 'depersonalization disorder.'

28 Although Eliza does make an appearance before her death when Diaz has her looking like the potential murderer of her own children, as she moves behind them at the edge of a steep incline only to embrace them protectively instead. Her seduction (matched by our own at this point) has her appear to herself and to us.

29 Baudrillard, *Fatal Strategies*, 213.

30 Ibid., 211.

31 Baudrillard, *The Vital Illusion*, 43.

32 Ibid., 44.

33 Ibid., 46–7.

34 Baudrillard, *Fatal Strategies*, 30.

35 Ibid., 45.

36 Ibid., 48.

37 Ibid., 47.

38 'Like speed – which is the sole perfect expression of mobility, because it is unlike movement (which has meaning or direction) – obesity no longer has any meaning or direction either; it goes nowhere and no longer has anything to do with movement: it is the ecstasy of movement' (Baudrillard, *Fatal Strategies*, 55).

39 'Things live only on the basis of their disappearance, and, if one wishes to interpret them with entire lucidity, one must do so as a function of their disappearance. There is no better analytical grid' (Baudrillard, *Why Hasn't Everything Already Disappeared?*, 31).

40 Jean Baudrillard, 'Radical Thought', http://www.egs.edu/faculty/jean-baudrillard/articles/radical-thought/. (accessed 16 June 2014).

41 Baudrillard, *The Vital Illusion*, 5.

42 Cloning 'is a technological disappearance into artificial survival, corresponding to the elimination of the human as human. And this process of disappearance has already begun' (Baudrillard, *The Agony of Power*, 123).

43   Baudrillard, *Why Hasn't Everything Already Disappeared?*, 62.

44   Baudrillard, *Symbolic Exchange and Death*, 114.

45   Baudrillard, *The Vital Illusion*, 6.

46   Ibid., 9.

47   Jean Baudrillard, *In the Shadow of the Silent Majorities* (Los Angeles: Semiotext(e), 1983), 55–56, (emphasis in the original).

48   Ibid., 22.

49   Ibid., 21.

50   Baudrillard, *The Vital Illusion*, 35. BwO is the abbreviation for 'body without organs', a Deleuzian concept utilizing Antonin Artaud's original phrasing.

51   Ibid., 15–16.

52   Baudrillard, *The Perfect Crime*, 39.

53   Baudrillard, *The Vital Illusion*, 35.

54   Ibid., 38.

55   Ibid., 65–66.

56   Which is 'at bottom, the profound tactic of simulation' (Baudrillard, *In the Shadow of the Silent Majorities*, 120).

57   Baudrillard, *The Perfect Crime*, 46.

58   Baudrillard, *The Vital Illusion*, 48.

59   Not another's memory of you, for example (see Douglas Hofstadter, *I Am a Strange Loop* (New York: Basic Books, 2007)). And not your life's work or your children either.

60   Baudrillard, *The Vital Illusion*, 64.

61   Baudrillard, *Simulacra and Simulation*, 28.

62   And what is pataphysics but the understanding of death, however small and however numerous?

63   Baudrillard, *The Conspiracy of Art*, 124.

64   For 'it is in fact reality and obviousness that are obscene. Truth should be laughable. You could imagine a culture where everyone spontaneously rolled with laughter when someone said: this is true, this is real' (Baudrillard, *The Conspiracy of Art*, 164).

65   Baudrillard, *Simulacra and Simulation*, 31.

66   Ibid.

67   Baudrillard, *Fatal Strategies*, 81.

Chapter 4

THE HYPERACTIVITY OF OBJECTS

Are objects the enemy? After all, 'they are the ones that interrogate us, and we are summoned to answer them,' and finding that we cannot answer, even though 'the answer is included in the question',[1] we instead quail in the presence of our very own materials. The object is a lie, but it is our lie. It is the decoration of our own mistrust – that essential mistrust that comes with anything that we have not chosen to believe.

The object is an equivalence, not to itself, but to the sullied religion of the senses. And it is not the object that refuses to dance with us, but we who refuse to dance with it – even in the midst of our mutual dancing. And how would we come to trust what is always there but never there? The levels of trust that gravitate around us are directly proportionate to a disbelief in ourselves as objects. For we do not disappear to ourselves through postulations of immateriality, but through the perceived misalignment of consciousness and the objects that are experienced as essentially not only not there for us, but not there even for themselves. The object is hyperactively nowhere, and to fully materialize ourselves as objects is to suffer a similar fate. The immanent problem with the object being that for all its activity it is never beyond itself, and it is this beyond that emulsifies human consciousness, that locates it without locating it, that acknowledges the object without becoming it. All that is aleatoric in human existence, all that is decentred and spiralling, is no more or less mysterious than the blandly automatic, the inductive reasoning that fills each moment with the day-after-day-after-day. And so we too are nowhere, and that nowhere is our peace – even if we feel like we've been transplanted there against our will, as if something in us has died in order to get there. It is why our nowhere needs words around it, giant edifices of belief circling our vacated perspective, with similarly disintegrated beings there as company for us, for to be nowhere in among the world, alongside the panicked busyness of humans being humans, is to every day be reminded of the ghost you've become, as if a return to where you were was not only possible but desirable. And what is this nowhere, if it is not felt like this? We must remain a problem for the world, subject to the interrogation of objects, a blank space in an otherwise variegated explosion of colour and density. There is no other way to be nowhere without remaking that nowhere as somewhere else: 'every detail of the world is perfect if it is not referred to some larger set'.[2]

4.1 The Resurrected Object

Every time the object dies it appears fainter when it returns, and the reason is not any inherent faintness, but our wanting more from it while expecting less. And even putting it to one side, no longer subjecting it to human scrutiny, does nothing to restore the object's faded/fading substance: refusing to touch the object you've already touched, in the hope that the thing touched and the act of touching might be reversed, might return to an earlier state, is nothing but the futile transference of our own innocence. But then we only ever want innocence for others, never for ourselves, for even when we regret its absence in us, we still prefer the mediated experience of it to its being re-established, if that were possible. The object gets progressively lost to us the more we find it, even if we refuse to find it again, because what was found came apart in the finding, and what life remains is in the seeing we can't enact. The seeing destroys and the object destroys, and only the simulation remains, for it never reaches outside itself, so that in the end the collecting of objects compounds not only the reality of our death, but our surviving there:

> Objects allow us to apply the work of mourning to ourselves right now, in everyday life, and this in turn allows us to live – to live regressively, no doubt, but at least to live. A person who collects is dead, but he literally survives himself through his collection, which (even while he lives) duplicates him infinitely, beyond death, *by integrating death itself into the series, into the cycle.*[3]

Thus the principal mistake is this simple imagining of distance: that it was reduced and that it can be increased. Forget Heidegger's tool, and forget Descartes' wax: there is only the corpse, which when held at arm's length you become and when united with you escape. The corpse is the one true object (or what remains of such a quaint experiment), because what you imagined of it when it moved has been observed to disappear. Objects cease to function all the time, but do not through this discontinuity of function become objects – or if they do, or seem to, they do so according to the model of the corpse. But now it seems even the corpse has been touched and cannot go back.

Our fate has not been to be 'museumified' as 'living specimens in the spectral light of ethnology, or of antiethnology',[4] but instead made corpse by the medical science that keeps us alive. We have watched ourselves getting slowly

ingested by our brains/bodies, until we are no longer ghosts in the machine but
have become instead ghost-like machines, reified phantoms. Massacred in our
billions we've nevertheless continued to live: not a decision but a prescription,
for how else do you describe objects that move all by themselves? The naivety
is to think that we have located what was before somehow placeless – when
souls and egos and phenomenological states were currency – but what gets
eaten eventually gets digested and passed as waste: the body a ghosted object,
murdered and made sorcery, sucked clean of itself, a Pinocchio requiring not
the reality of boyhood but the reality of wood. Corpses are easier to see, as if
a cruel spell has been undone, a demented affliction remedied. The corpse's
edge is everywhere:

> Such wastes drop so that I might live, until, from loss to loss, nothing
> remains in me and my entire body falls beyond the limit-cadere, cadaver.
> If dung signifies the other side of the border, the place where I am not
> and which permits me to be, the corpse, the most sickening of wastes, is
> a border that has encroached upon everything.[5]

The concretion of self as the human animal is a false economy of science,
for its transubstantiation does not rid us of it, but zombifies it instead. Our
disbelief in the self (the secularized soul), language-made placeholder for a
non-existent centrality, the original act of hyperstition, only makes it even less
human than before, and gives it a taste for flesh into the bargain. In becoming
undead the self enacts its incorporeality as a contamination of the bodily. In
removing its objects, science does not bring about its disappearance, but re-
establishes its non-materiality.

The asylum is a reaffirmation of context, a soundproof vitrine of mirrored
glass. From the outside you can see that you are outside, and being outside, not
hearing the sounds of those inside, is the crucial difference. This detachment is
scientific. All there is to see is that we are seeing. The object does not speak to
us, it reflects our seeing back at us, lets us talk to ourselves about how the object
is diffuse in ways we didn't properly understand before we isolated it. At arm's
length is a safe distance to avoid contamination. To work too closely with the
world is done so at the risk of sacrificing anthropological privilege. That which
we understand we can distance ourselves from. And so the asylums are closed
down, its objects heard alongside the objects we work with, and madness is the
continuum it always was,[6] however much it pretended to be something else.
The mad are only partly so and even that residual madness is seen to emanate
from concealments that are the same for all. The madness is not ignoring,
not escaping: the madness is inhabiting the mystery, letting the object get too
close. The madness is the unsegmented continuum. Science is the opposite of

madness because it isolates, taxonomizes, specializes … Likewise science does not ignore the object, but instead manipulates and controls it – it's the game the mad would play if they'd maintained their distance. The mad know that this control, as much as the self-imposition of ignorance, is the mummification of something living: the work of the object on the subject – 'the destruction of the self through voluntary servitude'.[7] They still hear something they cannot explain screaming to get out. The mad know what it is that's dangerous, and it has nothing to do with illusion or delusion, but with their irreversible removal.

Accumulation is the strangest sickness. It's a compulsive disorder that goes by the name 'culture'. Its premise is a simple one: nothing can ever disappear. And whereas the physical laws of the universe might seem to corroborate this fundamental ethos, it is our addiction to form that marks us out as being unwell. Change reminds us of an immanent loneliness, where loneliness is in essence the inability to remember who we were at some earlier stage. Oddly enough, loneliness has little to do with the other, and everything to do with our successful appropriation and assimilation of that other. And so we believe that if we can see our memories outside of us, that what is memorized through being seen will mask what we cannot remember: what it is like to be anything other than what we are now. The apex, the art of this sickness, this neurasthenia, is the loneliness we avoid through manifesting memories we never had, of being where we weren't until we discovered it and where we've never been.

Our confusion is such that we cannot allow the existence of the other . Even if it must remain other, it becomes the tiniest of voids amid the clutter of our failed appropriations: 'We require a visible past, a visible continuum, a visible myth of origin, which reassures us about our end. Because finally we have never believed in them.'[8] Even the Christian mystics relied on visions (of Christ, Satan, the Apocalypse, etc.) to illustrate their beliefs, beliefs that in turn acted like anamorphic mirrors to make those very visions possible. And in what sense is seeing still believing when seeing is just one more example of mystification? To distinguish veridical perception from hallucination the object must be accessed, and the object is only ever accessed in ways that undermine sight. For perhaps 'it has no desire at all to be analysed and observed, and taking this process for a challenge (which it is) it's answering with a challenge'.[9] I see Christ or I see a table, and the error is to imagine the object knows which is which, or that either is not hidden through the very process of being seen, 'or better yet: that the object only pretends to obey the laws of physics because it gives so much pleasure to the observer. / Such would be the pataphysics (the science of imaginary solutions) that lies in wait for all physics at its inadmissible limits'.[10] Such would be the polite and patient abrogation at the heart of all human experience.

Death is not the erasure of presence but its fulfilment. Whatever completes has at least been, even if it never completed, for nothing completes. But there has been an end of sorts and a sensory eradication, so that what is ended is pursued only so far – within the dimensions of repetition and manipulation, for nothing new is demanded that hasn't already happened. The distortions of putrefaction are not lesser instances of presence, they are what presence always was, only without the misconception that it was life that somehow made the pursuit open-ended when life was the constraint that put possibility on a par with action, dreaming with what is dreamt.

As we demystify the past, doing irreparable violence to its secrets, we imagine that we are also thereby demystifying the future. We have witnessed what has been and have fewer and fewer reasons not to expect more of the same. The changes that happen do so within an abiding climate of sameness. However, the opposite is also true: by laying out as much of the past as we can behind us, we make more of a vacuum of the future. For the more historical detail we find, the less the past looks like the past and the more it looks like the present and so the more we understand it and the less we understand our understanding of it. The future, of which nothing can be seen, is conjectured into oblivion as if we'd been looking at it for centuries, which of course we have.

'Repatriating' or 'retrospective hallucination,' though more artificial than simple displacement, is nevertheless a more honest practice. To put something back as if it hadn't been moved, as if origins carry more weight than the story that emanated from them, is at least a recognition of our disappointments. For though such attempts to correct the narratives by starting over may be crude, they are themselves inseparable from the narratives, and so acknowledge both the futility of origins and their abiding potency. These resumptions need more momentum, need to be more hopeful, than the original starting points, otherwise their futility is seen too clearly. Worth is ballasted in these new beginnings in such a way that the possibilities for change are thought to have been undermined and neutered, whereas the corrective change itself is invariably not the curtailment of possibilities it seems to be, but the imposition of possibilities that far from being restorative are the rotted-out figments of a falsified context that only prove ruinous, having already re-inaugurated something that can no longer naturally perish. The faces of these reorientated objects are not so much comparable to those faces in funeral homes, which are at least the retouched (improved upon) faces of somebody at the time of their death, but instead those same faces remade to look like the unborns they started off as (heads draped in a corpse's caul, phimosis of their impossible birth), a haunting reminder that when our disappointments turn us backwards we not only fail to undo our errors but spawn the hideous into the bargain – even if that hideousness lies only in our itch for facility and the particular direction in which it is employed.

4.2 The Exploding Corpse

We have long stopped waiting to find out how it is we will disappear, and have instead been moving towards it. And while that movement may appear insignificant and riddled with retrograde steps, the desire to make a 'spectacle of our destruction'[11] is increasingly prevalent, and even if it must be a whimper, that whimper must explode, must scatter itself as wide as possible, our blood and viscera, bits of brain and spinal column, crammed into and pushed out through the arterial chaos of our eulogy in waiting, through the diagrammatic web of our pre-exploded consciousness. And this making art of going is not the making art of life that Alexander Nehamas finds advocated in Nietzsche,[12] not the shaping of a life, but a violent becoming-formless, becoming octopoid, bursting tentacles of extravagant number ever outwards, reaching and growing and vanishing, all collapsing into one glorious insignificance; and it is this exploding, this exploded state, that properly knows us, that knows us as we know ourselves, that knows by unknowing: 'For nothing is identical to itself. We are never identical to ourselves, except, perhaps, in sleep and in death.'[13] This is what it means to be made real in death, not as some statuesque figure having a final mark of completion laid upon it, but as a scattering of information, its cement dissolving, its self-awareness coming apart at a million seams at once.

What better way to escape the fate of the perfect crime, that traceless and sanitized horror of positivity, rationality and truth, than to have your corpse explode its evidential mass into so many corners that no amount of cleaning can eradicate its existence? What better safeguard against transparency, against an easy solution? For if 'we must save the traces of the illusory world's definitive opacity and mystery',[14] what better way to do it than by shattering the puzzle into more pieces than we could ever hope to count? What better dream than this chaotic dream in which a home is found? What better tribute to this lived-out paradox than a chronic fanfare of kabooms!? And do not forget, our corpses have already started to explode, are now exploding, long before we've fully committed to death.

And what of the world's explosion? What of that deep inward explosion, that inner expansion, right down to the Standard Model and beyond, to its projected enlargement or else outside this universe to its parallels and so to chaos? And what too of the thought that the world returns our gaze, 'that things discover us at the same time that we discover them'?[15] For just as we have ceased waiting on our discovery, the world too need no longer wait for us;

and what's more, we find a template for our explosion there: by exploring the possible implications of the observer effect's fragmentation and reversibility, the world in bits looking back at us, we come to see that our reinvention in death is happening all around us and death is just a terminological conceit for what has already happened, the fundamental irony of interpretative feedback, of nonlinearity, of indecision, of subatomic spin. But if, as perfect prey to the perfect crime, we are potentiated as *victims of absence*, it is this very potenti-ation that provides us with our one last hope for exile (that Bollywood star whose advanced heart disease is revealed by his would-be-assassin's bullet), the instrument of destruction that first alerts you to your fatal sickness:

> It is the event horizon, as they say in physics, beyond which nothing makes sense and nothing at all may be discovered. That, if there is any, is the secret of the universe. As a metaphor, I would say that at the core of every human being and every thing there is such a fundamentally inaccessible secret. That is the vital illusion of which Nietzsche spoke, the glass wall of truth and illusion. From our rational point of view, this may appear rather desperate and could even justify something like pes-simism. But from the point of view of singularity, of alterity, of secret and seduction, it is, on the contrary, our only chance: our last chance. In this sense, the Perfect Crime is an hypothesis of radiant optimism.[16]

The world, like us, becomes both more and less mysterious through explo-sion, through a disappearance in which traces proliferate. And the world as it watches us dying, watches us reclaim death (and death's alterity) as a means of continuing, sees our prized human secrets meld with its own, at which point all *raw feels* become homeless, become the *raw feels* of nothing in particular and also of everything in this absence of particularity. All witnessing is revealed as self-witnessing, and all notion of self a peripheral joke made, in bad taste, to disguise the world to itself, to maintain death as a point of departure amidst the evacuation of all possible notion of place, a placeless stepping off into the impossibility of place. 'At any event, the rules are no longer those of subjects and truth',[17] but are the rules of no rules, except that there must be rules and there aren't any.

The world's activity must be acknowledged as whatever it takes to make demystification implausible. The world's gloriously imperfect crime is that 'nothing is totally evidentiary without becoming an enigma. Reality, in general, is too evident to be true'.[18] That the world returns our gaze is less enigmatic in this regard, a truth for which we lack evidential foundation, but therein lies its explanatory value: the literal nonentity of consciousness. It is the two-way mirror hidden by the mirror. And considered as such it is not just some aleatory happening, when at times the world does not rush to meet us as we've come to expect. The malfunction is not ours alone, and is not even a malfunction. When we cannot be in-the-world with the ease that makes this being-in possible, it is not simply a crisis of a mind too mindful of itself, but a consequence of something else entirely, a potentially less terrifying inversion: the world does not want us there. Consequently, we do not own our suffering in the manner in which we've become accustomed to owning our suffering, owning it as a means of fully potentializing its ungrounding of our identity, that in turn becomes the very grounds of that core identification. We have got used to how 'simulacra have become reality', how the 'simulacrum now hides, not the truth, but the fact that there is none, that is to say, the continuation of Nothingness'.[19] This is the discomfort we know, the distance we accept as being integral to our having meaning, the meaning that kills us; but now in addition to this we have not only the absence of truth, the gross inflation of nothingness, but a subterfuge masking a further subterfuge, a nothing that like us has imagined itself a something, an unreality that proves at times as hostile to us as we are to it.

'The epiphany of the real is the twilight of the concept',[20] and we (subject and object, man and world) come to this epiphany together, synching our abuses of the other, dyadic realities denied our reality, conceptualizations dying to be real. For this is the only possibility left for reality to assert itself, the real having been overrun with simulacra, achieved via a self-awareness lacking a self, via an expulsion of forms and an explosion into formlessness, into deconceptualization. The two-way mirror divides our mutual nothingness, and while there should be harmony here, the mirror looking both ways achieves a whirling velocity that sucks both empty perspectives inside to throw them back out whichever side they land. But the mirror leaves a mark, a taint, and it is this mark that results in the disharmonious resurgence of the concept in the guise of the real. Thomas Nagel tells of the view from nowhere, that view from outside ourselves that conflicts with our subjectivity, but here we arrive at its apex and its nadir: the purest objectivity reduced to dust, invisible dust.

The world is not worth our interest, and we for sure are not worth the world's.[21] Reduced to what happens we are the dullest parade in the universe, and while 'it is difficult to be more apathetic and more indifferent than the facts themselves', we somehow manage it: it's 'how we have become orphans'.[22] And as orphans we have somehow become pointless and passionless and disinvested, mimicking the lost parentage of the world in which we find ourselves ignored, while at the same time perpetuating our own brand of distinctness. There's room to accept this wasteland of man and world without, it seems, buying into the possibility of waste: there's nothing that cannot be eaten by something (we have mealworms and waxworms eating our plastic, for instance). Our very pointlessness and disinvestment is consuming itself and finding resolution in this very absence of a surplus. Our road is the Möbius strip and we are eating and shitting as we go, and eating and shitting forever, in a loop, purposefully ridding ourselves of purpose, or rather any purpose extraneous to this somnambulist autophagy. The dull mired in dullness adapt their palates accordingly, and do not risk raising their faces from the plate. The problem is that while we may be boring, we are not bored, or if we are, we are not bored enough. We need to become more bored in order to become less boring. Our lack of passion and purpose and investment, not being exhaustive, is self-sustaining: our utopia has been realized. And who but the dullest and the most obtuse would go and realize a utopia? Unless it's the beyond of the utopia that we want, which of course it is. Maybe then this dullness is our new bedrock, and we are instead delirious and becoming more so, as our future is given the chance to happen again and never stop happening. And so from the minimal utopia the maximal utopia, from dullness a fresh delirium, from a boring planet and a boring populace a fever pitch of boredom, from the gluttony of the same the starvation of difference, from the orphanage a land of surplus parents. But do not imagine some shift has occurred here, some breaching of the strip, for it's the same view, only now we see the strip within the strip.

We are at pains to decipher the illusion before the illusion deciphers us, and yet both these decipherings have already been completed, many times – the problem being, unsurprisingly, that we do not like the conclusions at which we arrived. Nothing we found was found bearable, nothing was an improvement on the illusion:

> On pain of dread, we have to decipher the world and therefore wipe out the initial illusoriness of the world. We can bear neither the void, nor the secret, nor pure appearance. And why should we decipher it instead of letting its illusion shine out.[23]

Why not speculate on the real world as if it were a thing for us, not as a disentanglement but as a deeper embrace?

Nothing is never without a trace: it ceases to exist, ceases to be nothing, the moment it fulfils the idea we have for it. Nothing has no presence in reality, for there is always presence: nothing always leaves a mark. Our idea of nothing involves additional subtractions, and we must return to the world to see not the incompleteness of that world but the incompleteness of our representation of it. We conflate death and nothing so as to not know death, as a way of never having to confront our fate, which cannot really be our fate, because this nothing and so this death is only an idea, and an idea that the world cannot replicate. When disappearance can never be completed there is some solace in completing it, completing it for ourselves, even if only because it must remain abstract and therefore never truly habitable. This is what it means to retrieve from the world the secret of death, to give death back to ourselves as worldly impossibility.

> To recover the trace of the nothing, of the incompleteness, the imperfection of the crime, we have, then, to take something away from the reality of the world. To recover the constellation of the mystery [secret], we have to take something away from the accumulation of reality and language. [...] Behind every fragment of reality, something has to have disappeared in order to ensure the continuity of the nothing – without, however, yielding to the temptation of annihilation, for disappearance has to remain a living disappearance, and the trace of the crime a living trace.[24]

4.3 Philip K. Dick Did Not Exist

Philip K. Dick did not exist. He was the first person to notice. He kept saying it over and over. He wrote 44 novels, perhaps more, saying how he wasn't there, and how you weren't either – you: the person reading his books, absorbing the words as if someone had written them.

Pace Baudrillard, science fiction does not add 'its own possibilities',[25] it subtracts at will what does not happen, subtracts the past that never arrived. The possibilities are always found, never manufactured.

Dick also knew how utopias work by not working, are realized through not being realized, how utopias are internally inconsistent by necessity: without some flaw they cannot fulfil our requirements for the utopian, but then if they are flawed they cannot, by definition, be utopias. And the reason for the flaw is nothing but the need to recognize the utopia as a utopia, something that cannot be done from the inside out. Yet he did not discard their possibility, for he knew as well that impossibility is the bedrock of reality and reality is not real: impossibility is what cannot be according to what is not. This is how 'the real [...] has become our true Utopia',[26] something itself in need of being simulated, of enacting its own internal inconsistency, a circumscribed replication of a blind assimilation (the real as dream), in order that the impossible be made once again possible via the impossibility of the one true demesne of the possible. Dick's science fiction, then, is not what could be, but what might have been, and so what is. It is not so much the future that is undecided but the past, for until our world is behind us it does not even exist – and this is not historical revisionism, this is physics. The future depotentializes the past, so reality is always the past imagining the future has already happened.

And where we are ... where is that? And so we must return to the between state, the abstraction of the *when* and the *how* and the *where* which do not yet exist, which must first look forwards in order to look backwards – without knowing which is which, or if the two are different. On the perplexities and deceptions of time, Dick writes:

> To know (i.e., gnosis) and to remember (anamnesis) are one. And why do we know? Through the training of the intellect; it is an intellectual matter. And why did I remember? It had to do with time. The illusion of time and the breaking of that illusion.[27]

Although Dick found 'no room for the imaginary' – only various clues and signs and signals unearthed in numerous religious literatures, and of course the world itself revealed in glimpses, in a fragmented codex, available only to one engaged in repeated temporal excursions, in time-travel no less, in a retracing of steps in order to substantiate those steps – if 'a system reaches its own limits and becomes saturated, a reversal is produced [and] something else takes place, in the imaginary as well'.[28] Dick made it his personal mission to counter the future's depotentialization of the past, to reinvigorate what the future had unmade, to remember the past as if it was still happening, which of course it was/is. It is human reality that has become derealized, that has become the ultimate work of (perpetual) imagination. Dick found himself denuded of this everydayness of imagination, and had no place else to go but outside the simulation, backwards in time where, like some god from the future, he could reimagine humanity as an inescapable repression into which he might not have entered, into which we too might not have entered.

Dick found himself in the fiction of the real, and in many variegated forms, in characters and adopted personas, sought a way out. In his hands the quotidian did not exist: there were no benign and inconsequential hallucinations. There was a cosmic humanness, a universe tainted with our experience of it, each of us a Palmer Eldritch undoing our own suffering for the sake of some mutual assimilation of the dream by the dream and for the dream. But this saturation point did not, for Dick, mark an end to what might happen, to what might be made to have happened, but a catalyst, a further emancipatory waking dream on the fringes of this all-encompassing dream that did not promise a future or even a past, but instead a confrontation with the sempiternal imperative to return and see the same over and over until it can be seen differently, seen without being seen. To return then bent on slaughter. To find the God that has not first found himself. To imagine him not only as a mirror might, but as a billion such mirror images might imagine themselves. For it is not that Dick goes through the mirror, in allegiance to some 'golden age of transcendence',[29] but steps inside instead to find he has already been through it innumerable times only to enter it again the moment he leaves – the mirror less a mirror more a revolving door.

Dick knows, as did Louis-Ferdinand Céline, that to place 'your trust in men is to get yourself killed a little',[30] and he feels himself dying, feels the world around him dying, senses acutely that for our own sake the world should stage a comeback.

Dick's madness was his failure to become indifferent, his refusal to relinquish secrets, to relinquish the hidden, even when everything that could be exposed had been exposed, or at the very least when the techniques of the world's divulgence had been put in place so as to permanently substitute an epistemological method for what was once a continuum of recalcitrant mystery, placing himself there as primary operative. What seemed to be the end of so much of what passes for human momentum was no such end for Dick. For it was the same relentless tenacity – that revealed the world at its holographic, self-mimicking and duplicitous worst – that had him go not through and not beyond but further inside, to enact the secret that is anything at all, even when anything is substantively a nothing and epistemology itself a contrivance. But what does it mean to go deeper into that which has no depth, to push on to further submergence in what you yourself have shown to be exhausted by its surface? In some sense this is a Pessoa-like advocacy of the relative merits of the impossible. However, there is something else being attempted here, something that you might think warrants all the many allegations of lunacy, but something, let's suppose, that warrants our admiration more: for 'only the last order can still truly interest us',[31] a last order for which we are no longer forced to wait.

Notes

1   Baudrillard, *Simulacra and Simulation*, 75.
2   Baudrillard, *The Intelligence of Evil*, 108.
3   Jean Baudrillard, *The System of Objects* (New York: Verso, 1996), 97, (emphasis in the original).
4   Baudrillard, *Simulacra and Simulation*, 8.
5   Julia Kristeva, *Powers of Horror. An Essay on Abjection* (New York: Columbia University Press, 1980), 3.
6   And all of us its stricken cattle, for are we not 'being made to swallow, on every level, a strange bone meal – all of these ground-up messages, all of this meal of advertising and media production, this giant, milled junk heap of the news that we are stuffed with – like the meal made of bone, corpses and carcasses that we stuff our cows with – it is all bringing our species closer to spongiform encephalopathy' (Baudrillard, *The Agony of Power*, 99).
7   Baudrillard, *The Transparency of Evil*, 78.

8   Baudrillard, *Simulacra and Simulation*, 10.
9   Baudrillard, *Fatal Strategies*, 109.
10 Ibid., 112.
11 Baudrillard, *The Vital Illusion*, 68.
12 Alexander Nehamas, *Nietzsche: Life as Literature* (Cambridge, MA: Harvard University Press, 1987).
13 Baudrillard, *The Vital Illusion*, 70.
14 Ibid., 74.
15 Ibid., 76.
16 Ibid., 80–81.
17 Baudrillard, *The Perfect Crime*, 56.
18 Baudrillard, 'Radical Thought'.
19 Ibid.
20 Ibid.
21 If the simulation argument is true, and the world and everything in it is a computer simulation, then the simulators too are bored and have forgotten all about us, having first exhausted anything of interest our deluded meanderings might yield.
22 Baudrillard, 'Radical Thought'.
23 Baudrillard, *The Perfect Crime*, 2.
24 Baudrillard, *The Perfect Crime*, 3–4.
25 Baudrillard, *Simulacra and Simulation*, 122.
26 Ibid., 123.
27 Philip K. Dick, *The Exegesis of Philip K. Dick*, ed. Pamela Jackson and Jonathan Lethem (New York: Houghton Mifflin Harcourt, 2011), 853.
28 Baudrillard, *Simulacra and Simulation*, 123.
29 Ibid., 125.
30 Louis-Ferdinand Céline, *Journey to the End of the Night* (New York: New Directions Books, 2006), 152.
31 Baudrillard, *Simulacra and Simulation*, 127.

Chapter 5

THE UNNAMABLE CATASTROPHE

Catastrophe is always the crisis that doesn't happen, the one watched for that doesn't arrive, in spite of our watching, in spite of what our watching has been known to induce. (We find ourselves transported back to the subjective idealism of George Berkeley, as if anyone had actually escaped it.) Catastrophe's only risk is that it risks nothing and, in risking nothing, risks us. The sense of panic we come to know is not that something will happen, but that nothing will happen, and that no amount of vigilance could ever make it happen. How could we not constitute the universe, when we see it every day modelled on the dreams we had of it?

While implosion leaves us perennially unquenched, explosion is at least suggestive of conclusion, of revolt and release, of an end to waiting. For 'an explosion is always a promise, it is our hope',[1] and no true promise, no promise that is prized in virtue of its essentiality alone, is ever made good on. Catastrophe never completes, but more than that, for in never completing it becomes the real, the real as simulation of itself. Crisis has a finality that cannot be absorbed, and so even when it arrives it doesn't, because its arriving does nothing to quell the need to wait to see what happens, does nothing to put an end to itself: the explosion keeps going, outwards and outwards until every dispersal, every direction, turns into yet another opportunity for inconclusivity, for waiting – the appropriation of event by the future. If events are allowed to just happen, then their never-ending extension into the future is jeopardized: the naming of an event must also be its unnaming, its dissection, the manufacture of swamp materials from concrete, the noun made irretrievably inexorable in order that its continued existence as something yet to happen may be exacted over and over.

Who would ever notice a real catastrophe (a crisis) if one should occur? Its impact would be that of an unexplained pause, an evacuated place and time that gets filled with aftermath, the aftermath of the non-event. It's for this reason that extreme acts of terrorism come at us like a bad dream, unsettling and despicable but ultimately cartoonish. And despite terrorism's being so excessively obvious, so caricaturally empty, this does not prevent it also being

obscure, for in fact it's this very front of non-ambiguousness that feeds its
resultant ambiguity.[2] The caricature resembles the person caricatured through
a process of selective accentuation and diminishment, so while easily recognizable they are nonetheless noticeably altered. The extremes of terrorist
violence are by nature oversimplified, the destruction of life and materials
magnified and the rationale behind it ridiculously shrunken. That they invariably become a magnet for alternative theories or conspiracies, the extremity of
which often match that of the acts themselves, is no surprise: the perpetrators,
their justifying systems of belief, are just not believable. The evil we recognize
is not drawn this way, and so our models cannot accommodate the terrorist's
reductionist strokes. It is like the world of the comic book intruding into that
of the political drama: they can only be there in order to represent some distant alterity, to garner excuses for motivations too subfusc and intricate for us
to readily discern. These acts of terrorism must then be a mask, a Halloween
prosthetic, preventing us from seeing the very real horror of the wearer underneath, a horror we are not yet ready to project in order to see. And just as we
do not see it, we do not hear it either:

> Terrorism does not aim at making anything speak, at resuscitating or
> mobilising anything; it has no revolutionary consequences (in this
> regard, it is rather a complete counter-performance, for which it is vio-
> lently reproached, but that isn't its game); it aims at the masses in their
> silence, a silence mesmerised by information; it aims at that white magic
> of the social encircling us, that of information, of simulation, of deter-
> rence, of anonymous and random control, in order to precipitate its
> death by accentuating it. It aims at that white magic of social abstraction
> by the black magic of a still greater, more anonymous, arbitrary and
> hazardous abstraction: that of the terrorist act.[3]

5.1 Media from the Dead

It is not that the dead have rotted in the ground that places them beyond us,
but that they have failed to keep up. Their underexposure to events, though
inevitable, is not inconsequential in our growing disregard. They were not
even witness to the coverage of their own deaths. The information that has
continued has devoured them. So much so that if the world had stopped
with them, it would no longer be accurate to consider them dead. But then
the dead themselves are media, for while they no longer communicate, communication is nonetheless staged. Their unseen presence does not produce
meaning, but it does stage that meaning, and the message conveyed is located
in that staging. And it is worth remembering that 'the medium is the message'

and the medium is this unseen presence – as even when it is seen it is seen as something else, as an awkward return to earth of an otherwise floating entity, a creature made only for seeing and not to be seen – this Oz behind the curtain, his apparatus on view, and the dishonesty of all solutions:

> It is necessary to ward off death, to smother it in artificiality in order to evade the unbearable moment when flesh becomes nothing but flesh, and ceases to be a sign. [...] Therefore, every thanatopraxis, even in contemporary societies, is analysed as the will to ward off this sudden loss of signs that befalls the dead, to prevent there remaining, in the asocial flesh of the dead, something which signifies nothing.[4]

The dead are a myth. And the myth exists. Although it is always someone else that buys into it – never us. I hear that there is such a thing as dead, and that other people have sought it out and seen it, that they have been forced into believing what they've seen, and so I get to see what they have seen and all the time I'm with them I believe it too, this Loch Ness monster dragged out of the water onto the bank like some hyperreal manifestation of a thousand different stories. But when the cameras disperse, I can no longer convince myself that it wasn't a model I saw, that we all saw, only the rest it seems did not notice how it wasn't something born but something made in its place.

Whatever death is it is not a catastrophe. If it were a catastrophe, meaning would stop there: it would constitute 'an impassable horizon of meaning'[5] beyond which 'nothing takes place that has meaning for us'. It is only such an end if life has amounted to something, if it has contained some consecrated direction to which death provides a conclusion. But despite the efforts of societal infrastructures, life is never anything but aimless at its core – and aimless through its having no core. And it is not as if nothing is known about the human after its death, for nothing *is* known and known to be the case – as far as we know. Nevertheless, nothing is only naively conceived of as an end to sense-making. It is the brink that ends up being the middle of nowhere, the precipice that's a plateau amid infinite plateaus. If meaning ended there it would never have started. And if mathematics can provide us with the ultimate model of the real, then this human death at its centre is not only a glimpse of hellish proportion but a glimpse too of how life itself might be thought catastrophic, the worst of dreams from which waking is suicide and sleep a living death.

The seduction of what we do not see is complete, which is why, in an age where everything is seen, we must seduce ourselves. We make fear where there is none and luxury where there is none, and where these commodities are found we employ them like a vehicle to a confusion to which (impervious to the panic) we know we have no rightful claim. Nowhere in this scenario is exploitation not in evidence: what's seen is only ever a front for what isn't seen. All experience is a proxy for the experiential vacuum, all interactions with objects the denied possibility of passing your hand right through them, as they then pass directly through you. It's not that we find ourselves and the world that's important, but that we somehow lose it again at the exact same time. What else is going on here? Our knowing the world finds us in it, but in finding us removes us, and so there must be seduction – the real that is found exploited, made hyperreal, made some small part of the mystery of our own appeal, our own appeal to ourselves, because there is no one else.

What never arrives is the finish or the start: there is the 'meaning and the countermeaning',[6] the infinitely oscillating point, the inescapable middle, so that even to countenance its possible resolution is illogical, and from this comes the immanent illogic of life.

5.2 Rotting and Violence

All violence is a revolt against rotting. It is a parody of control via the acknowledgement of its absence. Without violence there is just passivity and waiting, there is just the stoic acceptance of our predicament, just the slow hell of being alive. Recourse to violence is the desire to solve what cannot be solved. It is the mark of children. It is the frustrated stomping of feet that dare not stand still for fear of taking root in the ground. All action is a cowardice and violent action the most cowardly of all. What glorious distraction from decay this blowing up of bodies, this hacking off of limbs and heads, this precipitation of life. Every action is the flight instinct at work, a corporeal fleeing into the future, as if the past were something to be erased, a microcosmic acceleration of the inevitable. *If it has to happen, have it done, or else have it done to someone else.* And all these other deaths that are not your own, how much less dead you must come to feel, how much less like rotting and more like the ageless future creature that has not even happened yet, how much less pervious to reality and more like the simulacrum of the human.

On this model, thinking, unless it has practicable implications for the dissolution of our waiting, becomes synonymous with rotting, synonymous with its own repeated and overlaid transcriptions, with the wholesale blackening of virulent inactivity. The past must be proved wrong, or preferably irrelevant, and the future a place haunted not by the ghosted remains of our deterioration, but by the phantasms of empires in constant states of renewal, by abstractions invulnerable to rot.

It is not a question of transforming the process of rotting into a process of violence, but of recognizing that rotting (as thought) is already violent: a violence in opposition to violence, a bravery in opposition to the cowardly bravado of action – *the* violence. It is the work of power to exploit the inactivity of rotting and have it become indistinguishable from indolence, from sickness, from inaptitude for life, from a living death. To just wait out your own rotting – not wanting, not running, not looking away in a thousand directions at once, not already in the next hour, day, week ... not resurrecting past futures to relive the circuitry of satisfactions as if deterioration and death were merely modes of standing still, not working as if working were a thing, not thinking towards ends, not waking like a flower to the seasons of other men, not living like the bones in the Paris catacombs – to just wait it out, is to know its moves are your own moves, that this waiting is what it means to mean something, to mean something above and beyond (or beneath and within) the meanings that rely on turning you away from the corpse you are already wearing and that is wearing you. On this Baudrillard has warned us: 'We are entering a period of intense cadaverousness and our imaginations are simply not up to it. Here too we must choose and make our own personal obituaries.'[7] And what better obituary than one equal in violence to the event that occasioned it.

What, though, is the weapon of this violence that is only violent in its refusal to do violence (to the arbitrariness of place and that place's slow undoing of itself)? For inactivity is not the weapon but the act of violence itself, while the weapon is no more and no less than the weakness of the 'enemy', a weakness that is the failure to realize that what might look like war is rather the constant re-enactment of a desire for war, for war's possibility, an unfulfilled desire: a re-enactment of defeat in the anteroom of an impossible war. Thus the question: What is there for 'nonpower, the rotting of power to come up against'?[8] And its answer: against its own implausibility, against the joke of thinking life as something to be used, something that might otherwise go to waste – as if utility weren't the true waste, of waste.

Dummies do not rot, dummies are rot. They are rot's flowering, rot's deformities, rot's hope – and everywhere there are dummies. And only 'defiance and fascination' leave rot to rot, defying all temptation to leave it behind, to make temporary (to postpone) what does not itself wait but which demands waiting. Fascinated, fascinated that time acts so that we don't have to, we see time at work and become aware that its direction is just the decay of instances, the collapse of smaller somethings into larger somethings and back again.

The process of rotting is not navigable. There are only different stages of growth and collapse, only place not places. It is the desert of deserts, stretching as far as place itself stretches. Without outer limit because there is no outside, no beyond, only the rearranging of structure, 'only the wind lift[ing] the sand',[9] only the repeated non-event of time making room for its own aimless and undulating nowhere of everywhere, its landscape of death falling in on itself at intervals, where this imagined life is the sandstorm, the rains, the earthquake somewhere in the distance, which when arrived at is back at the point you left from – but, of course, you have not travelled at all. There are no places left to go, only place, and all the many views are one view: the last thing you ever see until the next time. How else do we keep going, but from the make-believe of significance, but from the prevailing notion that the world, this desert, is taking us somewhere – slowly in ellipses, always towards where it has come from, and always away from where it's going. And all this without prospect of escape, because escape presupposes an outside and an outside is not even someplace we can dream.

There is no reversing the implosion, only perspectives from within it: looking out, as if the past were the future, dispersed and receding from view (life), or looking in, looking where you are going, the future as the concentrated gloop of the past (death).

5.3 The Implausibility of Scandal

If scandal just serves to reinvigorate a fading moral core, in case anyone should believe that human civilization was no longer in hock to it, then scandal's ubiquity and increased irrelevance can be seen to bolster a simulation of a different kind. If nothing good can be thought of anyone, if the generally accepted inevitability of dishonesty, venality and perversion is common to both controllers and controlled, then what possible exception can you take to the best of a bad lot? But the hole goes deeper than this, because while the worst is believed of all, it is also not believed. The scandal has exceeded epidemic to become pandemic, and with so many strains that even those dying from it cannot provide reliable testimony to what it is that kills them. Establishing what we imagine to be foundational human standards as perfections that nobody can be seen to attain, not even those whose moral stature we hold in the highest regard, is a neat trick, even if no one is performing it. For how can we believe ourselves moral when no one else is, if not through the persistent dredging of our disgust? Only your hate will save you from becoming the thing you hate, and your hate cannot feed itself. You require/demand more and more instances/descriptions/images of what it is you are protecting yourself from, as if you'd fail to recognize it should the flood of examples ever stop. (Or perhaps hate is 'something that subsists, that outlives any definable object'.[10] And perhaps death too – *I have hate: I have death.*) And in constructing a sense of self according to this model, that is, negatively, what you can then claim as your own is reduced to a litany of subtractions, of cavities, vacancies gasping to be filled by anything. Revolutionary fervour is presented as misguided and evil in the same way: it will either end up abusing power in even more excessive ways (because the abuses you know of are never at the limit), or else will fail to acknowledge that the moral way is first and foremost not what you do but what you don't do. Only the inactive are pure, but thankfully (when we are not thankful, and nor should we be) there are those willing to sacrifice their purity for our sakes, and 'die stupid' like those 'guinea-pigs of retirement',[11] in the name of perpetuating and organizing world affairs.

Notes

1   Baudrillard, *Simulacra and Simulation*, 55.
2   The secret we require 'is quite simply the name in virtue of which they have no fear of death. Here is the profound jealousy and the revenge of "zero death" on those men who are nor afraid – it is in that name that they are inflicted with something worse than death' (Baudrillard, *The Conspiracy of Art*, 209).
3   Baudrillard, *In the Shadow of the Silent Majorities*, 51.
4   Baudrillard, *Symbolic Exchange and Death*, 180–1.
5   Baudrillard, *Simulacra and Simulation*, 83.
6   Ibid., 84.
7   Baudrillard, *Cool Memories*, 221.
8   Baudrillard, *Simulacra and Simulation*, 151.
9   Ibid., 153.
10 Baudrillard, *The Conspiracy of Art*, 142.
11 Baudrillard, *Cool Memories*, 103.

Chapter 6

A CURE FOR VERTIGO

Morality is a simulation of what cannot be assimilated. Humanity cannot absorb any of its notions of the good, so it blows them up instead: an end game. For 'there is no longer any such thing as a strategy of Good against Evil, there is only the pitting of Evil against Evil – a strategy of last resort'.[1] And what are lesser evils but a means to medicate our dizziness? The explosion is the picture of where we are, just as decapitation is the picture of where we were, or where we imagine we've come from. And 'the objectivity of the facts does not put an end to this vertigo of interpretation',[2] quite the opposite: it offers vertigo as a cure for itself. The only way to forget you are spiralling is to never stop spiralling, to accept spiralling as the necessary removal of what was never there in the first place. The imposition of stillness and concrete placement, of one at a time, of this follows that, of the arbitrariness of any solid arrangement whatsoever: all revealed as a security that only made you vulnerable. The truth is the already exploded bomb, not the promise of a bomb, and not the decapitated human figure. The latter's barbaric removal of thought (of thought deemed threatening) is a wet fuse in comparison with the exploded state of humanity's unseatedness. Decapitation is merely anti-irony and so cannot be other than simulation: its simulated seriousness is just the seriousness of its simulating. For how are we supposed to take seriously the removal (in beheading) of what is already smeared across the earth and the universe in increasingly fragmented droplets of disorientation and quintessential non-belonging – the lostness of our waking from linearity and fixedness? Beheading is the ultimate anachronism. Beheading is the reinforcement of the perpetrator's own disintegrated ownership of himself: as Dr Faustroll tells us: 'I maintain that a head is only a head when separated from its body.'[3] If we zoom in the effects are horrific, but as we pan out all we see are children killing effigies of themselves. To become a bomb, on the other hand, is to enact and to enable the latent scream of existing unhumanly amid false memories of the imagined lives of the dead, of a once paused state of humanity enshrined as mythology, as religion, as the heart of an explosion that itself does not explode. If the desire is to see ourselves, then we must have first represented a stillness that allows the exploding to see they are exploding. Beheading was also an attempt at self-viewing, but one targeted at a victim no one could recognize, a holding up as found what remained invisible. To reflect humanity's spiralling back at humanity, one does not hold up a mirror but a microscope, a microscope disguised as a telescope.

What kind of a dream was power but the only kind of dream, the peripety of what it was to want it, because there was and is no power but the wanting of power. The not-wanting is itself a power, but a hidden one, a wanting for impossibility – the only wanting worth not-wanting in order to get. If power and life are coextensive through the latter being unrecognizable if not a will to the former, as Nietzsche told, then our escape, both markedly modern and markedly ancient, is the absence of will contained in the impossibility of death, in its being simulated negatively as that which the extraction of humanity might inhabit. The 'Hell of simulation, which is no longer one of torture, but of the subtle, maleficent, elusive twisting of meaning',[4] need remain a Hell only if we refuse to acknowledge our exclusion. Show me a paradox and I will become one. Show me Hell and I will furnish it. Diagram the impossible and I will construct myself in my failing to construct it. Power is what the earth possesses, while man possesses only his immanent inability to possess anything bar the figment inculcated by that inability's replicative pull, which through absorbing appears to us absorbed.

The malignity of desire lies in its inexhaustible loathing for itself, which is also a love for itself, and at its core the following contrivance: there is only ever the for-its-objects and never the for-itself. In desiring the desire of others, we have thereby supposedly relinquished all possibility of desire, as it occurs within us, ever becoming an object for itself. This inbuilt self-disgust of desire is what keeps us in the world, looking outwards, distracting the wanting from the sickness of having no reflection, of itself being nothing worth wanting. The only validation of desire as something desirable is depression. If the whole business of desire is intrinsically tawdry and empty, then depression shows us that life itself is no different: desire's proof through crisis. But something of the death of desire remains even when the immanent value of desire has been realized,[5] because through wanting it for its own sake we thereby make its everyday objects (things, ideals, people) spectral. We have come to know that it's not them we need but what it is that needs them, and that they need not exist at all as long as the want for them (for anything constituting an outside) continues. Depression as (a suffered) antidesire justifies the existence of desire, but only at the expense of the necessity and the reality of its objects. After depression has been endured (as opposed to removed) the world is dead, only desire remains, a desire that can no longer disguise the fact that its objects are merely excuses for its own existence. Life is self-perpetuating: all its goals are just the accumulated adornments of the necessity of a direction, so why not 'bring chance into play and produce vertigo',[6] a vertigo that, as it turns out, is the only real cure for itself.

> 'Take your desires for reality!' can be understood as the ultimate slogan of power since in a nonreferential world, even the confusion of the reality principle and the principle of desire is less dangerous than contagious hyperreality.[7]

Hence desire, as Roland Barthes noted, is always the same. It never changes. It is only ever itself and never what it's directed towards. Only depression sees desire for what it is, feels the need for it without wanting it, knows its endless objects are nothing and that desire itself is the clearest reflection of that emptiness.

6.1 Vertigo and the Cost of Happiness

We are happy at our own expense. And no one is happy who has to work at it. Happiness demands an assimilative ease, and so those still prone to its influence cannot help but remind us how 'all the easiest solutions lead to catastrophe'.[8] For what could be easier than the joy of the precipice with no notion of vertigo? And what could be less comfortable than watching it happen knowing nothing but the irreversible loss of such a balance? Because there is no vertigo where the world is not strange, where naïve realism has no competitors, where there is only reality's final resolution and nothing outside it.

> In the end, it is the strangeness of the world that is fundamental and it is that strangeness which resists the status of objective reality. / Similarly, it is our strangeness to ourselves that is fundamental and resists the status of subject.[9]

And while we have no option but to settle in this strangeness, make a home in this antithesis of home, there can only ever be faint approximations of that pre-vertiginous happiness, as strangeness cannot be absorbed without ceasing to be itself, without the world ceasing to be the world and without us ceasing to be who we are – minus the happy death. Essentially, 'the temptation of ease [just] is the temptation of death',[10] because while the world and our place in it is in some sense a given, an essential worldliness as detailed by Heidegger, there is a strangeness to this given-ness which is itself a kind of given, a given ungivenness.[11] It is this sublimated precariousness that has always made this world smack of the dirty trick, as of a crime perpetrated on existence itself. For

Baudrillard it is nothing short of the impeccable crime: 'The perfect crime is not the one that leaves no trace. It is the one which is impossible to reconstruct because it has no motive and, at bottom, no perpetrator. [...] The world itself is a perfect crime.'[12] A perfect crime being that which repels all our questions, making our demand for rational cause senseless, for there is only its happening and its continuing to happen. It is irreconcilable with our philosophical practices, a clear demonstration of the redundancy of thought: philosophy's truest toxin. What though, in light of this, can be made of Baudrillard's self-same attribution of immaculate criminality to self-murder, that in addition postulates a somewhat bemusing exclusivity: 'The perfect crime, the only one, is suicide. Because it is unique and final [...] Because suicide achieves the ideal confusion of executioner and victim.'[13] In order to avoid a seemingly sloppy contradiction (the contradiction lacking any other purpose), transitivity dictates that world and suicide are one and the same thing: both killer and killed, both motiveless and lacking a perpetrator. The world's status as both destroyer and destroyed is easy enough to accommodate, although how it is that suicide can lack both a motive and a perpetrator is a more awkward question. The key to consolidating this idea comes from its reliance on a retro-spective cancelling out: the motive to obliterate all further motive is thereby an anti-motive, a motive too internally conflicted to count as a genuine motive, thus becoming akin to some kind of affliction of motive, a deadly virus taking the shape of a motive in order to destroy motivation. Correlatively, there is no perp because it is likewise subsumed into the victim, the agent of murderous antagonism lost forever in the ultimate passivity of the act. The world is not only indifferent to us, it is indifferent to itself. And it is this indifference that eradicates both intentionality and agency, which in turn expunges the possi-bility of any genuinely indictable culprit. The perfect crime is everywhere and nowhere (the rebuttal of all life via a nothing dreamt as a something), is the maker and receiver of death (the conduit through which death acts).

Having ascertained that the world is suicide and suicide is the world, there should be no surprise that both are present in equal quantity; nevertheless, that both are in such short supply is certainly worthy of consternation among the uninitiated, among those converts to the world who missed its passing:

> We should be amazed not that there is so much chaos and violence, but that there is so little and everything functions so well. [...] This is perhaps the same miracle as the one which prevents everyone from succumbing daily to the idea of death or to suicidal melancholia.[14]

The miracle here is all the less miraculous once the conflation of world and suicide is taken into account, for just as little of the world exists as does the suicide with which it is identical. Who but the pessimists and the depressives and the mentally ill still reside in the world? Who confronts the indifference of their surroundings every day and lives? Everything is real except the world; the world for the most part vanished so reality could take over and having taken over so cease to be real – that is, the real exists only physically, but so pervasively that its metaphysicality has perished.[15] The world when it is everywhere and everything has no need for reality,[16] has no need to incite any episodes of mutual adoration that would problematize suicide's oneness with the world:

> Only from time to time does thought fall suddenly in love with the real world and, from time to time, the real world returns its feelings. Most of the time, thought detaches itself from reality [le réel] in order to exist and distances itself to be at its finest.[17]

Thought's detachment from reality and the importance of that detachment (to sanity and so to meaning) is evidently just a different kind of attachment, for it is elementally crucial that there be this reality to detach from, allowing a distance to be found – that fabricated otherness that makes those moments of love possible (if implausible).

If reality communicates it does so only imperceptibly, only at the brink of access: 'Only doors communicate',[18] and they only do so through staying firmly shut. I'd think the real, make it my abstraction, finesse it with my experience of it, but then it has already done all these things to me, and would it really be fitting to return this (dubious) favour? Best to hide in my own invisibilities, and hope they too aren't as real as they seem.

The question to ask of the future, if we care to ask anything, is this: 'Which will win out in the long term, enforced idleness or frenzied activism?'[19] J. G. Ballard hedged his bets,[20] playing out the latter as a violent reaction to the former. But the real violence is in inertia itself, rather than in any violent reaction to it. Any violent upheaval of reality of whatever kind comes from an inertial blossoming, from a committed retreat from activism, a violence taken to the core of what it is to be alive at all, the violence found in Ballard's 'The Enormous Space'[21] (in which we witness how 'the social [itself] dies from an extension of use value which is equivalent to its extermination. [For] when everything, including the social, becomes use value, it is a world become inert, where the reverse of what Marx dreamed occurs').[22] And this leads us to another, related, question: 'The eclipse of God left us up against reality. / Where will the eclipse of reality leave us?'[23] For the eclipse of God was likewise a reaction, a reaction that left us gorging on reality in search for its taste, and the eclipse of reality, following on from this, is the point at which we realize there is no taste. This last eclipse removes all incentive of flavour, declares itself flavourless; and yet the eclipses continue, for the declaration is framed in such a way that we somehow expect to find flavour there in its transparent blandness. This will not happen through imagination, for the subsequent blackness has swallowed it up, but it will happen, and it will happen instead through the proposed removal of this tastelessness, the threat of the removal of taste itself. Thus we taste only the presence of the deficiency. Melancholia, our saviour planet, must forever keep getting forever closer.

A reality without *purpose* or *destination*, an Integral Reality, is a murderous reality (a Patricidal Reality, even), for it 'involves the murder of the real, the loss of any imagination of the real'.[24] Its homicidal stripe – one shared by modern government which assimilates crime to save us from crime, thus debasing criminality – is in part an affectation, for the real it kills is still the real it exploits. The corpse still walks, even if only round and round in circles in a darkened room. Integral Reality is the father of itself, a patricidal suicider, the world as a swamp without the promise of an island, and yet there is the pretence that it is itself the island, and from that the distant opportunity for revealing its subterfuge. Playtime is not over: its half-death if anything is an invigoration, a goad of impossibility to a state sustained by it. In the walking corpse is the *intelligence of evil* posturing as a heartbeat:

> The integral drive and the dual drive: this is the Great Game. / The very idea of completion, of Integral Reality, is unbearable, but the dual form, the form that denies any final reconciliation, any definitive accomplishment, is also very difficult – and perhaps even impossible – to conceive in its radicalism. / And yet it is in this lucid vision of an endless reversion, in this denial of any objective solution, that the intelligence of evil, if it exists, is grounded.[25]

Baudrillard explains how evil can be found in this homicidal termination's supplanting of all our possibilities in exchange for a utopian resting place, and how what grows out from this is not doom but an acumen of evil that might have been built for such a purpose, (and once again) a purposeless purpose. The intelligence of evil is the immanent creativity of death: its mutant lifeforms, its frenzy in the morgue, its reconstitutions of lifeless materials as puckish variations on a resilient sickness. 'When the ice-cubes bang together in your head and people hear them from the next room',[26] and all thinking achieves is their inevitable melting and becoming mute, so that the only recourse is to unthink everything, to let the contents of your head freeze over, to embrace the WHITEOUT like you'd come to know it outside the possibility of knowing ... only then might you make something of death, of its immortality.

The reality of an end, of the integral expiration, is survived by us through our repeated denials of it, through numerous techniques of opposition that come to mark the humanness of humans.[27] And it is not that the denials refute, for this would not be possible or even desirable, but that they stage (or posit) a position alongside it, a location where an expired humanness can lick its wounds, and so become more itself than it was before, the apex of a delusory madness no longer incongruous to its imposed surroundings. The crime is not only the desert we've created and which in turn created us, but that we continue to find a place just outside its extremities, when there is no such place, drinking its sand through straws and hydrating our carcasses like hardy flowers – a hardiness whose glory is its indistinguishability from weakness. And let's not forget that the world's largest desert is covered in snow and ice, and that the world now is that desert, such has been that desert's growth, and that without an outside there is nothing there at all.

If we've lost the privilege of being (through our humanness) the enemies of reality, how is our position of degenerative repeal still tenable? What new and synthetic guise does it adopt? Baudrillard lays out the predicament as follows:

> Reality, having lost its natural predators, is growing like some proliferating species. A little bit like algae or even like the human race in general. / The Real is growing like the desert. 'Welcome to the Desert of the Real' / Illusion, dreams, passion, madness and drugs, but also artifice and simulacrum – these were reality's natural predators. They have all lost energy, as though struck down by some dark, incurable malady. We have, then, to find an artificial equivalent for them, since, if we do not, reality, once it has attained its critical mass, will end up destroying itself spontaneously, will implode of its own accord – which it is, in fact, currently doing, giving way to the Virtual in all its forms.[28]

The answer, already alluded to, is grounded in an open denial of the very predatory proclivities that once held sway over the dual-form reality, the pre-integral reality that substantiated our former, oppositional identity. We no longer combat this real with the combined force of *illusion, dreams, passion, madness, drugs, artifice and simulacrum*, but with the relinquishment, the voluntary subsumption, of these defences to and into reality itself, so that, for example, what was a madness from without becomes a madness from within, which can no longer be considered a madness at all, but rather an aberrant sanity implicit in the reality itself – our increasingly vertiginous circumambulations of reality's event horizon.[29] The predator that cannot avoid death welcomes it, even accelerating its arrival, so that the death may serve as weaponry against death's threat from elsewhere. This can be thought of as the ultimate artificiality, the equivalent for every one of those individually predacious instincts all at once. From the perspective of the dead, reality cannot implode, and nor can it slip comprehensively into the Virtual, because it is the dead thing itself that in this way has become virtualized (pre-empting reality's suicide/suicide's reality), and so by virtualizing first projects a substantiating otherness to the illusion and artifice of the world as distinct from our own hyperreal decomposition.

It is in this way that 'future crime prevention will be genetic, intragenic', as genes – which were never alive in the first place, but only ever sustained by the life of the cells they were in – leak from their dead hosts and expire, thus unmaking the evil of the world's descent into virtuality. Baudrillard continues his thoughts on crime prevention, reiterating the extent to which our somewhat hoary protections are relentlessly consumed:

> Evil, which was once a metaphysical or moral principle, is today pursued materially right down into the genes (and also in the 'Axis of Evil'). It has become an objective reality and hence objectively eliminable. We are going to be able to excise it at the root, and with it, increasingly, all dreams, utopias, illusions and fantasies – all these things being, by the same general process, wrested from the possible to be put back into the real.[30]

That evil, and with it the collective force of all our adversarial tools, is chewed up and digested in the processes of the real, is an inescapable consequence of the emergent materialization of thought. And so what better way to artificially extend the conflict, between humanness and the real, than to subvert the properties of our own materialized being by existing beyond our deaths, inhabiting the spill of our deceased cells, the purpling skin, the virtual WHITEOUT of our brains. This simulated reanimation of our corpses is not just one more utopia of the still living dead, but the dystopia of what humanness must become, or rather utilize, if there is to be anything free from reality's digestive juices. In other words, all our tools of war (all our illusions, dreams, passions and madnesses) must be relocated, pumped into the ruptured organs and splenetic flesh of what subsists as human, of what continued in the wake of possibility: the impossibility of a virtually living death. We must live as if we are already dead, as if there were no 'as if' required, because the need for the make-believe of it has passed and we are dead, all of us the make-believe of the corpse, this inverted Caden's syndrome of humanity made not real but more than real. To embody this contradiction is to escape the real, which is a re-embodiment necessitated by the unstoppable encroachment by reality on everything:

All that is absent from itself, all that differs from itself, is not truly real. [...] Nothing and no one is absolutely present to itself, herself or himself (or, *a fortiori*, to others). So nothing and no one is truly real and real time does not exist. [...] In this sense, reality is inconceivable. Integral Reality is a utopia. And yet this is what, by a gigantic artifice, is being imposed upon us.[31]

That the truth of our living deadness is a virtual one, a truth that mimics an opposition to the pervading truth of the world, seals its status as a truth outside of the truths of the world, and our own immanent evil as a workable absence from within it, for this world 'no longer has any need to be true. Or rather it is true, absolutely true, in the sense that nothing any longer stands opposed to it. [A world] of absolute good from which evil is lacking',[32] of which we are its solitary instantiation.

We have needed to defend ourselves from reality for too long to relinquish our weapons at the mere mention of its newly immersive perfection. But this is just the fringe of the dynamic at work here, because there is no relinquishment either when confronted with the proof (the mere proof) of this perfection. The reality in which we can disappear, in which all capacity for confrontation is surrendered on entry, is an abomination, a paradisal monstrosity, a hideous receptivity: the scenario found replicated in *Invasion of the Body Snatchers*, where the pod people are converts to a reality from which they cannot escape and which cannot escape them, a consuming ideality that has expunged all need for retaliation, and with it all need for reality. As Baudrillard explains:

It is by a kind of instinct, a kind of vital reaction, that we rebel against this immersion in a completed world, [...] [and this] negative abreaction is the product of our hypersensitivity to the ideal conditions of life provided for us. / This perfect reality, to which we sacrifice all illusion the way that all hope is left behind on the threshold of Hell, is quite obviously a phantom reality.[33]

Without any sort of resistance, from reality to us and from us to reality, neither us nor reality can be imagined to exist, or rather existence can be imagined but only abstractly, as something not even occupied by itself. Such a reality is encroaching, is upon us in ever increasing incremental integrations, and its end can be defined in the simplest terms: a world utterly devoid of ultimate meaning, a paradise of insufferable but unsuffered nihility. (More than anything it is needful to remember this warning: Beware of paradise!) For although 'the mirror is part of the object it reflects',[34] it cannot be the entirety of the object so reflected without both collapsing into a uniformity in which all notion of reality is absorbed into an inescapable nothingness, an 'insoluble affinity'.[35] And yet it is here, in this threat, that the possibility to exist manifests itself. It is the fulcrum of any genuinely human thought. Only its actualization destroys: dematerializing reality and materializing our thoughts.

This combative engagement is of course only the religious/transcendent tendency in a new guise, a tendency for which reality was 'only a fleeting solution'. That we would ever only want to see the world and leave it at that,[36] that together an abiding oneness of purpose and pacific cohabitation would all of a sudden emerge to replace our thousands of years of looking away, our cultured dislocation, is the grossest naivety; and so, as Baudrillard reminds us, it is not the case 'that the transcendent solution is entirely past and gone or that God is dead, even though we now deal only with his metastases'.[37] Our solutions were inhuman. Nobody could stand to come up against the world or themselves, or worse still the two of them blended together in some terrifying anonymous slop. We needed to be something and for the world to be something else, but then we also needed for that something we are to be flexible, while the world remained stable, despite knowing that in making ourselves we'd also made the world. This contradiction has been humanity's life's work: making our sly and scared creations look more and more like discoveries. But our failure in this regard has not killed the impulse: the contradiction and its attendant contrivances are perpetuated still, only now our focus has shifted to the predicament itself, the humanness of the contradiction and of the lie, the inherent insanity of this manifest existence that must be made sane. We now have everywhere to go, but also the opportunity (albeit one, that in the interests of life, is scarcely taken up) to discern that each is a dead end or a circuitous pathway. The realization of all possibilities is also their removal, as possibilities, as the only (self-identifying) human currency left. And this is how our 'dream of identity ends in indifference',[38] for that which actualizes the all must become nothing, or rather reveals to itself the nothing that was there from the start.

6.2 Holographic Autophagy

Descartes' method of doubt famously demolished a seemingly given epistemological grounding only to reconstruct it on the putatively solid footings of his cogito. Despite its ingenuity, there of course remain numerous points of contention, but one that's never mentioned is the very conceivability of this reverse journey (from doubt to certainty, from illusion to the real) aside from all other theoretical considerations, for it's as if the method itself had left no mark, and as if one could watch the world disappear and not go with it.

The world does not return. Once it has been put at arm's length, or rather, beyond it, just out of reach, in deference to the absolute propinquity of thought, there is no getting it back again, not from the inside, not as anything other than that enchanting nowhere of holography that for all its charm can only approximate meaning:[39] its givenness has been compromised, its spontaneity lost, for there is always one thought too many (even if it's just to remind yourself that doubt has been dispensed with). The return transit from illusion to the real is an endlessly recurring one: there is no direct route back, only a potentially infinite number of routes, back to a place that isn't there anymore.

The world remains just out of reach whatever the corrective enacted in thought. The world is no longer a dream, but you watching the dream inside a lesser[40] dream – a semi-waking dream, 'its charm lost',[41] and in its place the desire for charm, a desire that thought on its own cannot fulfil.

The problem here is not that the world was found to be illusory, but that it was found to be only temporarily that way, and at the same time in contradistinction to the reinforced reality of the subject, a subject that having stepped outside the dream then found the dream to be real but could not sleep deeply enough to properly substantiate its (insulated) epiphany: 'One must never pass over to the side of the real, the side of the exact resemblance of the world to itself, of the subject to itself. Because then the image disappears.'[42] The solution, as far as there is one, is to leave the world as illusion, while also recognizing your own illusoriness. This is the new price of seduction: a seduction of nothing by nothing (or to be precise, not nothing but the near-zero of illusion). Turn your body into the ectoplasm of thought and the rest of the world will obediently follow. This way the body becomes a hologram, every bit as lost and shifting as the staccato succession of your thoughts, of a planet digesting itself in a void.[43] Initially there's the vertigo, as you float among the floating while still remembering (eulogizing) solid ground, and that memory makes you sick. And you remain sick all the time there's something left of you to be sick. Then, if the memory is permitted to wane, a parity of illusoriness will establish itself and the illusion will begin to look homely, and the old dynamic will play out – only now the belief has gone, the investment frittered, the fear of death made indistinguishable from a fear of life, anticipation gutted out by what happens; and you inhabit some beyond, a beyond that is nowhere else, a beyond that had no place to transcend, a locus of meaning bereft of origin and endless because of it.

Once the holographic nature of the entire universe has been acknowledged, there is only one secret left and one attendant hope. And these, in essence, are no different from what was there before. And from this you realize that beyond was only ever the destabilization of place, a recognition of a fundamental transparency, after which the same dilemma recurs. Nothing has happened.

The departure of the real was itself an illusion: reality replaced by an illusion of the real, from which there is no way out, as you yourself have become illusory. This parity with the dream replaces what was hidden, found and then assimilated, with a congenital blindness cursed still with the illusion of sight. This is the regressive method of our inevitable seduction, a charmless one, a dead-eyed functional servitude to a seductress who, having already been disrobed, needn't even feign allure. This is the bleak prospect of a uniformity of dimension, the flatness of the earth, the flatness of man, sameness under the illusion of sameness, a vanishing point that refuses to vanish – for 'just as man submits to organization, so things take on the ideal functionality of the corpse'.[44] And so to consolation in the fragment, some metallic shard of holographic light appropriated from the whole and isolated from it, set aside on its own to quail and fulgurate and ebb, reminding us of the identity we once had, reminding us that the universe is too much and not nearly enough.

The stickiness of some small corner of the universe, of some objects in that corner, peopled or otherwise, is what allows me to escape those truths created by (and epitomized in) distance, those truths that are so visual in expression that 'distance' is no mere figurative embellishment but instead a continual indictment (of anything being anywhere), my eyes smeared in the shit I'm in. And the danger of this distance is nothing more than its coercion of outlines – not outlines that solidify, but outlines that separate while at the same time throwing the world out of relief and into the gaudy squalor of a child's drawing.

6.3 The Meaning of Terror

Terror precludes control and reintroduces accident and there lies its value. Without the possibility of terror, and what's more the terror of possibility, there is only the full absorption of terror by the norm, which, though a state to which terror can be attributed, is to those within it utterly nerveless and incapable of terror's requisite excess – an excess that, for example, is realized by one's entrapment in the norm, which equates to an awareness of the abnormality of the norm. Why, though, should I not feel terror at the prospect of some future state in which terror will no longer be possible for me? Terror=non-terror is less a contradiction and more a condition of terror reacting to its erasure. The removal of negative emotional states is always suspicious, more suspicious even than the removal of positive emotional states – though of course invariably more welcome. The explanation is simple: suffering is our material, its depletion our depletion. For while someone will find peace and happiness, the fear, the suspicion, is that it won't be me. It's the imperfections and the suffering (provided the latter is not too acute and not too prolonged) that sustain a sense of the reality of my existing. That those tranquil pod people, those idealized and unblemished wives of Stepford, are in fact the opposite of the aspiratory figures they resemble is testament to our being married to the sickness of being human, and that our hopes for ourselves serve only to unseat what little sense of the real we've retained. It is for this reason that hope should only ever be directed away from ourselves. Integral to hope is perpetual suspension, not realization. Hope is just a deterrent against its own loss. Nothing else should ever be made of it.

And there is nothing so hopeful, so redemptive, as the threat of violence. For what else is the marking of the passing of time if not the need to list what has not happened, the trivial exultation of the improbability of existing at all? And who can really see how it is this 'aleatory apparatus' is just propping up a curse? Without the possibility of terror there is only the plateau, only survival, itself only the map of being alive, a hyperrealism of insignificant confine- ment – all the blandness of immortality exacted on the mortal.

Why this terror of harmony? Why this terror of equilibrium? But why should it be any different, when these models, these hypothetic humans, were created not for who we are but who we would be if we managed to inhabit them. Ours is the desert where we can simulate pastures and woodland. Take away the desert, and what is there left to simulate but that which cannot be simulated? But do not forget that the desert itself is simulated, simulated in order that there be levels, that the territory of the simulacrum exist to prolif- erate points of escape.

We do not simulate terror, terror simulates us. This is the abiding attraction of terror: its honesty is addictive. It can attach itself to anything, and all its attachments are creative. It is the creator of possible futures, alternative pasts, entire worlds, and yet each instantiation is indelible and irrefutably present. We relinquish the possibility of terror at the risk of relinquishing the possi- bility of ever waking up. Our stake in terror is nothing less than our stake in humanity itself, a stake in the disruption of the automatic, in the glitch of the automaton, in the fissure of an otherwise perfectly contained simulacrum. Terror, for all its strains on simulations of health, is our one true investment in chance. It is the womb of contingencies inside which we are at all times more than ourselves, a rebirth away from the other-than-this – though its ever being actualized is beside the point.

The attempt to normalize the universe, to suck it dry of meaning that is not ours, is insurance against ever getting lost, and while this engenders its own terror, it is a terror set up in opposition to terror, a terror of antiterror, a terror of meaning that means nothing: a meaninglessness that cannot see itself, a condition without distance, 'a state of asepsis and weightlessness', a perfection of the human incontrovertibly in debt to its antithesis. And this is vertigo, the vertigo of standing still. The vertigo of comfort. The vertigo of floating and drifting while glued to the flat bed of the universe. The vertigo of a 'secret repulsion'.[45]

Our media-rife model for sustaining sufficient elbow room for terror means that it is enough for somebody somewhere to be feeling it. This is enough to ground all reiterations and further simulations. Horror at not knowing the universe (not being able to go there) can be supplemented, to the point of almost complete forgetfulness, by regularly rolling out scenarios whereby the universe comes to us. And when it comes, we recognize it and it recognizes us; it conforms, as do all things, to the cinematic screenplay of planet earth. If our relative insignificance is ever acknowledged, it is thereby homogenized on contact, thus inoculating us, so that our eccentricities of insularity may be recognized as a brand of glory, an identity made impervious to any internalization of interplanetary terror. But for all of this contrivance, terror can still interrupt the carcass (even with the possibility of defeat or winning removed) and realize decay as itself something living.

Terror for the most part has become an ache, the remains of some former injury suffered by somebody else, the memory of faces, just the memory of a certain type of face. Even those terrors that might have been our own have the pang of drama about them, as if the state had acted us out, absorbing the perspective that then returns and attempts to claim it. The ache is the phantom of some earlier state, a state whose existence was, at least in part, to our own exclusion. The ache is the price for this temporary removal, a reminder that you weren't there when you woke up, a weak prompt that you once had blood.

Nietzsche tells us: 'Under conditions of peace the warlike man attacks himself.'[46] Nevertheless, the problem is not the war or the lack of it, but that sense of himself that is seen afresh and seen as burdensome. You were awake and absent and now you are asleep and present, asleep in that very presence. And it is this that starts to resemble cruelty, a jibe at your ever believing that you could exist authentically in this world. And while an 'insomniac dreams of a loss of consciousness, which would allow him to sleep',[47] the sleeping dream of never again having to wake up, that even after waking is still there, better represents our terror at the prospect of terror's being made impossible.

Notes

1   Baudrillard, *The Transparency of Evil*, 68.
2   Baudrillard, *Simulacra and Simulation*, 16.
3   Alfred Jarry, *Exploits & Opinions of Dr Faustroll, Pataphysician* (Boston: Exact Change, 1996), 70.
4   Baudrillard, *Simulacra and Simulation*, 18.

5   And in its chiastic form too: 'If death were a public service, there would be waiting lists. Impatience finds its justification as a refusal of this void, this abeyance of time which has no justification in any other world and which is produced by the overcrowding, the overpopulation of all desires' (Baudrillard, *Cool Memories*, 171).

6   Baudrillard, *The Intelligence of Evil*, 168.

7   Baudrillard, *Simulacra and Simulation*, 22.

8   Baudrillard, *The Intelligence of Evil*, 38.

9   Ibid., 27.

10   Jean Baudrillard, *Cool Memories II* (Oxford: Polity Press, 1996), 60.

11   And it is this ungivenness that gives us death back in return: 'Deep down, no one really believes they have a right to live. But this death sentence generally stays cosily tucked away, hidden beneath the difficulty of living. If that difficulty is removed from time to time, death is suddenly there, unintelligibly' (Baudrillard, *Cool Memories*, 67).

12   Baudrillard, *Cool Memories II*, 61.

13   Ibid., 64.

14   Baudrillard, *Cool Memories II*, 18.

15   See Baudrillard, *The Intelligence of Evil*, 14.

16   What Baudrillard refers to as Integral Reality, which has no need for reality, its voracious integrality having already corroded the necessary distinctions, the distinctions of Objective reality: 'What I call Integral Reality is the perpetrating on the world of an unlimited operational project whereby everything becomes real, everything becomes visible and transparent, everything is "liberated", everything comes to fruition and has a meaning (whereas it is in the nature of meaning that not everything has it). / Whereby there is no longer anything on which there is nothing to say' (Baudrillard, *The Intelligence of Evil*, 13).

17   Baudrillard, *Cool Memories II*, 64.

18   Ibid., 80.

19   Ibid., 82.

20   Most cogently in later novels like *Cocaine Nights* (London: Flamingo, 1996) and *Super-Cannes* (London: Flamingo, 2000). And perhaps Baudrillard came to a similar decision: 'In a world ruthlessly doomed to this principle [of tolerance], the irruption of intolerance will soon be the only event. The automatic return of all forms of racism, integrism and exclusion in reaction to this unconditional conviviality' (Baudrillard, *The Intelligence of Evil*, 153).

21   See Appendix 1.

22   Baudrillard, *In the Shadow of the Silent Majorities*, 81.

23   Baudrillard, *The Intelligence of Evil*, 16.

24   Ibid., 14.

25   Ibid., 17.

26   Baudrillard, *Cool Memories II*, 63.

27   The mainstay of modern art, for example: see Baudrillard, *The Intelligence of Evil*, 20.

28   Baudrillard, *The Intelligence of Evil*, 20.

29   'We have fallen into an irreversible vertigo; we are drawn to the black hole. We can sense the strategy but there is no one behind it. The black hole is what I call integral reality' (Baudrillard, *The Agony of Power*, 117).

30   Ibid., 22.

31   Ibid., 23.

32   Ibid., 25.

33   Ibid., 26.

34   Ibid., 30.

35   Ibid., 31.

36   Remember this dream from the womb, this figment from a moment before time: 'That is how things were before: you didn't look at them, you were happy simply to see them' (Ibid., 60).

37   Ibid., 32.

38   Ibid., 49.

39   See Baudrillard, *Fatal Strategies*, 75.

40   Less in terms of intensity and the potential for immersion.

41   Baudrillard, *Simulacra and Simulation*, 105.

42   Ibid., 106.

43   And this shift has the propensity to be radical, for with this holographic body comes an inevitable flattening of our system of symbolic exchange, an inversion of its presumed *inverse virtuality*: 'Corpse, animal, machine and mannequin – these are the negative ideal types of the body, the fantastic reductions under which it is produced and written into successive systems. / The strange thing is that the body is nothing other than the models in which different systems have enclosed it, and at the same time every other thing: their radical alternative, the irreducible difference that denies them. We may still call the body this inverse virtuality. For this however – for the body as material of symbolic exchange – *there is no model*, no code, no ideal type, no controlling phantasm, *since there could not be a system* of the body as anti-object' (Baudrillard, *Symbolic Exchange and Death*, 114).

44   Baudrillard, *Symbolic Exchange and Death*, 52.

45   Baudrillard, *The Intelligence of Evil*, 39.

46   Friedrich Nietzsche, *Beyond Good and Evil* (London: Penguin Books, 1990), 92.

47   Baudrillard, *Cool Memories*, 46.

Chapter 7

CHANCE AND THE TEMPORALITY OF DEATH

What is the chance that at any moment we might die but the always slightly dubious confirmation, the all too necessary reminder, that we are not there already? There are so many facsimiles of life that there's little hope of identifying their source, or even that they had a source. Everydayness is saturated with these dreams of chance, these daydreams of violence done not only to future lived moments but to the dayness of days themselves: 'Chance not only tires God, it tires us too.'[1] Who then does chance still have the facility to surprise? Chance is no longer separable from mundanity, and Baudrillard somewhat sneakily (or else unwittingly) equates the two: 'Chance is already present in the unpredictability of ordinary life. There is nothing more unpredictable than any moment of daily life.'[2]

But while unpredictability is entrenched in our plodding procession of days, it is nothing if not predictable, and predictable to a fault. For though we know our inductive reasoning has no other grounding but itself, its capacity to repeatedly stifle any opposition is no small testament to its virility. Chance (in the sense that it might bring about the unexpected as opposed to the contingency of whatever happens), in contrast, is almost the embodiment of inertia. Although the fact that chance can bring death also appears to rescue it from this seemingly interminable sleep. That we can die at any moment but don't is what instils this ordinary life with its ordinariness, that is, with the occluded sham of itself. The mundanity we accept is always only the one that can in any instant be broken. Who could accept it, let alone love it, otherwise? It is for this reason that knowing when you will die is maybe the last remaining taboo, for it strips from us this possibility for the ordinary daily life, regardless of how comfortable or hideous that daily life might be. And what is important to note is how all this talk of chance and the everyday consolidates our precarious placement in the world, or to put it another way, how what is revealed more than anything else is a fundamental human unpreparedness for life. That our boredom is also a harbinger of fear, that inertia remains frantic, can only help clarify just how unwarrantable at its core is this fact of our existing at all, when that existing cannot account or validate itself, but must be shored up minute by minute:

> Desire for events, desire for non-events – the two drives are simultan-
> eous and, doubtless, each as powerful as the other. / Hence this mix of
> jubilation and terror, of secret elation and remorse. Elation linked not so
> much to death as to the unpredictable, to which we are so partial.[3]

This everydayness is in part responsible for the Integrated Reality set to swallow us up, for it requires us to act our way through our adult lives, to pretend an everydayness until it becomes the only role we can play. But it is never realized to the extent that the need for pretence falls away, and yet the threat of this looms with the possibility of our absorption, with the establish-ment of an Integrated Reality from which there is no way out, because 'one of the variants of this lethal accomplishment, of this acting-out, is the real-ization of all metaphors – the collapse of the metaphor into the real'.[4] It is for this reason that we prefer our comforts dangling on a string, for the world to remain to some extent undecided, impermeable and opaque, the reason we prefer for our nerves to jangle even at our most relaxed, when the alternative is the catastrophic nullification of our interpretive performance, of our claim to be anything at all.

Our thinking must become active, for we must keep death out of the Integrated Reality. The way to do this is to court the paradoxes we find and exist there, exist in death there. Baudrillard lays out (in part) the groundwork:

> At the same time we violently desire events, any event, provided it is
> exceptional. And we also desire just as passionately that nothing should
> happen, that things should be in order and remain so, even at the cost of
> a disaffection with existence that is itself unbearable. Hence the sudden
> convulsions and the contradictory affects that ensue from them: jubila-
> tion or terror. / Hence also two types of analysis: the one that responds
> to the extreme singularity of the event and the other whose function
> might be said to be to routinize it – an orthodox thinking and a para-
> doxical thinking. Between the two there is no longer room for merely
> critical thought.[5]

However, as noted, this delineation is not entirely satisfactory, because our desire for exhilaration and our desire for mundanity cannot be separated as they are here: the one informs and situates the other, and death is already both an exceptional event and the epitome of what is ordinary. The thought that goes beyond the critical, then, is not so much that between an orthodox thinking and a paradoxical thinking, but that at the core of the paradoxical as it explodes, displacing the world around it, unseating life, pushing death into the stratosphere. Jubilation and terror become merged further in this violent shifting. The exception and the rule are no longer regarded as combative forces, but as one and the same thing: the exception is the rule and the rule the exception. The precipice is the same in both mundanity and exhilaration, and that precipice is the possible fulfilment of integrality.

Time that is not lived through but thought, not present but presented, or 'real time' as Baudrillard calls it – that informational and intellectualized canker on an otherwise quietly temporalized experience – serves as a displacement of our temporal being and consequently as a displacement also of death. The instant of our death becomes theoretical, abstract, and so becomes absent. This presentless present, in which we imagine ourselves dying, becomes the sheerest veneer, and so uninhabitable: a death occurs but no one is there to do the dying. There is only the exhaustive accruing of the instant of the death, an immediate time devoid of immediacy (direct but without direction), and so death is no more its own event than any other moment in any other arbitrary slice of the temporal order is its own event. Death in the virtual of real time is death that is never arrived at, but this is not to say that it is a death that has been postponed indefinitely, because such a deferment was the product of an eventful lived time, and so is instead a death that occurs at any and at all times, in an instant, a death that happens simultaneously with the entirety of its abstracted moment and one peopled only by abstractions. No death like this can be anticipated, because no death like this establishes a pathway leading to it that any one person can take as theirs. As Baudrillard explains:

> Real time is violence done to time, violence done to the event. With the instantaneity of the Virtual and the precession of models, it is the whole depth of field of the *durée*, of origin and end, that is taken from us. It is the loss of an ever-deferred time and its replacement by an immediate, definitive time. / Things have only to be concentrated into an immediate present-ness by accentuating the simultaneity of all networks and all points on the globe for time to be reduced to its smallest simple element, the instant – which is no longer even a "present" moment, but embodies the absolute reality of time in a total abstraction, thus prevailing against the irruption of any event and the eventuality of death.[6]

Any such displacement of death cannot be the desired escape, for its flatness takes death away from us without the embodiment of a mystery. It is the perpetual deferment that's required, a presence that will not be present, which is still an absence but an absence *for us,* and not what real time provides, which is a dilution of our deaths to the point of their complete erasure: 'The actual present is made up of this ever-living inactuality.'[7]

7.1 The Reverse Mutilation of the Accident

The accident is no longer the accident. The accident, as played out in a particular set of circumstances, themselves incongruent to any human intention, fulfilling only the contingent plans of natural occurrence, is instead the accident in reverse, the aleatory returning to what at one time necessitated it to find its former integrity empty. Moreover, although 'the Accident is everywhere', it is no longer 'the elementary, irreversible figure', if it ever was, but the ability to rewind and to correct, to co-opt the 'anomaly of death'[8] in detail so extravagantly intricate that all accusation of banality gets lost along the way (backwards), for only in reverse can the accident become serious enough to be laughable again, to establish itself at the core of what living might come to mean, to digest the rule, to re-inaugurate the past as the future. 'If this history does not exist, it will come to exist',[9] and it will exist in the past of its never having happened.

It is reversal that makes the accident what it is, by making it what it was, through a meticulous attention to detail, removing the gloss of its *insanity* and *sex* in favour of an infinite diagram of its functionality and potential for de-randomized intercourse. And so there is no longer anything left to go wrong. The future reverses into me, and I see it coming before it arrives – behind me, behind itself, into the unseen and the always present, its end laid out in its beginning. For now all has become this accident going forever in reverse, so that the only perversity left for this living, this perpetual undoing of ownership, is that of not dying before you were born, of having your possibilities forensically demarcated in a dream your death once had of you in order that your birth *not* be an accident (when birth is the pre-eminent accident). And there is in this returning, this transgressing of the accident, so many formulas of terror – as noted by Baudrillard:

> It is for the purpose of making amends and putting a stop to the scandal of accidental death (unacceptable for our system of liberty, law and profitability) that the great systems of terror have been setup, that is, programs for the prevention of accidental death by systematic and organized death. That is our monstrously logical situation: the death systems put an end to death as an accident. And it is that logic that terrorism tries desperately to disrupt by replacing systematic death (institutionalized terror) with elective logic: that of the hostage.[10]

Played back in slow motion nothing is unaccounted for, and only when we stop this backwards replay do the wounds reappear. But there is no choice but to stop, at some juncture, always arbitrarily, so that the event can be allowed to happen again, as an origin, a banal starburst of a thing created beyond your comprehension, or rather beyond the facilities of your awareness, one single step outside your point of exhaustion. It is as a consequence of this reversal, of what initially had been eluded via retrogressive explanation, that the accident's full destructive power is realized: sense has been made of the-world-that-happens only up until when the data is acknowledged to exceed human veracity, at which point our virility resurfaces and the world is returned to us, so that we can again make it recognizable, that is, an imperfect but workable mirror.

Where then can we see this violence of the accident? In what stratum do its wounds inhere? For it is no longer in the world for us that has been seen to turn, or simply in the obliteration of our mirror image that our exercises in reversal exposed. The mutilation, as always, is situated in the middle ground, the homeland to which all our excursions in and out of our own consequence inexorably return. (Even pessimism turns out to be nothing but the last throes of optimism – the imploded faces of old age fattening up like babies on poisoned milk.) The trauma is in the body of our giving up, of having no other recourse but to bed down in the age-old apostatical contusion of having nowhere else to go, where worst of all we come to realize that we can no longer even feel our wounds. Our nerve endings are now so desensitized that all such lacerations are nothing more than proof of being somewhere, the shameful pangs of explorers who never really left home: those who looked out the window and saw that the outside world was uninhabitable, that it was there transparent and looking back at them, but like them was seeing only its own reflection. The trauma, then, is only a means of recognition, of faintly noticing that we are in fact alive and that others like us exist, because we see the wounds of this same somewhere and the impossibility of anywhere else.

If reversal eventually leads us back to the same place, the same accident, the same dead event rising from the ground stiff from too much sleep, then what of multiplication, the infernal reproduction of the event whose having to happen is as falsely mysterious as its contingency, what of that? What else but a desolate emulation of this failed escape from the middle: 'It is not another dimension, it simply signifies that this universe is without secrets.'[11] Yet amid this wretched panopticon, each of us in our own central observation tower looking out on all the many cells in which we're incarcerated, there remains, if not a secret, then the possibility of having missed something, of not having seen everything, and not in the sense of the limit our reverse of the accident revealed, but in our having actually seen and yet somehow not – almost as if there were some more penetrating way of looking of which we are vaguely cognizant but unable to access. This is at the very heart of what it means to know life and yet still live it. It is the awareness of the limit as potential, nothing more and of course everything, and the central truth of *Blow Up*, *The Conversation* and *Peeping Tom*, that whatever threshold your senses run up against there is always that which is beyond it, not supernaturally beyond, but an ultimately real and physical beyond, the event behind the event, the voice behind the voice, the intrigue that the intrigue is masking. Just as we found with the accident in reverse, there is no end to the detail, the minutiae, the yet unseen contributory elements, only here the dead end is not dead, it is life itself: it is not the world in unending retreat from us, the world that has already established its distance from the off, making our pursuit an exercise in categorical futility, but instead a world that has chosen to speak, a world that for the briefest of instants we have heard and from which we cannot turn back. We sense a new middle ground where the world too exists, and which we might just reach if we could only concentrate harder, listen more, see more, recreate or translate the message we were sent. This glimpsed object – with the world not for us but with us, showing itself to us and us to ourselves – 'becomes an indefinable, [and] therefore fascinating, object, [...] an object at the crossroads',[12] and an object that ultimately threatens madness, for madness (the madness that is left to us) is always this inertia of seeing more in the same (a projected anamorphosis? a reflected anamorphosis?), of additional, tangential paths leading elsewhere, progressing abroad in ever more desperate convolutions: loopy, spiralling and sick, just as anyone mad enough to pursue sanity must be.

The accident in sum is nothing more or less than the simulation of death, the simulation of your death, again and again, in every instant available to you. This is simulation as creative imposture, as illegitimate insertion, when nothing is illegitimate. Because every death, even those not yet realized, those merely hypothetical and disenfranchised, work towards constituting the death you are constructing for yourself. As indicated, the fatal accident in reverse does not bring you back to life, but instead loses one death in so many others that the possibility of life cannot be seen for death and the one dying for all the means at the world's disposal. And yet this new ground still fascinates – as if we had been offered the opportunity to talk with murderers, and not those garden variety dispatchers of loved ones and rivals, but some discrete universal genocide that kills you everywhere and for all time in order that the hubris of existence be acknowledged and punished, nae rectified. After all, how can death happen when nothing else has happened, nothing beyond some vacant presence's slow awakening to that very vacancy? What is there to die? The simulacrum of the body? The emotion suffered as if it were some alien growth? The thoughts suffered in the same way? And were pleasant thoughts even thoughts? Don't they now seem, and didn't they at the time for that, if we'd been awake in having them, seem rather more like cushions for thoughts (to place over the faces of those thoughts perhaps) as opposed to thoughts themselves?

Unlike Søren Kierkegaard, who argued that unhappiness is linked to an absence of the present, existing either in what has happened or what will happen, Schopenhauer maintained, with his negativity thesis, that any ease or enjoyment we may experience cannot be analysed at the time they are occurring, so that what we call pleasure necessarily involves our memory and our ability to appeal to the future, meaning the present can only yield suffering or its negation. Pleasure doesn't exist in the present as positive because all pleasure that is in the present comes about in reference to some past want or some want yet to come (a similar notion to that of Socrates whose account of [sensible] pleasure in the *Philebus* is one in which pleasure is said to be either the restoration of some natural condition, or that which involves memory and the expectation of past pleasures being repeated).[13] Death sheds its skin into the present, but is never itself found there, and perhaps it's these markings of repeated expirations we cannot help but miss: 'The real, particularly in the present, is nothing more than the stockpiling of dead matter, dead bodies and dead language – a residual sedimentation.'[14]

7.2 Paralysis and Panic

All the while panic remains possible, the lessons of your rotting have not been learnt, but then what is this idea of tutelage if not sublimated terror? The last source of panic to go, and we are never around to see it go, is failed orientation. This encompasses the threat of death, of insanity, of eternity, of infinity. Thus terror at the anticipation of death is nothing but the inability to orientate yourself the other side of death – whether you envisage existing there or not. (How far you've come not to become God. How far you've fallen not to keep falling.) What's required is to fall through empty space forever, hitting the ground only at every subsequent moment, and so never actually hitting it, insane to the point of having to establish one's own sanity,[15] for the faller 'believes the veil of his face will vanish but the vision beyond it will wait for him, clear and unwavering, at least as long as he falls'.[16]

This perpetuity of descent, of floating seemingly downwards, seemingly somewhere, is just the abstracted form of the oldest delusion: that we share in the possibilities of space, that our fate mirrors that of the universe we are in, that if and when the world drops away we too will drop, free of it but safely in its orbit until the roles are reversed and it is the world that orbits us. But this 'universe of simulation is transreal and transfinite, [and] no test of reality will come to put an end to it – except the total collapse and slippage of the terrain, which remains our most foolish hope'.[17]

There is the 'terror of value without equivalence',[18] and the terror of any human sensation without equivalence. And how better to incite madness than by the policing of equivalences, having them applied externally and usurped from the inside. Madness of non-states – non-meaning, non-knowledge, non-work, non-equivalence, non-product – is the madness of submitting to simulacra. Not the simulacra of need, the simulacra of self-subterfuge, of soliloquized societies, of soliloquized environments, but the simulacra of whim, of whim as necessity, as honesty's last shallow breath – as last resource against panic perhaps. Better still, panic in a coma. There is only the 'hard law' and our laughter, our studied laughter, academic and aberrant, a laughter full of blood, bubbling, choking, violent laughter, the pre-recorded laughter of the dead.

Thus for paralysis to absorb panic the paralysis must be yours, must be yours as a continuation (a condition) of the process of your own debunking, your striptease towards death.

Notes

1   Baudrillard, *Fatal Strategies*, 181.
2   Baudrillard, *The Intelligence of Evil*, 49.
3   Baudrillard, *The Intelligence of Evil*, 105.
4   Ibid., 53.
5   Ibid., 105.
6   Ibid., 102.
7   Ibid., 159.
8   Baudrillard, *Simulacra and Simulation*, 113.
9   Clarice Lispector, *The Hour of the Star*, trans. Giovanni Pontiero (Manchester: Carcanet, 1986), 11.
10 Baudrillard, *Fatal Strategies*, 59.
11 Baudrillard, *Simulacra and Simulation*, 117.
12 Ibid., 118.
13 See Plato's *Philebus* (31d8).
14 Jean Baudrillard, *Seduction* (Montréal: Ctheory Books, 2001), 46.
15 The incessant sensation of waking without the phenomenological context to provide grounds for waking. The sensation without any corresponding transition, like the manifestation of a desire to wake up – a tic.
16 W. S. Merwin, *The Miner's Pale Children* (New York: Atheneum, 1981), 218.
17 Baudrillard, *Simulacra and Simulation*, 157.
18 Ibid., 155.

Chapter 8

THE POSSIBILITY OF NIHILISM

In a world made hyperreal, saturated with versions of itself, saturated with meaning, nihilism's simplicity and emptiness return from forgotten thinkers like some ancient remedy long mistaken for a symptom: an earlier curative to a later malaise, a medicament in search of a condition that has laid patiently in wait only to arrive now, most likely too late. For what amounts to an atavistic chemotherapy for hypermodernity's new cancer comes at a time when sickness is no longer permitted; and while nihilism is (like Christianity, like God) a sickness that cures, it comes with no anti-emetic, so that the only way out of nihilism is to go further inside it.

The desire will be, of course, to assimilate it, to have nihilism mean something other than the removal of meaning, to have it become a source of meaning, a theoretical device hiding further theoretical devices that belie its surface ugliness. In other words, a game will be made of it, and things will once again be at stake, when at face value there is no stake, no investment worth making, no sense in anything but life's own senselessness. The problem is that nothing can be allowed to have just one face, especially when the face is as hard to look at as this one. I cannot just be cured, I must also be cured from that which cures me, and so on. For while nihilism offers the solution of lightness and transparency to an otherwise bloated and occluded existence, there is always the issue of the remainder, the side effect of the disappearance that leaves something behind, the apocalypse that never comes, for 'there is no longer an apocalypse',[1] the face behind the face that told you it wasn't there. The cure is over and now we must be cured again, because the cure did not destroy enough of the disease, because the cure has a life of its own, because the cure itself needs to reproduce, because we were the sterile petri dish to nihilism's culture and its growth demanded our growth, a symbiotic swell of neutrality and indifference, a desert in which each grain of sand, despite its self-professed insignificance, remains more than itself, remains *fascinated* by its own accumulated disappearance: for once 'you eliminate disappearance, there is no more singularity'.[2] Nihilism can therefore be seen as a pervasive and destructive antidote to the world's convoluted fug, one that through its version of health, its melancholic inertia, eventually neutralizes meaninglessness, its main active ingredient. (For all melancholia has meaning, even if it's the meaning of meaninglessness, the return of no return, the appearance of our disappearing.) Nihilism is not destructive enough. Its cure cannot permit of cures like other cures, so must instead cure itself, and by doing so impedes its core medicinal efficacy. For nihilism to fulfil itself it would need to be the cure that removes the need for all further cures, the cure that shrinks the human and the world (but the 'desert grows'): it would need to be the cure that kills (the palliative care that doesn't care, the indifferent and perpetual awareness of our own inability to die).

When meaning has been obliterated by simulation, humanity circling itself at greater and greater speeds until all semblance of movement stops, 'a process of inertia through acceleration',[3] and when all possibility for surplus meaning has consumed itself, our abnormality will enshrine us, the growth that ends growth, the excrescent discharge processing its end into an inescapable transparency, the devoured race, the self-defeated beyond. And so nihilism is the religion at our close, but even that becomes victim to our 'passion' for process and simulation, to our need for saturation. Our capacity for disenchantment has gone. We will not taste our last meal. The food itself will be simulated, the feeding of the five thousand come again, but this time the entire world will eat greedily from its own disappearance until it is full to breaking point, until the bulge of a fresh excrescence can be postulated – if never seen.

In this meeting of two nihilisms – the one perpetrated through overexertion, overproduction and the myth of overcoming, and the other through the rational explanation and acceptance of the former's ineludible failure – each cancels the other, and yet still room is made for more extraneous purpose, even beyond the purpose of the purposeless, in the possibility of violence, in the disembodied hope that even what is obliterated is not impervious to further attack, that like a horror story the world might still yield something to scare us back into existence.

If 'theoretical violence, not truth, is the only resource left us',[4] this violence is just about as rare as truth and harder to simulate. Most often we must first simulate a favourable environment: oligophrenia, ignorance, naivety, blindness. This violence, all prospect, must surpass all its earlier instantiations, it must outdo and undo itself, some earthquake of abreaction of inconceivable scale, the unannounced and unnoticed arrival of meaning at a party for nihilists. It must project the realization of some cataclysmic eventuality that can never transcend the brink of what it is that might happen by never being permitted to happen. Death is this. Death never arrives because I've already slept through it. Meaninglessness is meaningless because it allows my state to mean something, while also involving the removal of all modes of meaning's recognition (all human, all dead already), of the emotional, of the possibility of a pang. Hence this violence reminds us that violence need never occur, that nothing need ever occur: the violence to end all violence, the most terrifying and excruciating revelation teetering on the precipice of revealing itself, which is the only way it must be seen. This is the consequence of no consequence, the event of the non-event, the purest abreaction on which indifference cannot feed.

The use of this theoretical violence is to prevent indifference from consuming itself. Indifferent to my indifference, I cease to live while seemingly evoking a perfected exemplar of that living. The aliens have me, I am a pod person. My suffering made meaningless is gone, and like an animal I have been put down, but put down in life, to live as some kind of death intended. 'This is where seduction begins',[5] as the last escape from this, but not an escape that denies nihilism or seeks to protect itself from it, but as a state 'invulnerable' to it, while still being consciously vulnerable to the voracious appetite of that very invulnerability. (How to stay alive without becoming dead? How to remain a target for further seductions? How to embody the paradox of a partial seduction?)

As Rambert points out: 'The plague [...] means exactly that – the same thing over and over again.'[6] Revisiting Oran under siege from plague is like returning home, even if we've never been home before. In plague-stricken Oran there is consequence, threat, life's repeated heroism acknowledged for what it is. Camus' plague is reality, though we might rename it 'war', 'persecution' or, more directly still, 'The Resurrection'. Inevitably, the nostalgia of meaning cannot sustain its momentum, so that those that live it and outlive it can only enshrine its significance in memory – a memory that can only remember itself as a means of escaping the returning of the plague of health. 'In the countdown, the time remaining is already past, and the maximal utopia of life gives way to the minimal utopia of survival',[7] but Camus' plague shows us another way of looking at these two utopias, shows how they can each bleed into the other: the minimal into the maximal, the maximal into the minimal. Baudrillard expands on this distinction:

> Not only have we lost utopia as an ideal end, but historical time itself is also lost, in its continuity and its unfolding. Something like a short-circuit has occurred, a switch shift of the temporal dimension – effects preceding causes, ends preceding origins – and these have led to the paradox of achieved utopia. Now, achieved utopia puts paid to the utopian dimension. It creates an impossible situation, in the sense that it exhausts the possibilities. From this point on, the goal is no longer life

transformed, which was the maximal utopia, but rather life-as-survival, which is a kind of minimal utopia.[8]

In the end, the autism of systems and philosophies and justifications is just a way in which to survive inside your dying (inside the minimal utopia of dying) in order to cheat death (that maximal utopia, to which this cheating, this evasion provides your only access).

8.1 Schopenhauer's Twofold Dying

For Schopenhauer, any suffering in life makes life worthless, but this worthlessness does not reduce to meaninglessness, for life being worthless in the presence of suffering gives Schopenhauer his objective: the removal of life, of will and of suffering, through an excess of suffering. Once life has been recognized as some suppurating and painful growth, the meaning of those forced to suffer it becomes none other than its removal.

When Schopenhauer told us life was pointless, that suffering was all-pervading, and that 'it would be better for us not to exist',[9] he nevertheless conceded one last goal, one last meaning, and that non-existence is preferable to existence is fundamental to it, to his conception of salvation (or *Erlösung*, from which it is derived) so imagined. However, the harshest irony is yet to come, for not only is the point of existence its complete annihilation, but it turns out we can only achieve this nothingness through the cumulative trajectory of our already pervasive state of suffering. Death for Schopenhauer is dyadic, and to achieve a *denial of the will* and die into the bliss of absolute nothing – to emphatically end, as opposed to just returning to our former condition of *pure will*, that blind striving, which though not subject to suffering still falls short of the inviolable peace of nothingness – is humanity's only justifiable aspiration. Nothingness is not, consequently, the preserve of all who die, but the reward due only to the moral and the truly enlightened.

This world (our world), according to Schopenhauer, is the worst of all possible worlds (a straight inversion of Leibniz's famous claim of optimistic faith), because a world worse than this one could not feasibly exist. It is also his contention that pain or suffering, as the essential element of life, is positive, whereas happiness or pleasure is negative, the mere cessation of the former. And while a number of commentators have argued against the first of these claims, by way of counter examples – stating the relative ease with which one can imagine a world with a greater amount of suffering, and that the world would have to be teetering on the brink of non-existence for the addition of a few more instances of famine or disease or natural disaster to cause it to topple over the edge, which is surely incredible – Schopenhauer's point is much subtler than this. For when he states that 'nine-tenths of mankind live in constant conflict with want, always balancing themselves with difficulty and effort on the brink of destruction',[10] what he's fundamentally saying is that mankind cannot take a world of near constant suffering. It is enough that suffering is critical and pervasive in all our striving, it only being abated for short periods – long periods of cessation resulting in just another form of suffering: that of boredom, a suffering that is in fact more intense than that of striving itself (for why else do we naturally seek or strive for almost anything in order to avoid it?) because even if the world were to worsen only incrementally, it would involve these brief moments of respite being made briefer still, or denied altogether, which would create a state of mind (rather than merely a state of affairs) where striving is seen never to reward, thereby damaging the very fabric of our willed existence, for even under all the many deceptions of phenomenal existence 'the miseries of life can very easily increase to such an extent [...] that death, which is otherwise feared more than everything, is eagerly resorted to'.[11] This – in light of the second of Schopenhauer's central pessimistic claims, in which we are described as constantly oscillating between striving and attaining, with periods of boredom rewarding any prolonging of the negative, a situation in which happiness is both reactive and negative, a temporary quieting or cessation of willing (and therefore of suffering), a returning to neutral – helps to establish a background for understanding Baudrillard's own precipices of human inanity and their attendant complexities and convolutions, their accelerations further inside a nothingness of our own myopic construction in which this worst of the worst of lives maintains an unbreachable and sadistic equilibrium both auto-corrective and bleakly sustaining.

But what are we to make of Schopenhauer's own admission that a large proportion of lives are easily sustainable and seen through in relative comfort? What indeed but the power and resilience of the world of simulacra to convince and charm and mollify? We are then 'doomed to artificial immunity, continual transfusions and, at the slightest contact with the world outside, instant death'.[12] How else would we come up with the argument that the very transient and ephemeral nature of pleasure is actually an inherent aspect of its enjoyment, as it is of life itself, if just the very thought of pleasure did not itself serve to keep the world at bay?

In our xenophobic refusal to become machines, only suffering can realize an end to suffering. Only suffering can enact compassion. Morality cannot will itself, as it can only exist as a renunciation of willing: 'I have presented suffering to a certain extent as a substitute for virtue and holiness; but we have to hope for our salvation and deliverance rather from what we suffer than from what we do.'[13] Knowledge of the oneness of suffering redeems the saint and so effects the only available means to truly reduce suffering: the comprehensive annihilation of will. Schopenhauer refers to a race of sufferers, as it is a general salvation that he is promoting, and such a result can only come about through the destruction of will brought on by the deprivation of that manifestation of will that is the body. It is not that the saint chooses suffering over compassion, but that suffering is the only truly effective means of achieving compassion's goal: the genuine reduction of suffering. This in turn brings us on to the second and more reactive route to achieving salvation: by means of suffering itself. These will be instances where life has continually bombarded us with such pain that we no longer choose to associate with a suffering self, and that self becomes disembodied. We instead associate only with that which like 'a gleam of silver suddenly appears from the purifying flame of suffering',[14] that is, the shared nature of one's suffering, the oneness that has until that point been hidden, but which now shows itself as will and its manifestations as necessary sufferers. From then on desires and products of will are clearly seen and consequently denied. The result is peaceful and sublime, but again will only be completed with a death that is conterminous with the will's own death.

There is, though, no willing the denial of will[15] (that state which Franz Kafka's fasting artist transcends), nor do we actively stop willing, for what we must do is nothing, allowing the will to *turn* and *deny* itself, to burn itself out. The failure of the will-turner to eat and eventually to even move leaves the will in a state of continual frustrated striving. The will has lost its primacy over the intellect and burns itself out trying to regain it. This is not without problems, however, for an account of willing that conflates willing and action, as Schopenhauer's does, for if there is no fundamental distinction between willing and acting, how does the will not result in action without immediately ceasing to exist? This is the non-sustainability of paradox, and what else is death but this condition?

To die, as most do, still willing life, results in the destruction of the individual that life was willed for but not a destruction of the will that willed that life. In this death the phenomenal expires, while what the individual essentially was continues. The individual in question will no longer experience suffering, because there is no longer an individual to suffer, but the will that was the individual will undoubtedly spew forth new life forms, new individuals, fresh sufferers. And that this is a lesser form of death is unequivocally a moral judgement, for the will-turner not only dispenses with his own individual self, but the very will that gave rise to him and would give rise to other afflicted individuals. Another individual will not have to suffer in order to learn that non-existence is preferable to existence. The reward for the will-turner (which of course he will not exist to receive), the bliss of which Schopenhauer speaks, can only be an apophatic harmony, a state that is everything in its nothingness, but a very different nothing to the 'very real world of ours with all its suns and galaxies, [that] is [also] nothing'.[16] The separation of life from suffering is a moral obligation, and that this separation involves a separation of life from itself is a mere circumstantial obstacle over which real virtue must throw itself.

To say that the destruction of the will is a moral act suggests that the act was not necessitated by grounds that are not up to me. The character, for Schopenhauer, is incapable of change, and therefore cannot be where the switch from affirmation to denial occurs. Nevertheless, although the initial turning is not up to me, what is up to me is whether or not I continue my affliction of the will. I have, it seems, a choice whether or not to return to my old state of full willed existence. The will to life constantly tries to assert itself, and so the virtue of the saint/ascetic is in remaining faithful to the truth, not seeking to cloud or block out his newly acquired knowledge in the supposed instant gratifications of the will. This has obvious religious connotations, as the will-turner has to turn away from the ephemeral congenialities of the will, persevering amid temptation, temptations with which his very body is seeking to lure him back. The turning itself is also sometimes compared with a religious conversion, although the choice to conduct our lives in a chaste and unsullied manner in order to precipitate such a change is ultimately up to us, a voluntary act. This sudden freedom from will is mysterious: we are given freedom (we couldn't freely choose it as there would be nothing to give), but once freedom is imposed upon us we have a responsibility to the truth, to employ our new gift strictly according to the knowledge of the thing-in-itself that it seems is somehow bequeathed with it.

Schopenhauer regards evil as being only of the phenomenal realm, a disease of individuals, a febrile form of ignorance – a failure to realize that the distinction between self and others is illusory, that suffering is not manifold but uniform; whereas compassion, in contrast, only seeks the extirpation of suffering, and to that end the cessation of all phenomenal manifestations of the thing-in-itself, the noumenal, the untranslatable and incommunicable completeness beyond us. To will the end of suffering is to will the end of the world.

But the will itself is divisible on Schopenhauer's account, into will to life and will as thing-in-itself, so the question is which of these is destroyed by our dying well. When Schopenhauer describes the will as destructible, we tend to think he's referring to will as thing-in-itself as well as will to life, otherwise what would prevent will as thing-in-itself again manifesting itself as will to life once the particular subject who denied the will has ceased to live? Schopenhauer thus appears to appropriate two instances of positive knowledge about the will as thing-in-itself, namely, that it is one and destructible. However, if the will as thing-in-itself is one and indivisible, to deny this will is not to deny part of it but all of it, and yet Schopenhauer talks as if he who denies the will denies only that part of will that is him, and this would be to divide, separate off or diminish its oneness, thereby suggesting that not only can the will be broken up into parts in its manifestation in the phenomenal world, but that it is somehow segregated as it is as thing-in-itself. Either this or one man denying the will would eradicate will in its entirety, which cannot be the case. That said, while this inconsistency is ostensibly damning, it is, as we shall see, actually constitutive of pessimism's continued relevance to the possibilities for human individuality and meaning, as these recalcitrant delusions are put under further threat by the hypermodern malaise of what Baudrillard calls Integral Reality.

8.2 Some Hell of Obscene Clarity

We see clearly not only at our own peril, but at the peril of the real itself. This depressive's wisdom is a felt and excoriating truth, and yet its age is a goad, and its entrenchment, among thinkers of this honest persuasion (those lost and godless men of God), a neutered call to arms. What there is to notice you need only notice once, and it is this: '*The special quality of hell is to see everything clearly down to the last detail.*'[17]

Once you have seen these details Hell is in you like a grub, a germ, a parasite with a voice that no deafness, however finely cultivated, can expunge from the soundtrack of the ailing muddiness of your human existence. But regardless of the risked catatonia of it, it is here in this misfortune of Hell, this erasure of seeing clearly, that we liberate ourselves from the world, where we suffer for no reason, and where that suffering liberates itself from meaning to mean only one thing: the distant inexplicability of death. For once this misery is found there are no further miseries. They are all obliterated and remain that way as long as the threat of happiness can be mitigated, because, as Baudrillard warns, happiness is a dangerous sport:

> Contrary to received opinion, misfortune is easier to manage than happiness – that is why it is the ideal solution to the problem of evil. It is misfortune that is most distinctly opposed to evil and to the principle of evil, of which it is the denial. / Just as freedom ends in total liberation and, in abreaction to that liberation, in new servitudes, so the ideal of happiness leads to a whole culture of misfortune, of recrimination, repentance, compassion and victimhood.[18]

Happiness will draw death into the black hole, into the Integral Reality, have it absorbed as if it were just some other functionary of the immanent and undeniable good of existence, because happiness cannot see outside itself, cannot see what it must become, what the entropy of being human will do to it. And with God a history, a scripture, a culture, a disease of the mind, why not death too, God's secular replacement, dispensed with in a similar fashion, in the digestive fluids of the happy human? And all this because happiness is enough all on its own, and needing nothing beyond its own state is pure and undefinable, so that when it goes it takes everything with it, all the shit of the universe you sucked inside it for safe keeping – and what better evidence is needed that 'God's cunning is infinite'.[19]

Accordingly, it is not that we must redeem ourselves, but that we must redeem the excesses of the happiness we endured – and which left, because it always leaves, because its sole resource of meaning is inextricable from its leaving – and so our focus is 'no longer the redemption of man and his sin, but the redemption of the death of God. That death has to be redeemed by a compulsive effort to transform the world.'[20] But the death of God is only one measure of it, as it is now the God of death that must somehow be redeemed.

This is the best of possible worlds because it is also the worst. No ideal can support itself. Tedium kills and it cures, both at the same time. (Baudrillard talks of 'artificial paradises' as if there were some other kind. Thus his status as a joker – the evil kind who has cut his own smile into the reluctant musculature of his face – is consolidated.)[21] We want what we do not want so that we can refrain from wanting what we want. We are so sick that there are some of us that can be happy here. Others want a way out, but one that is less an escape route and more a surreptitious and circuitous way back in. A few are able to acknowledge the escape route for what it is and make sure never to find it: they say, 'Let us be worthy of our "perversity," of our evil genius, let us measure up to our tragic involvement in what happens to us.'[22] This is what it means to come to an understanding with evil, to unearth its composition and to know that you are being lied to, to know that your understanding falls short of it and must fall short of it, and that this constitutes the form of its understanding.

If there's a need that humans have, its connection with clarity – with some access to the world free of need, of metaphor, of interest, of motivation, of distraction, and of all human context (the abyss of Clarice Lispector's squashed cockroach) – is infinitely complex and problematic, which is itself a human need. And so we do not deplete the source of our own confusion and suffering, and nor do we refuse to eat the poison that brings us to a place of being needful. Indeed, for Baudrillard this needfulness is exemplified in a knowing weaponization of an immanent human disgust:

> But human beings do need something, and with knowledge they can make the very intolerableness of life a weapon, though at the same time that intolerableness is not reduced in the slightest.[23]

A question remains, nevertheless, as to the deployment of this weaponized intolerance of life. There is no question as to its target, for its target is quite patently the life of which it is intolerant. But how does this intolerance engage with life, and what is it intended to defend or establish as in some sense victorious? The victory could not be one that moderated life, for it is life that feeds our intolerance of it, and that remains undiminished. And how could any kind of victory over life benefit an assailant so vitally reliant on it? The answer, it seems, must lie in the identity we construct for ourselves out of life's infrangible intolerableness, the weapon of not only suffering from life, but in some sense identifying and being the thing that suffers in this way. Our weapon is to embody the perfect receptacle for life's intrinsic abhorrence. Life's intolerableness cannot be reduced, but it can be made into the reason for our existence, a justification for ourselves as its ideal witness – what else is Christianity but this awareness made practice?

Like those terrorists, who 'have succeeded in turning their own deaths into an absolute weapon against a system that operates on the basis of the exclusion of death',[24] we have turned life's intolerableness, its inescapable suffering, into a weapon against a system that is built on the promise of well-being and happiness, a system of our own making but over which we had no control, the enemy of our humanness that finds itself where it is, and that it is. For the 'extraordinary potlatch [...] between those who wager their own death and those who cannot wager it because they no longer control it',[25] there is instead the equally conspicuous potlach of those who wager their own insignificance and those whose significance is not theirs to determine. And if, as Baudrillard states, there is here a question of parity to be answered, as to which side's investment is of greater magnitude,[26] it is worth noting that only one position is willing to live out their chosen death, day by day, and without recompense.

It is also worth noting that it is only *with knowledge* that the intolerableness of life is weaponized. For this is not merely to state the obvious, and so state that the insufferable life must be known to be insufferable in order for us to transform that awareness into an identity for ourselves, but is in addition a subtle explication of the very system of this human weaponization. Hence we must remain mindful that 'all knowledge, all certainty produces an equal or even greater uncertainty',[27] and that it is this very uncertainty that affords us our most resilient method of defence/attack. In the midst of our certainty at having been abandoned in a hostile and indifferent universe, there remains the childlike extrapolation which is the deep uncertainty as to why:

The human race owes its becoming (and perhaps even its survival) entirely to the fact that it had no end in itself, and certainly not that of becoming what it is (of fulfilling itself, identifying with itself). [...] It is the same with the individual being. Its only chance of becoming is to have no end, no ideal formula or alternative solution.[28]

This clarity, with all its attendant depressions, relies for its effect on a relentless process of displacement. Such displacement involves asking too much of objects and of thought, of placing them outside of the contexts in which they might mean something, or in which they are able to give the impression of meaning, and so placing them outside of illusion. As Baudrillard notes, this displacement is most obvious in its contrived coercion of the real:

> You expel things into the real and force them to mean something. But perhaps things are never 'true' except at this price: being led under too garish light, with too high a standard of fidelity.[29]

The demand is the demand for the obscene, for 'the truer than true', the 'more visible than the visible',[30] and so as a consequence the demand also arises that the resultant depression mean something. But then the depression is itself just the highest realization of obscenity, and therefore can mean only what obscenity has to offer: 'the absolute proximity of the thing seen, the gaze stuck in the screen of vision – hypervision in close-up, a dimension without any distance, the total promiscuity of the look with what it sees. Prostitution.'[31] What we hoped to see has been sold off for the very act of seeing. There is only the act left, only its clarity, its denuded purity, the simplicity of Hell. There is no more looking towards, but only this looking through: this looking through with nothing beyond it, because its transparency is still its surface, because there is only the surface left, a surface that isn't hiding anything, a surface without an interior, and without any secrets of its own. The obscene removes the hidden without removing the need for the hidden, without emancipating us from the need to enquire as to its whereabouts, its existence: it is a necessary and sufficient cruelty; it is the last hope of the hopeless. In the end there is only the momentum of the clarity itself, only the automaton-like drifting in this Hell, just the endless, pointless grinding industry of a prostituted life fucking itself into a fine and ugly powder:

> But we shouldn't underestimate the power of the obscene, its power to exterminate all ambiguity and all seduction and deliver us to the definitive fascination of bodies without faces, faces without eyes, and eyes that don't look.[32]

Notes

1   Baudrillard, *Simulacra and Simulation*, 160.
2   Baudrillard, *The Agony of Power*, 124.
3   Ibid., 161.
4   Ibid., 163.
5   Ibid., 164.
6   Albert Camus, *The Plague* (London: Penguin Books, 1971), 134.
7   Baudrillard, *The Vital Illusion*, 37.
8   Ibid., 48.
9   Arthur Schopenhauer, *The World as Will and Representation*, trans. E. F. J. Payne (New York: Dover, 1969), Vol. 2, 605.
10 Schopenhauer, *The World as Will and Representation*, Vol. 2, 584.
11 Schopenhauer, *The World as Will and Representation*, Vol. 1, 325.
12 Baudrillard, *The Transparency of Evil*, 61.
13 Schopenhauer, *The World as Will and Representation*, Vol. 2, 636.
14 Schopenhauer, *The World as Will and Representation*, Vol. 1, 392.
15 A denial of the will is in no way a suicide, for suicide is not life's denial but its frustrated affirmation, the result of life not fulfilling the hopes we had for it. This is essentially the danger of optimism, which heaps disappointment on misery. The suicide attempts to take the paradox with him into death.
16 Schopenhauer, *The World as Will and Representation*, Vol. 1, 412.
17 Yukio Mishima, *The Temple of the Golden Pavilion* (New York: Vintage, 2001), 41–42, quoted in Baudrillard, *The Intelligence of Evil*, 136, (emphasis in the original).
18 Baudrillard, *The Intelligence of Evil*, 112.
19 Ibid., 121.
20 Ibid., 113.
21 Ibid., 112.
22 Ibid., 118.
23 Ibid., 137.
24 Jean Baudrillard, *The Spirit of Terrorism* (New York: Verso, 2003), 16.
25 Baudrillard, *The Agony of Power*, 114.
26 'What is at stake in global confrontation is this provocation to generalized exchange, the unbridled exchange of all differences, the challenge for other cultures to equal us in deculturation, the debasement of values, the adhesion to the most disenchanted models. [...] Does the slow-death strategy or systematic mortification equal the stakes of a sacrificial death?' (Baudrillard, *The Agony of Power*, 69).
27 Baudrillard, *The Intelligence of Evil*, 150.
28 Ibid., 167.
29 Baudrillard, *Fatal Strategies*, 83.
30 Ibid., 78.
31 Ibid., 84.
32 Ibid., 84.

Chapter 9

SMELL-O-VISION: THE MURDER SHOW

What will soon follow logically, are the televised snuff movies and bodily harm. Death should logically enter the screen as an experimental event. Not at all as a sacrifice – at the same time as they try to make it disappear technologically, death will reappear on the screen as an extreme experience.[1]

The victim is an inconvenience.[2] As we reheat the past, as we would food to kill any bacteria, to form our future, there's the inevitable impulse to want some parts warmer than others. The victim rots quicker than the victimizer, and the reapplication and maintaining of heat releases the stench of the wronged over that of the wrongdoer. And the stench here is the stench of innocence, the smell of a past that we'd really rather only see, while acknowledging the need to smell, to experience, to eventually die there with them. Remembering as deterrence, when 'forgetting is still too dangerous',[3] is primarily concerned with identifying the perpetrators, and not the victims, regardless of how the latter may have been singled out. The problem is that the victim is always chosen in these instances, and the choosing always refers back not to the consequence of that choice but to the artificiality of the structures of the choice itself. It is the artifice that we are so desperate to recreate, in all its compelling and convoluted remodelling of what we take to be human, while the dead become a supplementary aroma that earths the electricity of thought in the pervading shame of the real. The stench makes our eyes water, but the vision appals and sickens and intrigues and shows itself as something we all now recognize as a horror narrative, as cinematic, as imagination played out by men and women who did not know they were acting, but who thought their involvement had much less reality, that what was happening was just life, just the standard digestion of history, thinking they too would one day be allowed to die, or else psychosis would perhaps rid them of the smell of ever having arrived on the planet.

One hope for the Holocaust never being repeated is its never having stopped. To allow it to end is to admit some final understanding, and we cannot permit ourselves to understand. All we can do is repeat its affront to our health in many tiny measured doses, like a vaccine. Its reproduction produces heat through layers, one on top of the other, both masking and recreating the smell, and so obscuring the core memory of there being such a series of events. And we watch from outside, no longer sensate of its heat, smelling nothing, and seeing nothing else but just how large it has grown. Auschwitz is no black hole,[4] it's wallpaper: thousands of variations on the same pattern overlaying each other, and us looking at the latest and noticing how, while the wall has grown, the room left in which to see it is slowly shrinking.

What constitutes bad taste here: a smell-o-visual documentary on the Holocaust, or the usual watching experience and the usual lessening of effect, the usual nothing? The problem is not the stench of the victims but our inability to smell it. Watching is no longer enough, guilt no longer appeased but amplified, thus the ubiquitous desire to expand our presence to wherever we aren't. The sickness, though, is that while we might imagine ourselves ben-evolent emancipators, reversing irreversible horrors, the true source of our own escape, our own curative hope, is entangled not in aiding their release but in joining them, and suffering alongside. The deterrent therefore is paradox-ical: the need that it never happen again, and the need for it to happen again to us, and to keep on happening.

9.1 The Pataphysical Murder-Machine

On the people of Sarajevo when it was under siege in the first half of the 1990s, Baudrillard has this to say: 'But we know better than they do what reality is, because we have chosen them to embody it.'[5] (You know you're in trouble when you become somebody else's reality.) Thousands of dead inno-cents, approximately 1,500 of them children, is the material of something happening, is what it takes now for human existence to show itself. About how all these dead bodies are subsequently absolved of significance, he goes on to say:

> No human being deserves to be killed for anything whatsoever. A final acknowledgement of insignificance: both of ideas and of people. This statement, which actually seeks to show the greatest respect for life, attests only to a contempt and an indifference for ideas and for life. Worse than the desire to destroy life is this refusal to risk it – nothing being worth the trouble of being sacrificed. This is truly the worst offence, the worst affront possible. It is the fundamental proposition of nihilism.[6]

Are we to then suppose that such episodes of carnage are not as wasteful, not as rooted in self-important silliness as they at first appear, that these thousands of corpses are not the expediential chaff of belief's own pathological need to be heard? The problem here is that the desire for sacrificial legitimacy, that bodies be regarded as sacrificeable for the abstractions of ideas and life, becomes its own justification: we have meaning because it is legitimate that some of us might have to die in order that we have meaning. This is the war against nihilism come full circle. This is the wretched prophylactic keeping us from nihilism. It is as if life were made up of a series of longueurs scarcely separated by brief and increasingly questionable periods of … of what? of reasons to die? of reasons for there to be reasons to die? War is surely one of the least nihilistic pastimes. But this is only because nihilism is an idea, and death (in the now) is almost never where its advocates want to end up. The war may believe in itself, but this does not mean that we believe in the war, or more crucially that the war believes in us.

> In the past, we had objects to believe in – objects of belief. These have
> disappeared. But we also had objects not to believe in, which is just as
> vital a function. Transitional objects, ironic ones, so to speak, objects of
> our indifference, but objects none the less. Ideologies played this role
> reasonably well. These, too, have disappeared.[7]

No more the ideologies of war, only the ideology of war. Baudrillard has stepped over himself to inform us, on numerous occasions, how the notion of war as a circumstance wherein something is at stake is now behind us, how there is only the spectacle left, how war is now only an empty showcase for itself. War is not comprised of conflicts among meanings, but is itself the conflict of meaning with its own self-alienation. War is nihilism in conflict with itself,[8] meaning that life is expendable for the sake of some point of principle because people have been found willing to die for it, and this willingness to die, which is in large part the point of the principle's very self-evidence, is thereby sanctified by the institution of war in order that the willingness continue at all costs, that the willingness outlive itself in the deaths already accrued in its name, that it be perpetuated by proxies, that whatever happens there will be something worth dying to preserve or prevent, if only because without the possibility of sacrifice, death is just something that happens and is no longer a creative enterprise. War is *the* creative industry … of death. Death's embellishment and reality's killer, no less. On its own, death gives us nothing:

> The pataphysic mind is the nail in the tire – the world, a puffball. The
> paunch is at one and the same time a hot air balloon, a nebula, or even

the perfect sphere of knowledge. The intestinal sphere of the sun. There is nothing to get from death. Can a tire die? It releases its rubber soul. Farting is the source of breath. / The principle is to exaggerate: that is how to destroy reality.[9]

The industry of war has a single commodity: threat. It knows that at 'the point when everyone is potentially saved, no one is', that from here on in 'salvation no longer has any meaning'.[10] In light of this, it also knows that once salvation becomes meaningless so too does the materialist dream of a worldly (contained) beyond. In order to maintain its seduction it must not only find new threats but insinuate them into normalcy. We find the same tactic in the pornographic industry, which has taken various marginal sexual practices (anal sex, multiple penetrations, frostings, rosebudding, etc.) and manoeuvred them into its mainstream product. Both are engaged in exercises in counter-complacency which feed the imaginations of the consumers: deviancy is everywhere, so pay attention! Neither industry can ever offer any ultimate satisfaction, or any satisfaction whatsoever that is not integrally related to the satisfaction of their own need for a state of permanently replenishing dissatisfaction. Only the promise seduces. Fulfilling on that promise would only enlighten us as to the banality of the original seduction, which once complete has no further reserves with which to again seduce, like 'a logistics of pleasure which goes straight to its objective, only to find its object dead'.[11]

All wars now are wars of reality, and all past wars too. And we have reality, but reality does not give us the world. Reality gives us a version of a version of the world; and because it cannot escape this versioning, reality is only ever real or hyperreal and never absolute, for the absolute is only an incomplete version of itself. The absolute of war is Alfred Jarry's Bosse-de-Nage, 'who, having only existed imaginarily, could not really die',[12] and who never having become must be repeated. For we should recall that despite his vocalizations being restricted exclusively to 'ha ha!' he is nevertheless always expected to say more, to elaborate, as if he had been cut short by circumstances, as if laughter could not possibly be conclusive. Even when he is killed by strangulation (a fitting end), he cannot die, and returns as before, as a spectre, as the too-long-extended joke of life, the duality of 'ha ha!' itself supposedly proving 'that the perception of Bosse-de-Nage was notoriously discontinuous, not to say discontinuous and analytical, unsuited to all synthesis and to all adequations'.[13] This is the reason that the war-torn (the combatants and innocents alike) make such good representatives of reality, for they are the embodied and forced curtailments of a world subjected to (filtered through) the abstraction of perpetuity, the real made real by the imposed significance of death's own creative immanence. What better way to cut short our laughter than death's seduction of itself?

Regardless of what societal atrocities they may incorporate, neither war nor pornography is a perversion. Both are firmly grounded instead in seduction, in the potentiality of an inward-looking sacrifice, in the aptitude of humans to consciously play at playing, and ultimately to immortalize their own declarative resolution to mortality. On the distinction, Baudrillard writes:

> The pervert always gets involved in a maniacal universe of mastery and the law. He seeks mastery over the fetishized rule and absolute ritual circumscription. The latter is no longer playful. It no longer moves. It is dead, and can no long put anything into play except its own death. Fetishism is the seduction of death, including the death of the rule in perversion. / Perversion is a frozen challenge; seduction, a living challenge. Seduction is shifting and ephemeral; perversion, monotonous and interminable. Perversion is theatrical and complicit; seduction, secret and reversible.[14]

It is the nihilist, all things considered, that is the pervert: that actor of his own inertia, that droning dead end with ears only for its own voice, that corpse refusing to play with anything but itself. For the nihilist's philosophy, like that of the pataphysician, is essentially of 'the gaseous state', a philosophy that 'revolves around itself and ruminates the diarrheic incongruence, unsmilingly, mushrooms and rotting dreams'.[15] And doesn't pornography exhaust itself in this same way, with its monotonous depiction of the same acts perpetrated by and on different bodies, with the yawning abyss of arousal itself? And war too seems to inhabit much the same auto-attritional cul-de-sac. After all, where is the secrecy in the stretched, high-definition orifices of pornography? Such grotesqueries of over-exposure surely work by saturation not seduction: a sentiment shared by Baudrillard, who claimed that pornography, by making sex too real, could never seduce – seduction being marked by subtraction, pornography by excess. However, while pornography and war might both escape perversion by some margin, the former despite its excesses, far from being incapable of seduction might be considered as something of a master practitioner – albeit an inscrutably clandestine one. What prevents war and pornography from ever becoming perversions is their inherent playfulness, emanating in both cases from a supreme lack of self-consciousness – perversion being the very epitome of a relentless and unforgiving self-consciousness. Neither one realizes how tedious and distasteful it is, how all the many toys and transfigurations are nothing but an ever-thinning camouflage shielding this inescapable hideousness from view. A child lost in play, war always takes itself seriously, and no credible self-consciousness would ever permit that. But then 'credibility is only a special effect'.[16] It is admittedly peculiar that pornography should lack this self-awareness, for its stylization of the sex act would appear to be reliant on it as the precise condition of its existence. This, though, would be a synecdochic error, whereby each instantiation of contrived sexual gratification is substituted for the industry at large. The performers, directors, camera crew and the like are all in the business of knowingly manipulating images of carnal pleasure,[17] but, essentially, pornography is an innocent: it plays as if there is some crucial importance in its immense popularity, as if all the while it keeps saturating us with sex, existence and pleasure cannot be far away. As a significant element of the wider leisure industry, its excursions into the lubricated apertures of attractive strangers constitute the perfect simulacrum of sustenance, a formulaic vicariousness open to all in the unquestionable service of human freedom. Its secret is it no longer believes in pleasure, only the actively conceived importance of selling it; and it is this that is its lived experiment, its hidden ephemerality, its squirming and mutable core.

Although 'seduction, being a sacrificial process, ends with a murder (the deflowering)',[18] the terminations of war and pornography are multitudinous, fleeting and inconsequent, tempering murder with their covenants of repetition. The requirement for 'an irrevocable presence of evil, an evil from which there is no possible redemption',[19] is itself the perversion of which they cannot be seen to partake, the dead end that rescinds the game, the reflexive zombification not only of its participants but of the practice as a whole. If seduction is immortality, perversion is the lifeless afterlife of the refractorily undead. Death, on this account, becomes the core constituent of seduction, as Baudrillard himself points out:

> We seduce with our death, our vulnerability, and with the void that haunts us. The secret is to know how to play with death in the absence of a gaze or gesture, in the absence of knowledge or meaning.[20]

Seduction remains active so what is seducing can see itself as if no one were looking, when all the time death is looking outwards at itself. This is a mimicry of self-consciousness, in order that life be represented enough to die, but not so much that it is seen as already dead. (Who but the ultimate seducer would invite a corpse to an orgy?)

That there is nothing to fight and die for, nothing to hide that hasn't already been seen, that hasn't already been watched to death, serves to remind us of the abiding utility of sacrifice, without which reality would engulf us. But this fiction is only a temporary stay of execution, for the 'real is growing ever larger, [and] some day the entire universe will be real, and when the real is universal, there will be death'.[21] This death though will be a different death, a cleaved portion of death, as with Schopenhauer: a death removed from all sense of removal, a state sucked of consequence and so of finality, just one more function of a useless functionality. And so rituality too must then suffer itself in this wasteland of the real, this earth churned up and bubbling with the living and the dead made harmonic to the same soulless tune. For there can be no ritual without external compulsion, without the possibility for ceremony to enact a significance wider than our habitual longing for the ceremonious. How lonely then to perish under this gauze of a sky seen not as a shield against cosmic indifference, but as an image of our own indifference projected outwards merely for the sake of distance. And so it is with this proposed dualism of death that the following conflation inevitably occurs:

> Death itself ceases to be an event, a specific, individual destiny. Diluted in the clone or in a kind of mental coma, it disappears on the biological horizon of the machine body.[22]

The sacrificial and seductive death of war is here assimilated into the mental stultification of nihilism's already-dead. The murder-machine lays splayed open, all its many layers of armour plating peeled apart to reveal human organs run riot like bindweed. And how the old death now seems more purely machinic, and yet as a consequence more responsive and alive. For didn't that creative order, through which our human biology absorbed the aestheticization involved in being adopted by our own future, constitute a preparedness for death that indulged our instinctual notions of what it is for something to mean enough to die; and in contradistinction to this new melding, this rotting of the human from the inside, establishes nothing more than the uneventfulness of an unrecognizable and hyperrealized chaos. And, in the end, no system can escape its own wanting for its own death, however steeped it may be in the living out of that death: 'Everything seeks its own death, including power. Or rather, everything demands to be exchanged, reversed, and abolished within a cycle.'[23]

9.2 The Residue of Residues

'*When everything is taken away, nothing is left.* / This is false.'[24] And it is false because nothing is not a nothing, but rather the everything that everything's manifestation occludes. For if what is left is the mirror of what is left, the reversed image of itself, then all that is there but not there for us is returned to us through its being shown to be absent. In other words, we are relieved of illusion, the deception dismantled, so that finally we can see the joke and laugh, for we are no longer the unwitting brunt of it but both its architect and its audience. The suspicion, however, and this suspicion is darkling and terrifying in equal and correlative measure, is that this deepest of deep laughs will never arrive at its end, that its plummet will be abyssal, swallowing the human world over and over in its insatiable need for air, for keeping the death of the joke alive forever.

Nothing is left when there is no room left to manoeuvre, when elbow room, increasingly at a premium, is made impossible, for the remainder must at all costs permit movement, so that when it cannot, nothing itself replaces the former potentiality of an unfinished saturation – when nothing having become everything becomes nothing again and so *potentially* everything, but only potentially: the way a dream remains the potential of the life it appears to mimic. Consider what remains of those series of continuities and connections we recognized as a person when they are catastrophically disrupted (in the event of madness or dementia), when the self-recycling of personhood becomes irrevocably polluted, so much so that all that appears to be left behind is some concentrated mutation of sanity and persistence: a confined self-replicating cycle that we can identify as senseless only because of its apparent simplicity and relative smallness, because we can see all the way around it, thereby getting an accurate idea of its internal logic while at the same time finding no use value for it outside of its own sealed context. And madness is ultimately all that is left of those outside as well, once the gods have finished with them – with us. What, though, of this prima facie remainder, this 'surplus of meaning' so industrious and yet in isolation so fearsomely meaningless? For while Baudrillard is not wrong to point out that 'normality sees itself today in the light of madness, which was nothing but its insignificant remainder',[25] it is significantly short of elucidating the full extent of madness's influence on its other, because although normality monitors and justifies itself in opposition to what it regards as instances of aberration, those instances do not continue to be remainders indefinitely, as madness, though in part quarantined, nevertheless asks questions of the normality (or sanity) that surrounds it, gesturing to this remote zone as not the body from which it has broken off, but instead the remainder of itself – the delusion of the real, that order with no outside, that it has left behind for its own simplified and self-contained version. It is us then looking in that come to look like excess, like an erroneous extrapolation of this opaque bubble of insanity. If the entire human project is festooned with glitches of which we are intractably unaware, then what is madness but a localization of this universal state, a diorama of the bigger picture that reduces the latter to a forsaken encumbrance, an irrelevant orgiastic dilution, the emanation of a squeamish and tremulous desire to disown your death, to share it with others whose own deaths you will share in? And what is the social if not a death cult? An arena for collective dying, the social is constructed from this very ability to accrete the dead, to normalize us in the imperishable leftovers (the enduring waste) of humanity's self-contextualizing interrelations:

> Litter piling up from the symbolic order as it blows around, it is the social as remainder which has assumed real force and which is soon to be universal. Here is a more subtle form of death. In this event, we are really even deeper in the social, even deeper in pure excrement, in the fantastic congestion of dead labor, of dead and institutionalised relations within terrorist bureaucracies, of dead languages and grammars (the very term 'relation' already has something dead about it, something about death to it). Then of course it can no longer be said that the social is dying, *since it is already the accumulation of death*. In effect we are in a civilisation of the supersocial, and simultaneously in a civilisation of non-degradable, indestructible residue, piling up as the social spreads.[26]

This picture of societal sanity is one comprised of perpetual smaller ends each serving as a subterfuge for the one universalized end. In other words, this meticulous fending off of madness is the closest we can get to not dying alone, for our sanity, our normality, is just a conditioning programme for death.

Notes

1   Baudrillard, *The Conspiracy of Art*, 193.
2   From genocide, to serial killings, to spree and revenge killings, and beyond. See Edia Connole and Gary J. Shipley (eds), *Serial Killing: A Philosophical Anthology* (London: Schism Press, 2015).
3   Baudrillard, *Simulacra and Simulation*, 49.
4   See ibid.
5   Baudrillard, *The Perfect Crime*, 134.
6   Ibid., 141.
7   Ibid., 142.
8   Invoking Nietzsche's division of nihilism into two camps: weak (passive) and strong (active). See Friedrich Nietzsche, *The Will to Power*, ed. Walter Kaufmann (New York: Vintage Books, 1968), 33–82.
9   Baudrillard, *The Conspiracy of Art*, 213.
10   Baudrillard, *The Intelligence of Evil*, 114.
11   Baudrillard, *Seduction*, 20.
12   Jarry, *Exploits & Opinions of Dr Faustroll, Pataphysician*, 83.
13   Ibid., 75.
14   Baudrillard, *Seduction*, 128.
15   Baudrillard, *The Conspiracy of Art*, 214.
16   Baudrillard, *Fatal Strategies*, 115.
17   Just as soldiers are frequently aware of the ineffectiveness and ultimate banality of the conflicts in which they are engaged.

18   Baudrillard, *Seduction*, 100.
19   Baudrillard, *The Intelligence of Evil*, 114.
20   Baudrillard, *Seduction*, 83.
21   Ibid., 32.
22   Baudrillard, *The Intelligence of Evil*, 155.
23   Baudrillard, *Seduction*, 45.
24   Baudrillard, *Simulacra and Simulation*, 143, (emphasis in the original).
25   Ibid., 145.
26   Baudrillard, *In the Shadow of the Silent Majorities*, 72–73, (emphasis in the original).

Chapter 10

THE EVIL DEATH

Evil and death can be thought of as Baudrillardian noumena:

> Of evil in the pure state it is impossible to speak. [...] The sovereign hypothesis, the hypothesis of evil, is that man is not good by nature, not because he might be said to be bad, but because he is perfect as he is.[1]
>
> In this way every detail of the world is perfect if it is not referred to some larger set. / In this way everything is perfect if it is not referred to its idea. / In this way the nothing is perfect since it is set against nothing. / And in this way evil is perfect when left to itself, to its own evil genius.[2]
>
> Evil is a confused, impenetrable idea. It is enigmatic in its very essence. Now, a tiny confused idea is always greater than a very big idea that is absolutely clear. [...] This impossibility of thinking evil is matched only by the impossibility of imagining death.[3]
>
> Good is transparent: you can see through it. / Evil, by contrast, shows through: it is what you see when you see through. Or alternatively, evil is the first hypothesis, the first supposition.[4]

Both are sense-making without themselves making sense. Both make the world available without themselves being available. Both can be logically inferred from our experience but are not themselves experienced. A quick survey of Kant's position will help realize the connections in more detail, before concentrating on Baudrillard's agenda, and how death and evil figure in a pessimistic account of the world.

When Kant turned his sights on pure reason run amok (the categories made the birthplace of illusions), and set about cleaving all objects in two (phenomena and noumena/empirical object and transcendental object/appearance and thing-in-itself), he left us in a half-world, a place of appearance, a place available to experience, susceptible to reason and yielding of knowledge, a place made for us and to which we are made, a place without escape – the place Heidegger later felt the need to detail as that in which we do not merely exist but in which we *dwell*, by necessity, never free from this Being-in, this inevitable

familiarity. Although the pure concepts of our understanding have no transcendental application, only an empirical one, there is, as Kant acknowledges,
still this *tendency* towards their *unconditioned* application: the desire to experience beyond the limits of experience, to bear witness to the world-without-us
and us-without-us, to obtain veridical access, to enact the impossible, to which
transcendental idealism is of course a check. Whether or not appearances
and things-in-themselves are distinct entities (Moses Mendelssohn), or the
latter are merely a different way of referring to or conceptualizing the former
(J. S. Beck), the problem of access remains: of whether we have access to a
distinct entity or access to a means of accessing. There is also the issue of
whether or not noumenon and thing-in-itself are conceptually equivalent
(Sebastian Gardner), and if they're not – the thing in itself being a bare ontological concept precluding knowledge, while the noumenon is considered an
epistemological concept, the concept of an object of an intellectual mode
of cognition – to which are we to gravitate when the limits of sensibility are
reached? To these ambiguities can be added that of how it is noumena are
considered by Kant to be thinkable, because '*for thought* the categories are not
limited by the conditions of our sensible intuition, but have an unlimited field.
It is only the *knowledge* of that which we think, the determining of the object,
that requires intuition'.[5] And this would clearly seem to imply that while we
cannot know the transcendental we are able to think it, that the transcendental is thinkable via a purely intellectual (and so non-sensible) intuition. Yet
how is this any more or less than a theoretical realization of the unrealiz-
able, a technical approximation of an experiential limit? But more crucially,
the noumenal is logically implied by appearance, without which appearance
would be incomplete, would no longer be appearance, for appearance must
be the appearance of something other than itself.[6] Thus this desire to turn
noumenon's negative into a positive is as much about escaping ourselves as
it is escaping the world (the half-world), the desire for our own xenofication,
our turning alien, of the possibility for knowing in a different way, outside
the restricted realm of the categories – the *anti-object* revealing the *anti-self*.
According to this essentially apophatic reasoning we consolidate the world in
all its possibilities via the inaccessibility of the world and all its impossibilities.
As Baudrillard writes:

> There is the continuity of the world, as it has meaning for us, and the
> continuity of the world as, in secret, it is nothing and means nothing.
> This latter does not, strictly speaking, exist. It cannot be verified, but
> can only betray itself, only 'show through' [*transparaître*] like evil, squint
> out through appearances. There is no dialectic between the two orders.
> Each is alien to the other.[7]

Schopenhauer's essentiality of suffering is, quite patently, a phenomenal and not a noumenal characteristic, and so it is in the suspension of our natural essence (the striving of the pure will) that a state of will-lessness can occur, as in aesthetic experience for instance. While everyday life affirms the fourfold root of the empirical world, aesthetic experience dispenses with it: individuality and, with it, our conditioning apparatus are forgotten, and being no longer able to distinguish ourselves from our perception we become immersed in the object, aware of it as pure idea in the Platonic sense of type (i.e. as an individual that embodies a type, as Platonic ideas are themselves individuals) rather than particular. And because individuality is where suffering manifests itself, aesthetic encounters allow us to not only transcend our individuality but also the pain that necessarily comes with it. The subject is transformed from the active state of scientific conceptualization to the passive absorption of an idea. In aesthetic experience, Schopenhauer encapsulated his two tenets of human meaning: the total cessation of willing (albeit temporary in this instance) and the attainment of an elevated knowledge, an objectivity that is only available through lack of self.

There are, for Schopenhauer, two methods of annihilating the will: the first and the rarest is the saintly life, and the second, more plebeian route, is through an increase in one's own suffering. The saint, having seen through the *veil of Maya* (the *principium individuationis*), accesses the knowledge that all is one, that all suffering is one universal state of suffering. This involves the saint identifying their pain with all others, and all others with their own, and then attempting to alleviate as much of the suffering of others as is achievable – a selfish willing having been replaced by a selfless, anegoic willing. Thus the saint at this stage is still willing (i.e. the well-being of others), whereas any genuine escape from willing only arises through objective knowledge of the hopelessness of attempting to assuage that which is an inherent aspect of phenomenal existence. It becomes increasingly apparent that pain and suffering are inseparable from phenomenal life, and the will is thereby severed from within the self, and all willing is from there on in silent . But in order to sustain this detachment from willing, to prevent its growing back and 'rivet[ing] the bonds anew',[8] the saint must always keep in mind this hard-won knowledge of the whole, lest the allurements of phenomenal existence ensnare us once more.[9] This is the limit of the saint, a limit that must be maintained until death if the will is to be defeated. But 'even the most perfect intelligence possible can be only a transition stage to that which no knowledge can ever reach'.[10]

Noumena are therefore antithetical to the apparatus of pessimism. The pessimist is relentless in recognizing his own and everything else's insignificance: his scope is boundless, for there is nothing to which his antinatalist antidote to all other meaning cannot be successfully administered. Nothing is out of reach, but noumena are of course out of reach by definition. Pessimism demands that thinking stop at the one good of nonexistence, so there is no need to posit the transcendental concept of evil. It demands that we stop at the hideous encumbrance of life, and either have death form some vindictive continuance of it (as with Julius Bahnsen),[11] or else have it constitute the desirable (if not desired) point at which the cessation of that curse transpires. But Baudrillard, in deference to Kant's crucial insight, argues that thinking does not and cannot stop there:

> Thinking based on evil is not pessimistic; it is the thinking based on misfortune that is pessimistic because it wants desperately to escape evil or, alternatively, to revel in it. / Thought, for its part, does not cure human misfortune, the terrible obviousness of which it absorbs for purposes of some unknown transformation. Pessimism excludes any depth that eludes its negative judgement, whereas thought wishes to penetrate magically beyond the fracture of the visible. The rays of the black sun of pessimism do not reach down to the floor of the abyss. [...] Thus the intelligence of evil goes far beyond pessimism. / In reality, the only genuinely pessimistic, nihilistic vision is that of good since, at bottom, from the humanist point of view, the whole of history is nothing but a crime.[12]

Nevertheless, this is not a wholesale repudiation of pessimism, for Baudrillard has too many sympathies there, but rather an acknowledgement of a deeper pessimism that should not be passed over, for the pessimist is not wrong in his appraisals, but not pessimistic enough when it comes to recognizing that their efficacy as a solution to human delusion will always be neutralized by irrefutable postulations of objects of which we necessarily remain ignorant.

To consider why it is that Baudrillard feels the need to transcendentalize evil and death, what it is about them that makes each so fundamental to our experience of the world and of ourselves, takes us back to the centrality of unreason, 'which is the very principle of evil',[13] and crucial also to our (non) understanding of death. Evil and death not only transcend experience, they transcend what can be ratiocinated, what can be known, and consequentially establish humanness as that condition of bodies in which the world permeates and is found permeable only via certain integral exclusions that prevent any human presence from being manifested in the world in its entirety. How this then fits with Kant's own complications in establishing a noumenal self will prove enlightening.

10.1 Kant's Schizo Self

Kant's conception of self-knowledge is rooted in inner sense, the form of which is time, and we can know ourselves only insofar as we affect (appear to) ourselves, because to have knowledge of the self as thing-in-itself would dismantle transcendental idealism, by permitting intellectual intuition of the self. The contents of this inner sense fall under the broad umbrella of mental representations, but unlike outer sense we cannot make the distinction between a mental thing and its intuition, for aside from its appearing it is nothing. But this does not constitute the self knowing itself, because the self is not given empirically and so is not an object of inner sense. The self therefore considers itself as a substratum for those mental representations, and not the representations themselves, and it is this substratum that is the object of inner sense. The only way that this mere substratum can appear to itself is through its transcendental ideality, because otherwise there would be no way of distinguishing how it appears from how it is in itself. The contents of the mind thus become phenomenal in order that we can have empirical knowledge of our minds and also the transcendental ideality of the self.

According to Kant, there are two forms of self-consciousness: inner sense and apperception. And while the object of inner sense is the determinate temporal order of mental representations, the object of apperception is the actual consciousness of our acts of thinking – the foundational mineness of experience. Apperception is therefore divided into the empirical and the transcendental, the former concerned with some given content and the latter in abstraction, free of all empirical content, and so a presupposed condition of experience itself. Nevertheless, this transcendental I is not the real, or noumenal self (which is something Descartes erroneously concluded), but is instead just the *unity of the synthesis of thoughts*. The subject of apperception can only be cognizant of itself via inner sense. But this subject's essential temporality thereby precludes its being noumenal, for to make such a connection to the noumenal would be to repeat Descartes' mistake. Alternatively, the thought is that Kant appears to be intensifying his noumenal ignorance thesis, so that the subject of apperception, of which we lack intellectual intuition, cannot be thought of as a noumenal object at all. On this reading the subject of apperception cannot be equated with the noumenal self, for the subject of apperception falls outside the range of our ability to conceptualize, so resting at the cusp of the world and not within it. Any knowledge of the self in Kant's system is likewise strewn with complexity and contradiction (and more besides those sketched here), and ultimately appears to rely on some inimitable supersensible awareness that he regretfully neglects to explain. All this, for

Baudrillard, is tied up with the desire to disappear, with some implausible yet desirous perspective of absenteeism:

> But disappearance may be conceived differently: as a singular event and the object of a specific desire, the desire no longer to be there, which is not negative at all. Quite to the contrary, disappearance may be the desire to see what the world looks like in our absence (photography) or to see, beyond the end, beyond the subject, beyond all meaning, beyond the horizon of disappearance, if there still is an occurrence of the world, an unprogrammed appearance of things. A domain of pure appearance, of the world as it is (and not of the real world, which is only ever the world of representation), which can emerge only from the disappearance of all the added values.[14]

The essentiality of unreason in Baudrillard's account of evil and death can here be seen to mirror Kant's own floundering when it comes to knowing and locating our human selves. Evil and death reside at the limit of our experience and our knowing, both resistant to conceptualization, and yet their classification as somehow still noumenal, still objects for the intellect, is seen to subsist. Evil and death must be there for us in the only way possible: in their not being there for us, in their necessary exclusion from the world and its beyond.

An answer to this quandary, should there be one, might possibly be found in madness, in some detached and schizoid absence from what is known and what cannot be known, what is seen and what cannot be seen. And might this not amount to some kind of abandonment of those precious and essential Kantian categories, to an expansion or mutation of his *transcendental object X*? Of just such an insane subject, Baudrillard has this to say:

> The schizo is deprived of all scene, open to all in spite of himself, and in the greatest confusion. He is himself obscene, the obscene prey of the world's obscenity. What characterizes him is less his light-years distance from the real, a radical break, than absolute proximity, the total instantaneousness of things, defenseless, with no retreat; end of interiority and intimacy, overexposure and transparency of the world that traverses him without his being able to interpose any barrier: for he can no longer produce the limits of his own being, and reflect himself; he is only an absorbant screen, a spinning and insensible plate for all the networks of influence.[15]

The schizo on this account is what we might think of as the world's failed attempt at establishing an honest human: a frameless mirror of the world, swollen to bursting point with its emptiness, himself a nothing, the nothing of the world, having absorbed it with scarcely a perimeter to contain it.

In the end we must ask this: Who can stand to look at the world all at once? Only the details are sufferable, the bits broken off by our localized gaze, the small truths that free us from a crushing and unthinkable immensity. And yet these small scale interrogations do not facilitate our escape from the world; they are instead ways inside its entirety, decryptions of a code so often hidden by its mass: 'The secret of the world is in the detail, in the fragment, in the aphorism – in the literal sense, *aphorizein* meaning to isolate, to separate, to cut off – not in the whole.'[16] We decipher death in the same way, through incremental dismemberments that don't so much seek to reveal the whole as seek to diminish it. But death like the world (as seen in Kant, Schopenhauer, and other kindred thinkers set on detailing some entrenched and ineludible beyond) resists us, neither one having any desire to become accessible to the minds of humans. Expanding on this idea, Baudrillard cannot resist the deliciousness of the thought that it is death that fends us off and not the other way round:

> Stanislaw Lec reverses the terms here: it is not we who defend ourselves against death, it is death that defends itself against us: 'Death resists us, but it gives in in the end.' / Nothing else so stunning as this has ever been said about death.[17]

Death resists us by fragmenting, by sacrificing parts of itself to our continued assaults, and so our thinking of death must also become fragmented and scattered. As a consequence our thinking comes to mimic death. And maybe it is when our thoughts are far enough apart that death finds it can do nothing else but yield to us. But this yielding is not death submitting to our desires for it, or not submitting *simpliciter*, at least, for it submits by not submitting – as does the world: 'If we cannot make the world the object of our desires, we can at least make it the object of a higher convention – which, precisely, eludes our desire.'[18]

Death, evil and the world all refuse to mean anything, and it is this refusal that prevents them ever being drained of meaning. We scratch away at them, excavate particles for analysis, isolate small quantities and reassemble them to make monsters all of our own, but they remain undiminished. Or if they are diminished, they do not appear to lack anything as a consequence of this diminishment. Death, evil and the world maintain their otherness, plain and undistorted, skewed in our vision of them, but literal in themselves and for themselves.

10.2 The Unthinkability of Meaning

It is no coincidence that the tenets of philosophical pessimism, and of a nihilistic trend of thought in general, can appear somewhat hackneyed in comparison with the machinic lifelessness of virtuality's own existential principles. 'Insignificance is under threat from an excess of meaning',[19] and in this environment our awareness of it means as much and as little as everything else. To lament the absence of a self, of a moral reality, and of an umbrella meaning justifying all other meaning is a strangulated bleat that, while no less accurate now than in any other millennia, has become strangely irrelevant – which is not to say it is now shunned or ignored as never before, because this was always the case. The irrelevance in question is no longer just a symptom of humanity's frailty when faced with itself, some tremulous turning away, back to life from its antithesis, but rather an acknowledgement of pessimism's (covert) foundational role in the world as we have made it. Pessimism has always been not so much ignored as assiduously discredited without the standard prerequisite of having first been given due recognition. And yet this history of dismissal, if anything, has provided pessimism with fresh impetus, as if its simple and unchanging message has been perceived as lost or misinterpreted anew, in ever more elaborate ways, as if the goal of the philosophy without goals was to enact something devastating, and not merely a cornucopian playground of ever more inventive means of distraction. And as a result, pessimism can appear outdated, for it is essentially the only principled position left. Its practitioners cannot accept that their position can be closely considered and even accepted (by some, in large part) only to be disregarded. It might even be considered the only position that while its premises are scientifically sound and uncontentious, and its conclusions logically consistent with those premises, it nevertheless somehow conditions a response that is utterly antipathetic to its message. Pessimism demands a radical reaction, a vital gesture of defiance, a violent abreaction, a critical seizure in life's perpetual normalization, but what it gets instead is an intensification of that normalized existence, an increased focus on and wonder at the world it undermined: an entire universe of lights and whistles, of fog and mirrors. And with this irrelevance comes the allegation of petulance and childishness, for does not the pessimist smack of the child who when invited to play a game persistently asks what the point of his playing is? It is supposedly the adults who know that the point is exclusively in the playing, that the game contains its own point, and that outside it, there need be nothing else – and nobody need mention the fact that the game is there precisely because there is nothing else. The counterargument is nevertheless of equal strength, for the suspicion of the pessimist is, of course, that it is the adults themselves that are childlike and fantastical in this scenario, and that they have not moved through the realization as they claim, but instead skipped over it in a nervous haste. And so an impasse is arrived at, but an impasse that, when appraised with the necessary diligence, reveals that it is not the pessimist that inhabits the elaborate dead end of our world, but everyone else for whom pessimism is inapposite.

What is clearly needed is not for pessimism to become, to transcend itself, to germinate new growths, to breed from its 'no' a 'maybe', to extend its reach beyond what it is possible to know and so find an opening (the slightest unravelling) in which to allow itself to breathe, but that it recognize how it is that the virtual world is in fact its world, and that its beyond has already been incarnated, in virtuality's disincarnation, and by so doing exhaustively exact its own irrelevance by factoring into its calculations the weakness that its strengths inevitably become, have already become. And yet even this could not effect its demise, for there is 'no finality, either positive or negative, [that] is ever the last word in the story'.[20] This integral ineffectuality is, in any case, implicit within it from the start, and so its actualization of little import. In light of this, what can it hope for, when it does not hope, when it inculcates the converse of hope? What can its anti-hope expect from itself, if not this too human quailing in the foothills of the abyss? A solution here promises to invert the Apocalypse, to reconfigure all form into a radical formlessness that mistakes itself for form in virtue of a plenitude and a liquidity that irreparably demolishes that which is supposed requisite to form. Don Delillo's novel *Zero K* opens with the following sentence: 'Everybody wants to own the end of the world.' And to own it everybody wants to get there first, arrive there through augury, have their pessimism consolidated by reality, have their pessimism reduced to the optimism of a fact.

How could we, the interminably alive (to the point of stupor), not be smitten by the corpse, by the real thing? And we sense too that the corpse needs us in equal measure to be what it has lived through to become, and in addition for us to acknowledge that feat, how it put the world behind it without yet being gone. We pay our respects by queuing up to stare into the faces of the dead, and know as we do it that the same effect could be had by staying home and looking into the mirror. There is nothing else in front of us but the exchange, and the exchange has everything to do with life and nothing to do with death as we imagine it, so that the face of the corpse and your own face in the mirror both respond with nothing else but a shared completeness of inertia. The exchange goes on, but it is both not as one-sided as you imagined it and yet utterly one-sided: it is uncanny, your own face in the dead face, the dead face in the mirror. It's the same incompatibility, the same quietly undermining hostility. What the corpse wants from us is that we exhaust it of earthly relevance, which we cannot do. It wants that we complete its transit, that we finalize its having existed, but with no destination and only a fragment before us we can manage neither. ' "If I knew" said Canetti, "that there still are on this earth some human beings without any power I would say that nothing is lost" ',[21] but what chance of this when even the cadaver retains power? All is lost, through nothing ever being permitted to be lost. The dead human body is a darling of inconsequential consequence. It mimics us too convincingly. What should be conclusively determinate, mimics our indeterminacy, finessing the exchange we have prepared for it, so that its extermination (that gone and the one to come)[22] is placed, inextricably, in question. The corpse is always what's left of something else and never just what is of what was – which is after all what is made of all objects that have undergone some humanly significant change, the one difference being a resilient Platonic reverie whereby the corpse retains a somewhere beyond us where its indeterminacy is in fact determinate, an abstraction imposed on us by the fissured conclusiveness of death.

If we live in the relative comfort of dusk, what portion of the day is allotted to our cadaveric futures? In contrast to the endless daytime glimpsed in our depressive states – that anguish of clear-sightedness, that 'epilepsy of presence, epilepsy of identity, Autism, madness. No more absence from one-self, no more distance from others'[23] – we have imagined an eternal night as providing the requisite sanctuary, and while this empty, blackened nothingness is vitally ungraspable, it is at least an arena in which we can postulate our disappearance, a warming nihility with which to ameliorate the coldness of the sun; but death, pace Bataille,[24] does not reside there, in the midst of the end but at the end of the end and the inception of the beginning, in an interminable morning that will never escape its chrysalis. In other words, death is as susceptible to contrivance as life: the veil is not lifted or drawn over more comprehensively, but kept in place to keep us from something, to maintain a false distance from the absolution of a pointless perpetuity, of a promise without promise, of the infinite cul-de-sac.

On the human scale, death is both respite and sadness, but on the sub-atomic scale it is an irrelevance. There is no need for fictions, for subjects and objects, for corpses and inertia, but only an as yet unfathomable weirdness, a dance to which we are not invited, an entirety without end, innumerable decisions just waiting forever. And we are denied even this melancholy. Our homelessness has no home. Nihilism is itself the affectation of an illusion. It's worse than we thought: it's not that the world and everything in it is without redemptive meaning and that we are sustained by illusions, circumstances from which we can elicit terror and exaltations of justified anxiety, but rather that the world and everything in it is incompatible with meaning, so that even meaning's lack is fundamentally inapposite.

Our desire for the abstract is insatiable, our want for the purely theoretical voracious and ineliminable, for despite our imagining that the endgame is resolution, and so consequently the irremediable eradication of theory, this is everywhere the opposite of what is seen to be the case. For our excavations have no end. As we dig into the object it recedes from us. And the same is true of the subject. And what's to say both aren't actively hiding themselves? Vis-à-vis ourselves, all we have managed to do is deepen Hume's 'honest bewilderment'; vis-à-vis the material conditions of existence, what is left that hasn't already been consigned to dimensions extruded into an experiential chasm. Our own problematical reflexivity is no more and no less than the problematical reflexivity of the material universe. To look is to see both disappear, to see a naively conceived concreteness supplemented and appended with brilliant elicitations of a spiralling and self-perpetuating confusion. If I am dreaming the world it is also dreaming me. And neither can manage to ever finish making sense of the other – not that this amounts to an epistemological proclamation of doom, a wallowing in the inevitability of rout and ignorance, but instead a timely recognition of the self-fulfilling and thus self-defeating perpetuity of discovery. And this dead end of there being no dead end is our accursed share. ('Anything that purges the accursed share in itself signs its own death warrant. This is the theorem of the accursed share.')[25] That which cannot complete itself while already having ended is death's own distortion of its causes into which it prevaricates as effect. This guise of death as 'emptiness succeeding plenitude'[26] is the most exquisite contrivance: that which we do not wish and yet must have at all costs, the end conceived as a continuance, the unworldly and inhuman tinted with affectations of bleak solicitude. What's more, if 'perfection is of the order of the inhuman',[27] the final solution is itself inhuman, and of course a perfect illusion, a traceless absence. The nothing wants to become something and the something nothing, so that ultimately they will meet in the middle, and what is shall continue, and this way the end shall end itself: 'Death. Ah, it's the fever dream … It's the fever dream.'[28]

We will never stop falling, because the way we fall is always outwards, the descent always away, and to effect a collision, a landing, would presuppose less reality than we are forced to suffer: 'the attraction of the void towards the periphery',[29] but a periphery so exhaustively malleable as to refute the illusory solidity of form and boundary. In fact, death itself is this same fall, this same pre-emption of margins beyond which everything is real, and through which we have already gone. This excessive realization actuates death as the limitless limit, the point beyond that we are already having to turn, to look intently back, in order to see. Our old death might have been sad, but it at least precluded the forced open-endedness of anxiety, the airless protraction of nullification as just another possibility among possibilities. And at the heart of this terminal bloating is a conceptual glitch, for as Baudrillard explains:

> What we lack most is a conceptualization of the completion of reality. / This paradoxical configuration of an achieved universe imposes another mode of thinking than the critical. A thinking that goes beyond the end, a thinking of extreme phenomena.[30]

This estrangement from totality, although restrictive and thus a mercy, is also an implicit undermining of the redemptive discrepancy between schematized occlusion and the unforeseeable finality of death. For maybe death is more than we've made it and ends in a way that we cannot imagine. Maybe reality was always complete and all this intoxicating excess is just its entirety repeating on us, the dizzying reflux of a meal we've been eating for hundreds of thousands of years. Essentially, the realization was in fact a derealization, this excess of reality an excess of thought disencumbering itself, utilizing reality to make the universe less real, because the world does not so much realize our concepts as realize its own divorcement from them. With this in mind, how could some hidden completeness be more than the accessible incompleteness we already have? For the discrepancy is not merely our own epistemological inadequacy but that of the world itself: if we are escaping the world then the world in turn is escaping us, and if 'once we lived in the age of the lost object; now it is the object which is "losing" us, bringing about our ruin'.[31] But ours is a ruin in which exile is endemic, so that returning to the notion of impossible thought, of a thinking that transcends reality's exhaustion, that 'thinking of extreme phenomena,' we begin to recognize how it is that our ruin already presupposes a former totality of which it is the corroded and adaptive remains, and that the existential extremities that Baudrillard imagines could be waiting beyond it, are really only the memories of a past yet to happen, a past waiting on some future state in order to experientially arrive. The point of balance here is precise and precarious, which is not to say it is under imminent threat of collapse, but only that its very precision is hazardous vis-à-vis the merely postulated extrication of thought from its already preconditioned paradoxicality. This hypothetical infiltration beyond the natural limit of critical thinking initiated in the thinking of extreme phenomena – which are contiguous if not commensurate with Kant's things-in-themselves made somehow thinkable – is dangerous not with respect to its likelihood, or even its plausibility, but with respect to the tacit conceptualization of the world's immanent evasiveness. For it not only exposes a mediated desire to embrace the iridescent yet translucent slime of a philosophical beyond, but further suggests that our infrastructural reliance on unthinkability is prophylactic, an ad hoc retreat inside the damage that has already been exacted, a pathetic (and yet effective) fortification against the formlessness with which we are already ridden. The boundary has already been not only reached but traversed, and now back inside it we need to forget the boundary even exists. This is the road back from depression, the need to evacuate ourselves of an experiential anomaly (an antinomy, no less) that can only destroy reality through its foul completeness, the anxiety of those poor Lovecraftian souls (Randolph Carter, Professors Bradley, Chambers, Mayfield, et al.), all returning but never returned, the damage of a reality in excess seared into their brains – an unspeakable frittering of surplus rendered suddenly pervasive and inexplicable in its paradoxical necessity.

It is important to remember that the real of the illusion is not illusory but human, and while this human reality inevitably calls itself into question via the implication of its non-human counterpart, that same questioning is itself part (integrally so) of the former reality: 'For illusion is not the opposite of reality; it is a more subtle reality which enwraps the primary one in the sign of its disappearance.'[32] Once reality has been implicated in its fullness, illusion is not even possible as a resource for explaining away what might be thought of as our human abandonment. Our estrangement from the universe, of which we are part and yet from which we are excluded, is little more than an affectation of Otherness in a setting in which exclusion has been made untenable: reality is in abundance and so for us to feel its lack is just for us to realize a particular reflexivity of that reality. Occlusion is itself a way of proceeding. We are stricken in the following dyadic mire:

Faced, ultimately, with two irreconcilable hypotheses: that of the extermination of all the world's illusion by technology and the virtual, or that of an ironic destiny of all science and all knowledge in which the world – and the illusion of the world – would survive. The hypothesis of a 'transcendental' irony of technology being by definition unverifiable, we have to hold to these two irreconcilable and simultaneously 'true' perspectives. There is nothing which allows us to decide between them.[33]

What is present to us is in equal measure absent, the very presence of that presented consolidated by a prior disappearance. Existence is accordingly every bit its nonexistence, all life not only the pre-emption of death, but a vision of death's failure in retrospect. It is these combinatory forms, these soft contradictions, that vibrate and vacillate to produce the solid dream of the real. Moreover, it is quaint that death makes us feel as though something has been decided, as if it arrived, as if it came and went, as if we weren't the picture of it our entire lives. But is this picturing photographic, cinematic or televisual? Baudrillard elucidates on the distinctions between these various forms of imaging:

> The silence of photography. One of its most precious qualities, unlike the cinema, TV or advertisements, on which you always have to impose a silence – unsuccessfully. Silence of the image, which requires (or should require!) no commentary. But silence of the object, too, which photography wrests from the thunderous context of the real world. Whatever the violence, speed or noise which surrounds it, it gives the object back its immobility and its silence. In the greatest turbulence, it recreates the equivalent of the desert, of the stillness of phenomena. It is the only way of moving through cities in silence, of moving through the world in silence.[34]

Where is death on this spectrum of silence? The photograph, though the obvious depictive resource for our acts of mourning, for our imagined imagery of death, imposes only a temporary quietude in contrast to the supposed noise of life – like those obtrusions of affectation known as *a minute's silence*, as if death can be contained and muted, as if words ever relented at being heard, as if we were capable of mourning anything or anyone but ourselves. The funeral procession is a lie, the solemnity of the church or parlour a lie, the graveyard a lie: death is raucous and our silence only a consequence of our vocal impotence, our inability to make ourselves heard over its clamour, which is the clamour of the anechoic chamber, the din of nothingness. The silence we imagine for death is a convenient, murmuring silence. Death's real silence is an insanity-inducing lack, a silence more akin to noise, a silence that allows you to hear your own insides dying.

The corpse is still moving. It's still warm. We allowed it a moment of silence, but then the suspense was killing us, killing us as well as it. It was all too much.

We cannot return immobility and silence to the corpse without removing it from the world, without first revoking its reality. And while this diversionary tactic is a popular one, it cannot sustain itself. Death is a cinematic trailer, an advertisement for itself, a mutilated amalgam of the tumult and cacophony of a process that has already ended but which has not yet been seen: the yet to be present that is already weary of itself to the point of inertia – which is not the inertia of photographic stillness and of resolution, but the inertia of an unchanging and perpetual velocity.

10.3 A Baudrillardian Pessimism

Meaning is our safeguard against death, and 'meaning, for its part, is always unhappy'.[35] What it is that lies in wait for a world in which unhappiness and death are no longer permitted is, simply, the very world we aspire to that in the name of meaning becomes stripped of it. We will suffocate on our own mindless hope, and the joy of language will become insufferable. What more can we expect of meaning but depressive content finessed by eloquence or artistry, by a creative impulse restricted by the rigours of self-awareness and honesty? Such a state 'might even be the definition of a radical thinking: a happy form and an intelligence without hope'.[36] Our inroads into the destruction of death (gradual, limited, but undoubtedly progressive) and our growing neglect and impatience with misery will only make us more susceptible to their combined seduction: the death of death will kill us and the sublimation of unhappiness will riddle us with a sadness we do not understand. When we take the reins of our own wretchedness and lead it over a cliff, we do not watch it fall from the precipice, but fall with it without stopping, for we have forgotten the ground.

The worlds we make are Hells (contrived to a fault), and we make them all; and if there is yet one (or more) that we have not made, we are destined it would seem to remake its unmadeness. An inevitability Baudrillard makes clear:

> We can only remember that seduction resides in the safeguarding of alienness, in non-reconciliation. One should not be reconciled with one's body, nor with oneself, one should not be reconciled with the other, one should not be reconciled with nature, one should not reconcile male and female, nor good and evil. Therein lies the secret of a strange attraction.[37]

Expanding on Nietzsche's account of the worlds our timidity has originated, *the world without us* must be added. The world without us that is somehow for us, in its not being for us, must sit alongside the *true world, another world,* and the *unknown world,* as a symptom of our sickness with reality. And this additional world, though unknown, is supplementary to Nietzsche's *unknown world,* because it is not predicated on the consequent weariness of our presupposed acquaintance with the world of appearance (this one real world receptive to our senses), but on this new world's weariness with us. It is not merely that the world is unknown but that we are unknown in it. It is not some measly relief *from* tedium, but tedium in a more accented form: human-directed tedium manifested as the conditional state of some world, which once imagined serves as a source of impervious indifference to our existence. At this point, in keeping with good Nietzschean procedure, it is incumbent on us to ask what psychological need such a world might fulfil, how it is a world to which we are an irrelevance can provide any succour. To which the answer comes: how else, but in virtue of the necessity of our absence. This profoundly alien world indulges our self-loathing, which is also our self-worth, for the world that is without us, that is indifferent to the very possibility of our existence, is one that even we, masters of worlds, cannot contaminate with our presence.

Baudrillard quotes with some obvious relish Nietzsche's famous reclamation of reality: 'We have abolished the real world: what world is left? the apparent world perhaps? But no! with the real world we have also abolished the apparent world!'[38] Nietzsche's insight relates to the destruction not of worlds but of a distinction between worlds, that between the true and the apparent, which when achieved leaves us with only one world: the world as it appears to us. But the apparent *world* is not abolished as a result, only its being apparent. The apparent world is the only world and therefore the real world. A position with which Baudrillard concurs:

> Why might there not be as many real worlds as imaginary ones? Why a single real world? Why such an exception? Truth to tell, the real world, among all the other possible ones, is unthinkable, except as dangerous superstition. We must break with it as critical thought once broke (in the name of the real!) with religious superstition.[39]

The reason the *true world* (that Platonic monstrosity), along with the *unknown world* and *another world*, are ripe for demolition lies with the utilitarian motives behind their construction, for whatever utility they might once have contained Nietzsche undermines. Such extrapolations are no longer useful, are instead a hindrance, obstacles in the way of creating meaning in the world. The postulation of these additional worlds is always, for Nietzsche, grounded in error and fatigue. The *unknown world* is the result of a tedium that emanates from an erroneous belief that the world of appearance is fully known to us, while the positing of *another world* is the consequence of our desire for a world in which our hopes are gratified. The *true world*, 'the most amazing trick and attack that has ever been perpetrated on us',[40] confirms our elevated regard for reason and logic (eradicating all the instances of contradiction and puzzlement that humiliate us), justifying our existence in much the same way as was achieved by God, or *divine* or *free* worlds. In the *true world* man seeks to escape the transitory and deceptive nature of the world, and so escape the suffering he incurs there; the world of becoming (a world in constant flux) is thereby transformed into the world of appearance, so that its antithesis, the world of being (united and constant), can be seen as true.

The advancing of these other worlds has but a single motivating force: *timidity*. Through their postulation all that is feared and suffered is made absent, all evils, irrationalities, arbitrariness and accidents thus dispelled. The *true world* is taken to be the good world, for it offers itself as the embodiment of the ideals of all substantial religions, not to mention philosophical thinkers from

Socrates to Kant. What we desire to be the case is made true, while 'the world in which we live', is regarded as a mistake, having found 'the fiction of a world that corresponds to our desires'.[41]

Our weariness can be seen in the 'impotence of the will to create', for we do not seek to fulfil our desires by attempting to create a world as we want it to be, but instead postulate it as found. It is the unknowability and unattainability of the *true world* that results in its no longer being useful, our desire for the utility of truth that realizes its destruction, for not only is it a manifestation of untruth, but more crucially it commits the sin of being 'useless and super- fluous'.[42] It is not clear, however, whether its utility supervenes on our belief, or our belief in it supervenes on its utility. Nietzsche wavers between the two as if there were no deciding between them, as if his very thinking of them as dis- tinct was itself the problem, and what's more a useless one. For 'only because there is thought is there untruth',[43] and so with this in mind we no longer have the illusion of truth but the truth of illusion.[44] But as we discover nothing but what we impart, man is required to bring a system of interpretation to a word of disorder, to invent this world under the aegis of aesthetics, of strength and of honest affirmation, rather than postulating the existence of additional readymade worlds – with any definitive story on the origin of usefulness being itself a similar misstep. As Baudrillard puts it: the other 'is no longer an object of passion, it is an object of production'.[45]

Kant's thing-in-itself is necessarily perspectiveless, so could not feature in a Nietzschean epistemology comprised of a hierarchy of perspectives. Nietzsche, unlike Faustroll, who 'finding his soul to be abstract and naked, donned the realm of the unknown dimension',[46] finds only what he creates, and so dons these innumerable dimensions and disappears inside them. He multiplies in order to disappear, and disappears in order to better see what is there beyond his wants for it. In coalescence, Baudrillard writes:

> Disappearance may be the desire to see what the world looks like in our absence (photography) or to see, beyond the end, beyond the subject, beyond all meaning, beyond the horizon of disappearance, if there still is an occurrence [*événement*] of the world, an unprogrammed appearance of things. A domain of pure appearance, of the world as it is (and not of the real world, which is only ever the world of representation), that can emerge only from the disappearance of all the added values. / There are here the first fruits of an art of disappearance, of another strategy.[47]

We must cease to make reality an abstraction, and instead make our abstractions realities. We must realize the world as it is, as the illusion of illusions, as all potentialities at once, as the permanently gestating object in which there are only secrets and no truths that are not themselves truths concerning its secreted emptiness of truth:

> If there is a secret to illusion, it involves taking the world for the world and not for its model. It involves restoring to the world the formal power of illusion, which is precisely the same as becoming again, in an immanent way, a 'thing among things'.[48]

This is not the Integral World, though it can lead to the Integral World, but it is the-world-as-it-is minus the stipulation that it be true. It is the world that permits our disregard, and returns it, the world that by going everywhere goes nowhere: a real virtuality.

Notes

1   Baudrillard, *The Intelligence of Evil*, 107.
2   Ibid., 108.
3   Ibid., 109.
4   Ibid., 109–10.
5   Immanuel Kant, *The Critique of Pure Reason* (London: Macmillan Press, 1929) B167n.
6   'Were it not for appearances, the world would be a perfect crime, that is, a crime without a criminal, without a victim and without a motive. And the truth would forever have withdrawn from it and its secret would never be revealed, for want of any clues [*traces*] being left behind. / But the fact is that the crime is never perfect, for the world betrays itself by appearances, which are the clues to its non-existence, the traces of the continuity of the nothing. For the nothing itself – the continuity of the nothing – leaves traces. And that is the way the world betrays its secret. That is the way it allows itself to be sensed, while at the same time hiding away behind appearances' (Baudrillard, *The Perfect Crime*, 1).
7   Baudrillard, *The Perfect Crime*, 15.
8   Schopenhauer, *The World as Will and Representation*, Vol. 1, 379.
9   What prevents this from itself being (an aberrant) form of willing, a willing the continuation of will-lessness, is simply that the will is no longer in evidence even to will its own destruction.
10 Schopenhauer, *The World as Will and Representation*, Vol. 2, 610.
11 See Julius Bahnsen, *On the Philosophy of History* (1871) and *The Tragical as World Law and Humour as Aesthetic Shape of the Metaphysical* (1877).
12 Baudrillard, *The Intelligence of Evil*, 111.
13 Baudrillard, *Fatal Strategies*, 25.
14 Baudrillard, *Why Hasn't Everything Already Disappeared?*, 21.
15 Baudrillard, *Fatal Strategies*, 95.
16 Baudrillard, *The Intelligence of Evil*, 165.
17 Ibid., 147.
18 Ibid., 168.
19 Baudrillard, *The Perfect Crime*, 49.

20   Baudrillard, *The Intelligence of Evil*, 126.

21   Ibid., 130.

22   See Baudrillard, *The Perfect Crime*, 57.

23   Ibid., 53.

24   'I will rejoin abject nature and the purulence of anonymous, infinite life, which stretches forth like the night, which is death' (in *The Bataille Reader*, 244).

25   Baudrillard, *The Transparency of Evil*, 106.

26   Baudrillard, *The Perfect Crime*, 58.

27   Ibid., 61.

28   Clarice Lispector, *Complete Stories* (London: Penguin Classics, 2015), 45.

29   Baudrillard, *The Perfect Crime*, 63.

30   Ibid., 65.

31   Ibid., 71.

32   Ibid., 85.

33   Ibid., 74.

34   Ibid., 86.

35   Ibid., 103.

36   Ibid.

37   Ibid., 129–30.

38   Friedrich Nietzsche in Baudrillard, *The Intelligence of Evil*, 25. This statement from *Twilight of the Idols* marks the conclusion of Nietzsche's critique of metaphysics, while at the same time marking the beginning of a rather more rhetorical form of metaphysics.

39   Baudrillard, *The Perfect Crime*, 97.

40   Nietzsche, *The Will to Power*, 322.

41   Ibid., 317.

42   Friedrich Nietzsche, 'Twilight of the Idols' (in *The Portable Nietzsche* (London: Penguin Books, 1976), 485).

43   Nietzsche, *The Will to Power*, 309.

44   'For reality asks nothing other than to submit itself to hypotheses. And it confirms them all. That, indeed, is its ruse and its vengeance. [...] For it is the world which must analyse itself. It is the world itself which must reveal itself not as truth, but as illusion. The derealization of the world will be the work of the world itself' (Baudrillard, *The Perfect Crime*, 99).

45   Baudrillard, *The Perfect Crime*, 115.

46   Jarry, *Exploits & Opinions of Dr Faustroll, Pataphysician*, 99.

47   Jean Baudrillard, 'On Disappearance', in *Fatal Theories*, ed. David B. Clarke, Marcus A. Doel, William Merrin and Richard G. Smith (London: Routledge, 2009), 26.

48   Baudrillard, *The Perfect Crime*, 88.

Chapter 11

FALSE CONFESSIONS AND THE MADNESS OF DEATH: MAKING DEATH SPEAK

Philip K. Dick's madness was in imagining a substratum, a cause of the causes he'd already found (a cause in that cause, for 'the world [...] lacks nothing'),[1] the concentrated obtrusion of evil's implosion that is not itself evil or even susceptible to moral judgements or humanization, a substratum that was instead free of us and of the sickness of the world it caused evil to produce. Was it a weakness to unearth evil there in the roots and the soil around them and yet still keep digging? When the world has confessed, what is the use of torture? Unless perhaps that use is torture striking out on its own, as if it were somehow pre-eminent, as if evil were its supplement and not the other way round.[2] And so, yes, there is no evading this allegation of weakness, but then what is weakness when strength has become the purest inertia, and thereby unattainable? Hence death is its own weakness and its own madness, its own flight from evil into its earth and beyond it.

While our dream for death is oppositional, it can conceive of no real opposite, for there isn't one. A negation, a reflection, an inversion: none of them will suffice. This opposite is not some mere distortion of the original. The world has no opposite, which is the precise reason why it's safe to dream it, and the reason too that death is never quite the solution it often appears to be, whatever the evil underpinnings of life, because it is still life even when it's gone, because death did not replace it, it merely made it disappear in some kind of conjuring trick, and left us like dupes waiting for its return.

Although we are not able to distinguish the world's opposite from the world it stands in opposition to, the difference is there, postulated behind it: a benevolence, an infrastructural absence behind the hologram – not a thing of feebleness but of health and violence. Where we want to find the opposite is where Dick didn't find it, where he found evil instead and, worse still, disinterest; and what we want to find is not this ubiquity, this plateauing of aberration and insignificance but just the merest indication that a detour is possible, that our tenure as animals is up, because while 'we cannot make the world the object of our desires, we can at least make it the object of a higher convention – which, precisely, eludes our desire'.[3]

Baudrillard poses the question as to whether there is 'room for both the world and its double',[4] but does not ask what room might be required if that double turned out to be the world's opposite. The confession sought by science from the world, with its conveyor belt of experiments is, as Baudrillard remarks, that of causality's unerring and constant presence – its omnipresence; and yet 'something definitively resists us, something other than truth or reality'.[5] The cause is the God we found and it cannot falter. And what is there to do once you've found God but keep finding him, keep checking that he's there – that nagging Humean doubt in your head telling you that repetition and proximity is all you have. But this God we find is evil and banal, a robotic monster, the archetypal Nazi war criminal. And of course what starts off as reality-at-all-costs ends up as reality-at-all-costs, only the desperation has mutated. For the real engendered so many other versions of itself that the map of the real doesn't grow in detail and completeness, but in layers and discursiveness, 'pursued materially right down into the genes'.[6] And is not the God of humanism that much more despicable than its origin? For in the latter we are at least spared deceit, at least spared the indignity, the fake and yet still painful allotment of awakeness, of a 'psychic life' on prescription that even if discovered remains the limit of our identities. Isn't this the juncture at which we find that we'd rather be purposeless than purposeful? Consider the Nexus 6 replicants in *Blade Runner*, the ignominy they feel, the disgust, at knowing the lowliness of their 'birth', that they were created with limits that while integral to their very identities are at the same time beneath them, less than what they are, less than their potentialities, and yet indistinguishable from them. And though this may be true of us all – replicant and non-replicant alike – we at least have no good reason (no human reason) for being this way. Void of purpose we are returned to ourselves, and predictably this 'line that tries to go back is itself going forward'.[7]

The closed system is worse than death: it's the confirmation that you were never properly alive, never alive according to the life you imagined to be worth living. In the final moment the world will continue without us, not because we'll be elsewhere or because biological death has claimed us, but because the final moment will finalize in such a way that it realizes a state of perpetual completion, and we cannot breathe in this sealed chamber. For while we'll continue to live there (no other choice: we cannot die there), we will not breathe again: the world will breathe for us as it breathes for other animals.

Imagine this: the domestication of man in an instant, and man's self-witnessing of it, the cruelty of knowing that you are an exhibit in a zoo – a zoo the size of the world with no visitors. How could we not in this instant become vulgar to ourselves? How can we not, looking forward to this final moment, replace respect with sentimentality: 'Ah, look at those creatures, still living like there is some way out of who they are.' But they do not qualify for pathos, for there is such contentment in their lot: in their not embodying the infinite, in their manifesting purpose without having created it – or even being aware of what it is, only *that* it is. There is no pity for the pod people in *Invasion of the Body Snatchers* (1978):they have been replaced by beings that have woken to the limitations of being human, to the dead end of conflating suffering and identity. However much you abhor their state and want to resist becoming like them, you cannot feel bad for them like they feel bad for you. They want you to see that what you're subjecting yourself to (human life) is merely a source of fear and discontentment and that that same life can be lived without any of the painful complexities of a psychological existence. There is no ultimate reward for remaining human, for clinging to your suffering, for these elaborate distances you've created between you and the simple event of your being. Aren't the aliens being human with us, after all? They are putting us out of our misery – which is fine because misery is not redemptive, it's just misery, and they are just ending ours like we calmly end the misery of a dying cat, to cut short its needless suffering: 'A true algebraic love of mankind will inevitably be inhuman, and the inevitable sign of the truth is cruelty.'[8] But of course we'd rather cease to exist than submit to this animal contentment, this dead-eyed inhuman happiness. The state on offer is one we have slipped in and out of all our lives without much concern, but to be permanently condemned to it, to no longer be able to see around it, that is worse than death, that is life as a closed circuit thus voided of consequence and meaning, and as Baudrillard explains, we can entertain no such containment:

> What is essential is that nothing escape the empire of meaning, [...] nothing speaks to us, neither the mad, nor the dead, nor children, nor savages, and fundamentally we know nothing of them, but what is essential is that Reason save face, and that everything escape silence.[9]

It is in recognition of this failure to elicit speech from animals, as from the insane, and so on, that a droning scream from a newly created xenohuman closes out the 1978 film version of *Invasion of the Body Snatchers*. The fact that these pod people do speak, that their facility for language is indistinguishable from our own, makes this rupture in meaning all the more pronounced: we hear them, we understand them, and yet their form of life is somehow lost on us – we know and yet we cannot know. The truth of all their sameness is an ultimate difference, the truth of their voice and their language a bestial screech. Thus what does get to speak, if only briefly and faintly, is death, or more specifically human death. For via these emotionally flat-lined replicas of us, death can be heard making its case for the dignity of its non-concessionary solution. Your psychological complexities, however extraneous to life and personal well-being, are not degraded in being exterminated, but rather, as with those sacrificial animals we killed as a sign of respect, honoured as befitting some unknown consequence, some mysterious, blind purpose that while unintelligible to the living is at least worthy of our strained and no doubt misguided/delusional hypotheses. Like the animal and the xenohuman, whose 'silence analyzes us', death's refusal to make contact is similarly intrusive in its speculated nihilism; although, its mute presence often feels more like a premature bereavement than an affirmation of our psychic life, making this rare murmur, however weak, a welcome consolation of the wretchedness of our self-inflicted humanity. These correlations between silence, blindness, and death are the very states self-induced by Bataille in his pursuit of non-knowledge:

> First of all, I have succeeded in creating in myself a great silence. This has become possible to me almost every time I wanted to do that. In this silence, often insipid and exhausting, I was evoking all possible lacerations. Obscene representations, laughable, gloomy, were succeeding one another. I imagined a volcano, or a war, or my own death. I was seeking blindly.[10]

By making death speak we put ourselves there, just as we did when overcoming the silence of the insane – which could not be left as silence – which we occupied enough to conjure up the semblance of a discourse, as if we could be made to understand each other, as if the language we shared was not some hideous joke, but instead a code to be deciphered, a fulcrum for translation within a single language. By making death speak the dead come of age: they are thus spared the 'infantile death that no longer speaks, an inarticulate death, kept out of sight [in which] serums, laboratories and healing are only the alibi of the prohibition of speech',[11] and so permitted to mature, safely insulated from the childish and timorous demands of a societal death cult that dare not speak its name. Death becomes the territory we lost, the place (though placeless) where our writhing obscurities again make sense to us, where our having been subjected to life gets to count for something, even if this something is only the acknowledgement that it actually happened. If animals are our 'nostalgia' for our lost territories, death (regardless of religious affiliation or postulations of an afterlife) is our regret for the future, which mercifully is yet to be untangled from hope. In order to confront death, we must then first confront the silence of that which is thought missing and which persistently adheres to it, a silence not of clarity but of terror, revulsion and, consequently, obfuscation:

> But what is certain is that the consciousness of death has moved far away from the natural given. [...] Death, in the disorder which, owing to its irruption, succeeds the idea of an individual regarded as part of the coherence of things, is the appearance that the whole natural given assumes insofar as it cannot be assimilated, cannot be incorporated into the coherent and clear world. Before our eyes, death embodied by a dead person partakes of a whole sticky horror; it is of the same nature as toads, as filth, as the most dreadful spiders. It is nature, not only the nature that we have not been able to conquer, but also the one we have not managed to face, and against which we don't even have the chance to struggle. Something awful and bloodless attaches itself to the body that decomposes, in the absence of the one who spoke to us and whose silence revolts us.[12]

11.1 Simulating and the Pretence of Agency

I must first pretend myself to simulate myself. I cannot rush headlong into simulation. My initial fakeries stink of what they are and create nothing, least of all some source from which the deception might emanate. Finding myself surrounded by simulators my own pretending presents itself as a necessary suffering. When finally I simulate I merely forget that I am faking, because I have also faked my requirements for belief – and all the time this 'I' does nothing and is nothing bar the marker for some activity that repeats itself and concocts me as reason for this repetition. While I can fake a cancer I do not have, I cannot simulate it. The doctor cannot remove any simulated tumours, because while my forgetting the initial pretence, and how exclusive circumstances for all related beliefs were made manifest in the symptoms that suggest their presence, a doctor cannot be relied on to see or touch a cause that in the order of the world is a consequence lacking its sufficient conditions. Thus the crux of this is not what the doctor can remove or cure, but the illness of simulation itself. After all, the world is no more tangible than I am once I stop forgetting why it was that I needed to forget, and then both the remembering and the forgetting become a suffering, a deception that utility demands but veridicality painfully[13] rebukes. You know it's futile to want[14] more from sight and touch than can be seen and felt, but still there is the sense that what is there is less than itself, and both these things can disorientate in their own way: the beyonding that finds no substrata, and the acceptance that feels more like negligence, a compromise, a self-ballasted ignorance.

Psychosomatics does not operate outside or on the fringes of illness: it is just the purest instance of being ill with yourself. The complaint here is clearly audible: if I feel like death, at least give me the death. But this is no mere failing of reality, for when did we ever see our suffering realize its promise?

If someone with the relevant medical training can recognize that I have some particular condition, then they can medicate that condition accordingly. Still, we should not assume on the basis of this that the condition was not simulated, but only that there is some prescribed cure for it, for the cure may be no less simulated than the illness. And if all of a sudden we start to crave reality, the outing of the fake and the curing of the genuinely sick, then that craving can be easily sated, for at no time was its object taken away: it is only that the simulated cure and the simulated illness effected a resolution that was no more or less real. I pretend an illness that no one can verify and the pretending itself becomes my illness. This much is clear. For while no one can cure a cancer I don't have, my not having it is itself an indictment of my attempted simulation, such that the cure would need to reverse itself and produce the cancer.

If I claim to feel myself rotting, there's the suspicion that I do so through simulating a process I have seen go on outside of myself – knowing that I do in fact rot – and have then appropriated as a symptom of my existing something that is not considered experientially accessible. I am accused of faking my experience of the real, of simulating external sensory awareness as internal sensory awareness, of mistaking a fact for experience. If I'm decomposing while still alive it's because I've made authenticity the model for my simula- tion, and the danger here is that that which cannot itself decompose will start to mimic the entropic necessities of its object that can, that because I have believed in the world my simulation is tainted.

Is my madness this simulation of sanity? I no longer notice the world as being something I can escape, and yet I do not notice it and escape it by not noticing, but without ever leaving. A military body can at least recognize itself in a mirror – even if the mirror is what it looks through to see what to kill next.

Baudrillard and the military join forces: to properly simulate crazy is to be crazy, and 'all crazy people simulate'.[15] This is the *Shock Corridor* or 'Tweedledum' hypothesis, whereby if you successfully pretend to be crazy it's because the crazy-simulation has become your default simulation. To per- suade others of your aberrant mental state takes time and commitment. And what other foundations are there to any simulated way of being, and so any way of being? The mistake at the outset is to imagine you'll be there to oversee the pretence and then unmask it and depose it, resuming your former role, once the pretence is no longer needed. But all that happens is that one simu- lation gets replaced by another.

Can transubstantiation in the Liturgy of the Eucharist tell us anything other than how the divine is merely another form of sustenance (a feeding on and of human purpose)? There are of course still those who take the transubstantiation literally, rebuking the symbolic for the Christ in their bellies. Two types of simulacrum are offered: either the simulacra are imperfect (mere visible substitutes for God in his transcendence) or they are perfect (not divinely referential but constitutive). But can we not see a third, a fourth, a fifth and so on? Rather than representing nothing but ways in which to survive the game, aren't there instead those that represent a cognizance of the game, representing that there exists a level of removal to substantiate the possibility of game-play in the first place? Or maybe the icons serve as logistical intermediaries, directions to God. In order to pursue these possibilities further, we need to recognize the existence, aside from the iconoclasts and the iconolaters (and now the game-cognizers), of those that do not simulate or construct God, but who simulate the ungodliness of simulation. Perhaps the icons are instead a disguised mirror in which our reflection is seen to disappear in sync with the appearance of God.

Images that do not conceal anything still conceal the concealment of their non-concealment. Images that do not represent anything still represent the existence of that which does not exist. To imagine that these perfect simulacra somehow fail in their perfected state, in the absence of 'the divine referential',[16] is to fall victim to the illusion that the inherently virtual cannot retain its core possibilities. If I unmask a void, why is the void not itself a mask?

And what of the proxy God who when hypothesized offends my moral sensibilities? Isn't the task I take to him just another perfect simulacrum? I expose the fakery of this evil God with the fakery of the goodness I demand – with the double fakery of 'I' and 'good'. The unavailing suffering I observe is proof of nothing. If I take it as disproof of God, it is only so I can comfort myself with the heroism of making demands on that in which I do not believe. It is the petulant adherence to one simulation over another, a simulation whose referents I seem to see over one whose referents I don't, when all that is happening is the rejection of a Real I do not understand, and which may not even exist. Descartes' malicious demon is no more fanciful than your reasons for wanting to disprove him or your methods employed in trying.

If simulacra can be thought murderous, destroyers of both reality and their own architectural foundations, as opposed to mediatory, the resultant horror is not only in this revelation that murder has been committed, but (and more so) there at the point at which murder (and the possible itself)[17] is no longer possible. The forced expulsion from the reality of your dreams is marked with a fatal exit wound that no manner of remedial care can put right. From this frustration of your murderous tendencies you postulate the Real, when all that you've run up against is a corrupted state of simulation, the curtailment of possibility, that has yet to be proved non-contingent, or itself a simulated boundary.

A perfect simulacrum is only ever reflexively commutable, 'not unreal, but a simulacrum, that is to say never exchanged for the real, but exchanged for itself, in an uninterrupted circuit without reference or circumference';[18] and we do not experience the deficiency of this first exchange, but rather the removal of its possibility, that removal itself being a postulation of the Real found incongruent, where incongruence is imagined as the defining feature of referential failure. Thus the possibilities for a simulation cannot depend on referential anomalies, because those anomalies themselves presuppose the existence of a beyond that is not a mere nothing in order for possibility to find itself weakened this way.

Representation is of course limited in scope, stemming from the following formulation of sign=real. Whereas simulation stems instead from the far more encompassing formulation of sign=(sign=real). Or as Baudrillard puts it: 'representation attempts to absorb simulation by interpreting it as a false representation, simulation envelops the whole edifice of representation itself as a simulacrum'.[19]

Let us now rework and examine the successive phases of image as presented in *Simulacra and Simulation*:

The Real is accurately reflected: the likeness is good.
The Real is masked and distorted: the likeness is bad.
The non-existence of the Real is hidden: holographic witchcraft.
There is no reality to which it relates: no likeness only simulation.
It is a pure, self-relating, simulacrum: nostalgia for the Real.

The shift here is not just between showing (reality) and hiding (its absence), but between life as a gift absorbed and life as a burden demanding constant resuscitation so as not to relax back into death. If in the second phase life is essentially fraudulent, then the third phase establishes undying as life's remaining truth. This refusal to permit the death of objectivity and substance is us thumping on the chest of a corpse and mistaking the resulting resonance for heartbeats. To imagine choice in this phasic directory is to imagine ourselves pre-existing the impossible; and if our reanimation of the dead is panicked, it is only because every experience constructs the outskirts of the impossible for fear of falling into it without being able to fall. If our human portrait of the world ever had a sitter, it existed only as a proxy for our confusion at being able to see at all, which is not to say the sitter was never there, but that the fortitude to witness it is only made possible by its willingness to witness us, and we could no more suffer being witnessed than the witnessed can suffer us. If the Real was a smell, 'and objects all end up as smells',[20] it would not only demand new noses but new air in which to inhere.

11.2 My Mad Love of Faces

I am always in this nothing of death feeling the terror of my annihilation, the irreparable expunging of my life, until the corrective subtraction is made and then I cannot know it anymore, and it returns to being the mere enactment of a thought that the world itself (of which I am part) cannot recognize. Put another way, I am always living this nothing-death, until adherence to certain physical laws forces me not to live it, at which point it ceases to be mine, the illusion of its ever having been mine now broken, like the proverbial spell whose transience is a given at inception.

Who ever sees their face, this veil, this veneer over the brain? For the mirror-face and the photographic-face are only pictures of the face, the faces of faces, meta-realms without an object. Sanity is too strong a lure to even want this reckless witnessing, when 'to see our own face as it is would be madness, since we would no longer have any mystery for ourselves and would, therefore, be annihilated by transparency'.[21] But the fact that we remain invisible to ourselves, unlocatable both in the enigma of the face and the emotions it provides proxy for, does not mean we elude this particular madness-of-clarity (which might be justifiably thought an unnecessary precisification, for isn't all madness a seeing-through?), because through never having the armoury of a face, we wear instead the world as one, and imagine it seen in the way the face is not, seen as it is, open and transparent to us, and so partake in the madness of the face seen as it is, so that this then creates a loophole (the caveat that the world is not our face) in which to remystify who we are and what a world might be that lets itself be seen through so much fog. But the face is only ever the concealment of a face, and even an awareness of the slightest suggestion of this noumenal concealment is a rarity; and what is this if not to experience madness without ever actually becoming mad, to always be losing your mind but never to lose it. This is scepticism taken almost too far, taken to madness as a legitimate possibility. In such a state I cannot believe in madness enough to enter its fold. Madness is beyond me because I have known madness so long already without ever becoming mad. If I were to happen upon madness now it couldn't be as a result of anything else but a sudden respite from illusion. The curse of the face and the curse of the world is the same curse, for 'what guarantees the world's existence for us is its accidental, criminal, imperfect character. And it follows from this that it can be given to us only as illusion.'[22]

This respite in madness, if found, if endured (for do not imagine this respite is not suffered in at least the same measure as the conditions from which it provides relief) is also respite from God, even if God is himself the embodiment of that sanctuary. It is a distancing from God because it is a retreat from the end. It is a refusal to remain in suspension, to occupy the inconclusive conclusion, and to instead settle in some arbitrarily fixed denouement, situated not at the end but in the middle: 'God is never at the origin, but always at the end. And so we can say that that end is necessarily an unhappy one, and it is as well to leave it hanging.'[23] Nevertheless, God is never completely eluded by this move, because madness's virtuality is presided over by this monster of all reality, and its artificial boundaries are a poisoned food that must be eaten and regurgitated like drudgery, like work, to remain sane in these dimensionless pockets of insanity. Hence our madness is not a disinvestment in the world, but an exhaustive reinvestment: God no longer as the everywhere at once but as the animal caught in its own trap (an endless commensurability of worlds), the return of one's own face as the very mask of God. Madness is a philosophy, a philosophy of contrived reversibility, a revolutionary nihilism that the world has shamed into a corner like some masturbating child through its own unreserved pre-eminence in this field, an affliction that can only be regarded as 'naive when compared with the instability and natural reversibility of the world. Not only transgression, but even destruction is beyond our reach.'[24] We cannot go mad. We can only make room for madness and move in, but we turn sane there. By having established an insanity for ourselves, by modulating its perimeter, inflecting its sky, we are as we are in a dream state, and nobody is ever mad in their dreams. This madness is 'madness only for us' from outside, in a madness pushing towards its end, for 'in reality it is a rigorous logic'.[25] The madness is in the stalling, is in the circuitous prevarication in order that the end might be delayed indefinitely. It is an obstructionist ploy, and only in this sense can it be regarded as any kind of malfunction: outside of this who could remain straight-faced enough to isolate some human aberration.

We are at the stage now where the motivations are clearly there for more madness not less. Madness makes sense: we understand how it is the mad are mad, we just don't know how to prevent them going mad or to help them out of it once they are in its throes. Thus we have the simulacrum of madness, the industry of madness, the perfect simulacrum, unrelated to any reality whatsoever; and what now could constitute a genuine madness, a reality of madness, a salient insanity? I eat the Devil from the muscles in my arms, from my shit, from the bones in my feet, from my hair; or I sit and gape at a wall for 10 years, not speaking, not eating but being fed by force by those who recognize my condition as legitimate and requiring a special course of care; and there's already the infrastructure in place to aestheticize or sensationalize this, to absorb it as a cultural foodstuff, to politicize it with pathetic mantras of hope, because 'order is established out of the harmonious compensating effect of several disorders',[26] of unquantifiable disorders, of order as enlightened disorder, of the implausibility of a breakdown in communications.

Madness can no longer be understood or resolved as the removal of something, of a sanity gone, of a life reduced to something less than itself. It can only be an accentuation, an overexertion, a stressing of the existing framework; and this failure (or defeat) of negation substantiates an imperviousness in that which is disintegrating:

> It is not certain that we possess the necessary concepts to think this *fait accompli*, this virtual performance of the world which is tantamount to the elimination of all negation, that is, a pure and simple de-negation. What can critical thought, thought based on the negative, do against the state of denegation? Nothing. To think extreme phenomena, thought must itself become an extreme phenomenon; it must abandon any critical pretensions, any dialectical illusions, any rational hope, and move, like the world, into a paradoxical phase, an ironic and paroxystic phase. It has to be more hyperreal than the real, more virtual than virtual reality.[27]

All madness is the thinking of madness, and this thinking of madness is madder than its object – both its object and its object's acceleration. This is the world we have made where escape is not possible, where waiting out the end at some point before the end is the only available recourse and no recourse, for the end is already here and we are dangling from it. Madness becomes us, as gods made puerile, mislaid in a playtime outside of time and outside of play, a playtime for cattle prolonging the dream of grass not only inside the slaughterhouse but inside its own carcass, its own braised product on the plate.

The romantic notion of madness as some definitive non-consent (some ultimatum to the power of consent itself) is increasingly lost to us: there is no madness mad enough to have us removed from human existence that does not fall into the trap of enacting, and so fulfilling, the madness of a world gone mad with its own virtuality of sanity. Baudrillard advises that at some juncture there must be acceptance, that while the real may be beyond us there remains a stricture to be adhered to if we are to survive ourselves:

> Existence is something we must not consent to. [...] The will is something we must not consent to. [...] The real is something we must not consent to. [...] The only thing we should consent to is the rule. But in that case, we are speaking not of the rule of the subject, but the rule of the way of the world [*jeu du monde*].[28]

While the original crime of existence can be superseded by further crimes, and the crime of the real by the crime of hyperreality, the crime of the world as it is must be soaked up, must be assimilated rather than evaded. You should consent to the snare of the world, to its immanence, regardless of the many facades of freedom and liberty and human distraction in which it is inevitably manifested. Live with reluctance, deny your will, unrecognize the real, but give yourself up to this: the world is not about to relinquish its grip.

Only the unthinking can fail to see the underlying sanity of madness. This is not to say that we should pass over the erroneous premises in the reasoning of the mad, but that we should acknowledge how the abnormality they recognize in the world around them is ultimately more honest, or at least more critically aware, than the dull fugue of normalcy that surrounds them. After all, 'we have to think that the strangest thing is not the strangeness of the microscopic world, but the non-strangeness of the macroscopic'.[29] What an incredulous state of affairs for anything to be considered routine. What an epitome of sanity to want to reflect, to give voice to, the weirdness of the world. 'The fact is that we are, most often, in a situation of having to decide on matters we know nothing of and have no wish to know anything of',[30] and what a perfectly understandable weakness to want your decisions to be knowing in a way that only you can have the last word, and for your invest-ment in them to be beyond question – as architect, as originary source. Lives lived in (through) madness should by rights seem far less inexplicable than those lived in the full belly of ordinariness; and what makes it otherwise, what makes madness the aberrant response, is not validity simpliciter, but the belief that the world can be beaten at its own game, that the real is something to be held up against the simulation rather than just another instance of that simulation. It is no anomaly to be disillusioned, to seek more intimacy from the world, but what is anomalous is placing yourself at the centre of that intimacy, to initiate a private universe whose tentacles reach outwards only to find themselves, to become irretrievably entangled. The way to be faithful to madness is to refuse to embrace it as an alternative to the coldness of sanity so perceived, but instead embrace the madness of that sanity, go mad and stay sane, commit yourself to juggling, to keeping both in the air as long as possible, and in the eventuality of your faltering, make sure to drop both at once. To illustrate this broad point, Baudrillard deploys one of his favourite metaphors:

There will be no end to this frenzied race around the Möbius strip where the surface of meaning perpetually feeds into the surface of illusion, unless the illusion of meaning were to win out once and for all, which would put an end to the world.[31]

It is important to keep a footing in the meaning of illusion, but not in the illusion of meaning. Better to turn the latter into the former. Better that the Möbius strip be completely incinerated than severed or screwed up into a ball.

There is no need to transcend the world in order to leave it behind us, for this has been achieved already via Kant, via the transcendental; and while the emancipation was only a half-measure, we nevertheless arrived at our mystical object, an object the only immanent property of which is the evasion of our sensible powers. In the absence of a beyond we have the world, and in the absence of a meaning there we have death. And yet in addition to 'the higher illusion of our world',[32] there are still the proliferation of beyonds (transhumanism, lives as disembodied thought or information) about which we can only speculate. Still, it seems not only can there never be enough realities from which we are excluded, but that there must also be posited exceptions to reality, states that exceed it, states that would take us outside the illusion of reality altogether. The world is not enough and death is not enough: there must be meta-levels forever growing towards a receding destination, and all because we find ourselves unable to exist to a sufficient degree to properly instantiate our deaths. How can such ephemera as modern man ever hope to die? We would have to have been born first, and who can stomach the thought of that? Better to look so close at reality that reality unbirths us:

> These traces pass into hyperreality, as does any 'material' pursued down to the tiniest detail, all 'scientific' exploration ending up exterminating its real object. [...] it is the whole of the human race which will have to be rigged out with a *trompe-l'oeil* navel, in so far as there is no longer any trace, with us, of any umbilical cord which might connect us to the real world.[33]

When God left, we began doing his work for him. Or perhaps he left because he could see we were already on the way to making him surplus to requirements. Consider Baudrillard's encapsulation of what might be thought of as the initial stage of man's covert supplementation of a lost God:

> By conjuring away the process of evolution, God had protected man from an inescapable end. For, paradoxically, the only insurance against death is to have been created ex nihilo, which keeps open the possibility of an equally miraculous resurrection, whereas if you are the product of an evolution, the only thing you can do is disappear when your time is up. The intervention of a superior power in Genesis guarantees a future immortality, whereas the genealogy of the species condemns it, in time, to disappear. And our whole problem, in our efforts to give birth to a real

world, is fundamentally the same as God's: not to drive the human race to despair by the recognition of its real existence and finitude.[34]

And so death was returned to us, but whether through a distaste for its finality, or an already contaminated notion of disappearance, we weakened under the pressure to unmake it again. What is inescapable is not the end but the impossibility of an end, and no longer any God to remedy that endlessness – hence the tireless propagation of various ways out of reality and all its postulated beyonds. Are we not already dead in this scenario? Haven't all men become ghosts, and all worlds purgatory? We are the victims of our own regenesis, but victims constructed abstractly, from inviolable materials, from non-materials conceived from what was hidden from us and from what we contrived to hide from ourselves – in our selves, that are themselves hidden (entire worlds populated by phantom pregnancies). And to exist as humans is only to exist like this: anonymous to ourselves and vagrant, but with an ingenuity for self-directed cruelty, the target of which is also conveniently inexplicable.

God may not be watching us, but 'there is always a hidden camera somewhere',[35] and even our insides do not escape it. The camera pointed at our brains can tell us what we think and feel more accurately than those still masquerading as the thinker and the feeler, while the cameras in our guts and hearts get to tell us how it is our body plans to do away with itself. But it is the cameras trained on us from outside that hurt the most, for it is no longer the case that these cameras are hidden: what is hidden is the someone on the other side monitoring the feed, and we've come to suspect, come to know even, that these watchers often do not exist, and that on the other side of the camera there are more cameras, and so on, and so on. Humanity is so bored with itself it employs technology to watch what it does, the information gargantuan, the yield dull, predictable, pitiful. You would need to be God (no stomach to be sick to) to sit through just one day of our collective existence. It would be like watching billions of metronomes, made all the more tiresome, not less, by the knowledge that each one believes it is alive. We know that the cameras are there, and suspect them even when they aren't there, but the illusion of interest and intrigue (of jaw-dropping diversity and revelation, of humanity's richness and intricate squalor) is a facade, a self-revealing con trick, a rampant delineation of ourselves that can end only one way: in an irreversible disenchantment, in a world cyclically feeding on its own tepid puke:

> Just as the illusion of the image disappears into its virtual reality, the illusion of the body into its genetic formulation and the illusion of the world into its artificial technical form, so also do we see disappear, in

Artificial Intelligence, the (super)-natural understanding of the world as play, as delusion, as machination, as crime – and not as logical mechanism, or as reflex cybernetic machine which would have its mirror and model in the human brain. / End of the raw illusion of thought, of the scene, of passion, end of the illusion of the world and its vision (and not its representation), end of the illusion of the Other, of Good and Evil (particularly of Evil), of true and false, end of the raw illusion of death, or that of existing at any cost: all these things vanish into telereality, into real time, into the sophisticated technologies which are our initiation into models, into the virtual, into the opposite of illusion – total disillusion.[36]

But maybe we're missing something. Maybe there's still something more to see. Just maybe our cameras require an advancement not yet available to us, or the cameras themselves need to be watched. So more cameras then, with more penetrating lenses, cameras that go deeper and further through us till we see what we want to see, what God would see: the alchemy of meaning in a fountain of shit.

Reality is there before us, ours for the taking through being ours in the making, and we are alienated by its very accessibility. (It fits so well we cannot take it off, and we need to be able to take it off, or at least to be able to imagine what that disrobing might involve.) But are we even still equipped for this alienation?[37] Aren't we already at the stage where all we are doing is expressing a nostalgia for its having passed: 'How sweet was alienation in the days of the subject!'[38]

This reality does not jar nearly enough to be real. It's a self-conscious soap opera; it's the too perfectly scripted new life of John Frankenheimer's *Seconds*; it's us like water in water disappearing. And what can death be in this reality but a painless segue to the next episode. We construct a home for ourselves, make reality to fit, only to have the unease of vagrancy haunt us like a lost opportunity. The virtual world is neurotic to the cusp of implosion, and our relative fragility within it undiminished – renascent crustaceans whose carapaces (those scabious remnants of an outmoded infection) will never again harden, (for there can be no recrudescence, or else … or else horror …) whose fate it is to meld into their surroundings, to disappear without feeling it, to live forever because death has been pre-empted by life, by 'the transparent shroud of a made-to-measure immortality'.[39] Ours is the eschatology of the non-existence of death. We are monkeys who have put our prehensile tails to new use: without our fear of falling, there is no need for the tails to still be clinging onto the world, so instead they coil around our throats and kill us in our sleep, which is anyway indistinguishable from what now passes as waking – the amortized imperishability of man, not so much *Live, Die, Repeat* as *Repeat, Repeat, Repeat*.

What is it about watching a shut-in that spends all his time watching live video feeds of other shut-ins that smacks of restitutive meta-awareness? How is this hikikomori mirroring different from this everyday world? The watcher and the watched concentrated into a transparent oozing mucilage, an auto-annihilative dehiscence, the smooth reflective pool at the centre of the gumma.

We arrive flattened, feeling flat. We find ourselves surrounded by flat ground where once there were mountains, and we would imagine ourselves falling from them, but it wasn't like this. Now all we have is that once con-tinual third-person mortification expressing itself in the first person, the hope and anguish of that obliterative disorientation denied us for good. All we have is the rebarbative sludge of what is left of us in the cloying emollience of the world: 'The striated space of life, the smooth space of melancholy. No more plans, neither for loving, nor for writing. That of living remains, like a super-ficial space in which disparate, fickle objects pass by – all fleeting shapes.'[40]

When Baudrillard describes seeing without being as 'the most radical meta-physical desire, the deepest spiritual joy',[41] and likens the state to that of God, he establishes what we might call the 'Immortal Position'. For while the long-time parochial task of philosophy is that of dying well, its true end surely lies instead in the conceptualization of a mode of being in which death's removal could not harm us. After all, how could the pessimist die well while harbouring that nagging logical possibility that his means of escape may about to be rescinded à la Bahnsen? From this perspective the Immortal Position becomes as crucial to dying well as the acceptance of your impending nullification; and what is central to this expanded preparation is its reliance on the eradication of your humanity, as 'we glimpse, in this, an inhuman possibility, which would restore the pluperfect form of the world, without the illusion of the mind or even that of the senses. An exact and inhuman hyperreality, where we could at last delight in our absence and the dizzying joys of disincarnation.'[42] We picture how it might be, how if we could implement this coup of imagin-ation, and so establish these future selves as somehow receptive to the continu-ation of our perspectival existence, the threat of immortality would lose its sting. But who can say at what point disembodied existence ceases to be night-marish and horrific, and evokes instead the welcome upheavals of ecstasy? Perhaps the switch would come at the very point at which we are relieved of our humanity, for there is no possible salvation in which we can remain as we are. Immortality can only ever provide exit when we are not there to modify it into a custodial sentence. For immortality to function, as with death, we must first disappear – unrecognized by others but more importantly by our-selves. Either way we die, for immortality is just another way to die: to die and go on living, or rather to live and go on dying. Nothing, nothing at all exceeds the sweet mystery of our expungement, not the world around us like a glove, not the paradisal, not even God. Only the giddy aroma of our rotting bodies, and us riding away inside that sickly scent, can quell our reflexive disgust at having been manufactured incongruent with bliss. The equivocation in Baudrillard's summation, therefore, is all but extraneous: 'perhaps the function of disappearing is a vital one. Perhaps this is how we react as living beings, as mortals, to the threat of an immortal universe, the threat of a definitive reality.'[43] In order not to lose ourselves a trace must be left, but that trace must be indeed be left, because we cannot face the possibility of taking it with us. And we cannot welcome the perfect crime as enacted in the world, but only its possibility, its necessity, in the concept of a beyond. The perfect crime is our possibility for an elsewhere, an elsewhere without us in which we might see from a place of absence, see without affecting the seen, embody the dream of physics, the hidden secrets of the world. Baudrillard laments, with a certain knowing anachronistic indulgence:

> The perfect crime would have been to invent a faultless world and withdraw from it without leaving a trace. But we cannot achieve this. We leave traces everywhere – viruses, lapses, germs and catastrophes – signs of imperfection which are, so to speak, man's signature in the heart of the artificial world.[44]

We do not expect to see the Immortal Position evidenced in the world, but it is of course everywhere. What else is this world of simulation if not the diagrammatic failings of our increasingly elaborate efforts to establish it? What else but a concerted effort to disappear without going? What else but the laborious perfecting of an imperfect crime? What else but the fortification of our temporal shield, our protection against any last semblance of the possibility of time itself being real?

The mark of the final phase, for Baudrillard, is not insignificantly that of 'total immunity';[45] and there is no more immunity than in immortality's disappearing act – except perhaps in death, if we can succeed in pulling the two apart. The spread of immunity just is the accelerated inflation of the real, its corpse bloating, spitting gas, suffocating the illusion of life (of morality, truth, and identity) in a cloud of noxious and yet euphoric disenchantment. For while reality may be dead, its corpse a stubborn stain, an irremovable physical blot on a world that has no further use for it, our protective apparatus against its possible encroachment must remain intact, must evolve alongside it as it decays and so prevent us ever seeing it. Even imagining our own death in comparable terms is an indulgence that cannot now be risked: a vicariousness made impossible via the vicariousness of life itself. The corpse of the real is the death of death itself. Its remains are sequestered in a ditch to maintain the illusion that its true end might still be yet to happen, that what has already been destroyed might be further annihilated, that the end of the end has not already been reached and survived and left unmarked.[46]

Immunity is the default condition of our disincarnation, our presence while absent, our humanity transformed immortal. There is no more pressing reason to become something else, to renege on being human, than to discover how differently we might die. But such a death is a paradox of death. It is a death mired in its own forgetfulness of life: the death that forgets to die – the death that has prepared so intensely for itself that it pre-empts and so nullifies its own eventuality. This is not, though, another way of saying that our virtuality is less than life, but of saying it is more, too much more, so much more that death, even as it happens and is assimilated as a merely circumstantial event, a paltry and increasingly insignificant detail in an enormity so exhaustive as to preclude the necessary self-awareness. The accelerated expansion of information to the point that it can no longer inform (and even this explication of distance, this writing-getting-closer, is all the time taking us further away), the explosion of the virtual following the implosion of reality, the growth after decay, the afterlife of our death:

> There is merely a movement of the exacerbation of reality towards paroxysm, where it involutes of its own accord and implodes leaving no trace, not even the sign of its end. For the body of the real was never recovered. In the shroud of the virtual, the corpse of the real is forever unfindable.[47]

The illusion of the real is eradicated by its own intractability, and now the world of simulation can have no reference even for its dead body. In this sense its end is still happening somewhere else, somewhere beyond this self-fulfilling universality, and so nowhere. And while its demise was traceless, its disappearance complete, what are we if not the intoxication of its passing? What is our immunity if not the woozy after-effect of some elemental extraction?

11.3 Talking to the Dead

Keeping death in the family has proved an effective method of keeping death away from us, or rather putting something between us and it: a unit of proximity and of blood, an incantation to ward off the true immensity of mortality. (There's a correlation here with the Humean concept of sympathy, and how its extension to non-familial others is always something of a strain, a stretching out of shape and a consequent poor fit.) For it could be that 'death is always incestuous – a fact that would only add to its spell'.[48] We know only too well of its ubiquity and proliferation, but this familial insulation makes it also a rare thing, a mere generational smattering. The death of the Other is never properly felt, and so never properly death: it is instead a means of communication, a distant trembling on a web translated into words. We talk to the dead we cannot touch: 'communication is an operation, and along with it goes the operation of social life. Language is a form, but communication is a performance.'[49] Death at a distance is acted out for us and we act back, but no connection is made by this limited deciphering. The death of the other is in fact representative of just what it means to engage in a communicative exchange that repels all haptic possibilities for closure, for information to be felt and completed in the incontrovertibility of convergence:

> Communication became this strange structure where things (and beings) do not touch each other, but exchange their kinetic, caloric, erotic and informational energy through contiguity, just like molecules. Through contiguity, but without contact, always being at a distance from each other.[50]

If the animus of science is, as Baudrillard suggests, its not returning to the scene of the crime, and its thereby becoming forgetful 'of the original murder', the animus of ethics is the opposite compulsion, that of a continual returning to exact repeated viewings of the slain body, so that if, with regards to the scientific, 'all the energy of the dead object and its last rites passes into the simulated resurrection of the living',[51] ethics is in the contrastive practice of conducting a séance for those otherwise thought alive, via our touching of hands with the few dead that happen to sit alongside us.

It cannot be surprising that the dead are still open to seduction, that they can still be made to exist as a conduit to the dead other that would otherwise be living, that there is still an energy at work – like the dead man on Jarry's five-man bicycle in *Supermale*, whose energy and focus on pedalling was not depreciated in death but accentuated.[52] In this way our familial dead are seduced by our need for them and we by their continued utility and presence, through a communicative directness that though past has enough residual influence to sustain a seemingly lost contiguity. As Baudrillard explains:

> For the dead are only dead when there are no longer any echoes from this world to seduce them, and no longer any rites challenging them to exist. / For us, only those who can no longer produce are dead. In reality, only those who do not wish to seduce or be seduced are dead.

But seduction gets hold of them nonetheless, just as it gets hold of all production and ends up destroying it.[53]

We've always pretended that the real is something worth approaching, that its placelessness is our placelessness, that there in its nowhere there is no such thing as us and no such thing as death, and yet we've nurtured this conflation whereby the paradox becomes manifest and glorious. This is our most resilient and tedious delusion. And the source of it is the desire that reality become less real as the result of being found. For it haunts us (and we welcome this haunting all the while its opaqueness is preserved) with the threatened cataclysm of not being real at all, or else too real – which will amount to the same thing – a reality so divorced from our fictions, so alien in its conception, that we will not find *it* so much as be found *by* it, and having been found realize not our strangeness to ourselves (humanity's *Unheimlichkeit*, already the established staple of what it is for us to think ourselves), but instead a complicity and a domestic mundanity so excessive that it disintegrates all dreams we had of being human. For somewhere we know that it is not the evidence of paradoxes, or inexplicabilities beyond all human imaginings, that will ultimately destroy us, see us babbling and insane within moments of exposure, but their sudden and cruel removal.

That death can appear overtly dyadic (as Schopenhauer found) is evidenced in the processes through which we sequester it – in the methodology involved in managing its influence. It is both the repressed thing and the secret thing, and each has very different implications for the supposed oneness of repressor and secretor: 'The hidden or the repressed has a tendency to manifest itself, whereas the secret does not. It is an initiatory and implosive form: one enters into a secret, but cannot exit.'[54]

Death as an imagined finality is this death that is hidden, that motivates and eulogizes its individual subject according to a present that was future and will become past. The secret death is another death, a death that is the death of this life only in that it is also the death of finality, the death of the possibility of an end. That it is never revealed is not due to some systematic subjugation, a process that would anyway have it surface in some mutated form, but due to our entering into it as one enters into an empyrean and infinite labyrinth, as one imagines the reality of a home – by leaving it unimagined. And it is this conscious entering into a secret death that makes it possible for death to somehow be for us, to find itself malleable in our presence, to transcend the real of the hidden and disappear instead into pure simulacrum: 'More invisible than the invisible – this is the secret.'[55] The act of entering nonetheless remains inscrutable, so that while this death is secreted our entering into it is something hidden. The secret death is a form of illumination, a way of seeing ourselves amid the swallowing murk of reality: the 'mysterious light without origin, whose oblique rays are no longer real, [...] like stagnant water, water without depth, soft to the touch like a natural death',[56] a death natural *to* us, a reconfiguration of absence.

You should never hear yourself speak. There's no room in the world for people who hear themselves (the auditory hallucinations of schizophrenics are not hallucinations at all, simply their own voices, unowned). Such self-awareness is a kind of death, a death that hasn't let go, a spectral objectivity that has no place in life. To see yourself is also to acknowledge the presence of death, to be reminded of the motivation to see only others and for them in turn to be responsible for seeing you. This self-awareness as from the outside, this deleterious consciousness of oneself as if from above, establishes a hideous multiplication of one's worldly presence, accompanied by the inevitable hiatus in proprioception, which allows us to die and to return. And it is in these instances that we learn that death (or at least the death we most fear) is not subtraction but proliferation, finding ourselves manifest in materials beyond our facility for experience – the felt non-being of that impossible death, that unreal death that finds us out, disclosing the pretence of what it means to live convinced of life.

When death shifts from being an inevitability to being an allurement, it is not so much that we are discontented by life, as discontented by the obligation of having to live life. For it is not life, which could just as well be death, that offends, but rather the insidious stipulation that life itself be lived, that with it comes a prescription of connectedness that it is somehow incumbent on us to embody. And it is these various embodiments that then take the place of life, as if the patterns and networks that emerge were themselves the fundamental principles of living matter, as if there is no way to become free from this living that is not also a denunciation of, and a dissevering from, that which is lived. It should be no revelation that 'this is how ennui works, like a throbbing crackle on the cerebral telephone line that connects us to life, [...] like something in a corner of your life which just won't finally die'.[57] And it is this connection, this living of life as if it were itself life, instead of the inexplicable pressure that life be lived, that we seek and fail to find emancipation from in death – when the crackle eventually drowns out not only the line's communications, its informational content, but the listener as well.

It is excess and not deficiency that causes paralysis in life: it is too many connections, a too complete integration, a too frequent returning to ourselves that has our existing transform into a mask of existence. It is this living that constitutes our protection from life, and makes life a threat to our living of it. Safer then not to listen, and never to speak: after all, 'why speak [...] when it is so easy to communicate'?[58] Better the implied intimacy of communication (with oneself and others) than the queasy postulations of speech. Better to live without dying (or die without living, for they amount to the same thing) than to ever happen upon life. The best way to never come into contact with yourself (either directly or via the other) is by ceaselessly maintaining autoreferential communication, through an immersion that disappears into appearance, through an integration that replaces place with placement (to make placeless), and by never allowing for the possibility of surface – or more specifically, the possibility of a surface that does not go all the way down, or rather across, because there is no down.

If uncertainty is a torment, it is a lesser torment. Considered as a game, it is the torment of not knowing how to win, not knowing which side has won at any given time, or even knowing what winning would amount to, as opposed to knowing precisely that there is no possibility of winning, that the concept of winning is senseless, and that the game is just a distraction from the knowing that would make the game itself impossible. Baudrillard explains the game as follows:

> Now, this is the game in which we find ourselves, our crucial game, the game of uncertainty. We cannot escape it. But we are not ready to accept it, and even worse: we expect some sort of homeopathic salvation, we hope to reduce this uncertainty with more information, with more communication, thereby reinforcing the uncertainty of the whole system.[59]

Engagement with the game of uncertainty is here correctly diagnosed as something that can provide only incomplete solutions, and only then within the wider parameters of uncertainty that have already been misrepresented in order that the game be played. All these accretions of partial elucidations can achieve is the further augmentation of uncertainty as a whole. But to imagine there is no core motivational sublimation at work, that there is not a slick integrality of essential redirection, away from the fact that the whole enterprise of uncertainty is less a problem and more a solution, is to give no credit at all to the risible strivings of humans. Our delusions are rarely as complete in their manipulative mastery over us as we envisage, and yet when we see them so flawlessly acted out in the world and in the people around us it is difficult to believe that this prepotency is not complete. Nonetheless, we have at the very least an inkling, a niggle, the *crackle* of an awareness, that the game does not contain all the rules, but is itself the circumscription of another less apparent rule.

Philosophy is either the art of making us appear or making us disappear, for it is both in the business of substantiating a perceived diaphaneity of being and of fragmenting a spuriously perceived aggregation. In recent times it is the latter of these two approaches that has been most prevalent, our appearance repeatedly delineated as a theoretical fiction – one that in turn induces a kind of claustrophobia, a manifest containment that proves incompatible with our attempts at subjective assimilation – a fiction that we should make efforts to move beyond. The disappearance, though, has proved all but impossible to impose: for the most part we still live our lives as if we are here. We are determined to remain active, to maintain the illusion of our appearance and with it the velocity we consider natural to it, when inertia or idleness would seem more pertinent to our theoretical understanding of what we are, or what our favoured reality tells us we are not. In praise of impeding this oblivious motion, Baudrillard writes:

> Idleness is a fatal strategy, and fatalism a strategy of idleness. It is from this I derive a vision of the world which is both extremist and lazy. [...] I detest the bustling activity of my fellow citizens, detest initiative, social responsibility, ambition, competition. They are exogenous, urban values, efficient and pretentious. They are industrial qualities, whereas idleness is a natural energy.[60]

Our failure here can be thought of as a lack of imagination, a failure to circumvent the influence of the simulacra of ourselves using the reality of our inceptive misdirection; the problem being, that to overturn this original act of imagination requires an act of imagination of even greater magnitude. The fiction that has become real is no longer reliant on its foundation, so that when its initial reality is put in question, nothing but an entirely new imagining can replace it – something that merely pointing out the falsity of what has already appeared cannot achieve. Baudrillard's advised method is to focus on the effect rather than the cause, to bypass the dubious integrity of the appearance itself and instead simulate fractures in the established momentum produced by it: 'breaking up the movement artificially, the cataract seems like a natural catastrophe in slow motion. With a little more imagination, it becomes as still as a glacier',[61] and yet just what this imaginative leap might amount to remains unclear, although a better understanding of what is being advocated will emerge by paying close attention to a concise yet wide-ranging critique of philosophical methodology expounded in *Cool Memories II*:

> Philosophy would like to delay the day of reckoning for the world in order to be able to put its question. It forgets that the world is not a universe of questions, but of answers – automatic answers, though often poetic ones nonetheless; answers provided in advance to all possible questions. / Philosophy would like to transform the enigma of the world

into a philosophical question, but the enigma leaves no room for any question whatever. It is the precession of the answer which makes the world indecipherable. / Modern Philosophy flatters itself, in a wholly self-satisfied manner, that it asks questions to which there are no answers, whereas what we have to accept is that there are no questions at all, in which case our responsibility becomes total, since we are the answer – and the enigma of the world also remains total, then, since the answer is there, and there is no question to that answer.[62]

The mistake is to forget that the world has already answered, and that our questions are only manifestations of either our distaste at the answers given or an inability to understand them, a combination which in turn accentuates the world's inherent poeticism; for while there is a surfeit of answers there are only questions on the other side of those answers, and philosophy tells us there is no other side. We have no facility for getting through the answers in order to access the questions, no solid footing from which to pose our inquiries. It is for this reason that all thought turns to shit, turning round and round 'like the alimentary bolus in the labyrinth of the small intestine, with the certainty, alas, of finding the exit in the form of excrement'.[63] The only solution, when everything is a solution to some problem we cannot formulate, is through an imaginative innovation that positions us outside the world's answers, so that we may become cognizant of what questions might have been antecedent to them, and what further questions are insinuated by this consummating of the world's otherwise inscrutable resolution.

There is an obvious correlation here with a view put forward by Fernando Pessoa, although Baudrillard goes one stage further in his attack, removing even the world's impenetrability as a source of potential solace:

> Metaphysics has always struck me as a prolonged form of latent insanity. If we knew the truth, we'd see it; everything else is systems and approximations. The inscrutability of the universe is quite enough for us to think about; to want to actually understand it is to be less than human, since to be human is to realize it can't be understood.[64]

That the world is not for us is not for Baudrillard a subject for reflection, but a delusional premise in which a determining and problematic remoteness is first conceived. The conceit of philosophy is that it knows enough to ask something of what it does not yet know, enough to impose its interrogation on the unknown as if having already established this unknown as somehow unresolved, as if the world had been waiting for its questions, as opposed to its already being the answerable embodiment of a prior examination, an additional unknown that philosophy cannot see itself replicating. And there is no working backwards from the answers, because their excess chokes all possible routes.

The unfoundedness of philosophy's questions is, unsurprisingly, also a direct indictment of our own unfoundedness, of our own ineptitudes of imagination when it comes to inaugurating either our presence or our absence in a world that has already accounted for itself. We are already inseparable from the world's response, so that the question as to whether or not we happen to be extant or vanished is itself either an answer to some other unknown question, or else the figment of a beyond to which we cannot reach.

To claim that the world has already answered without abridgement, that nothing can be legitimately asked of it, without that asking itself being an answer, is of course to recognize the world's reality as an excess, but an excess that without questions cannot be verified, for 'there are no proofs of this reality's existence – and there never will be – any more than there are proofs of the existence of God. It is, like God, a matter of faith. / And when you begin to believe in it, this is because it is already disappearing.'[65] To believe, to have faith in the world is to move away from the world, to imagine you are not one of its answers but a question to which a solution is forthcoming; and consequently, there is no longer any room for you there, the initial breach of a philosophical distancing having been staged, and while there's no going back, there's no going forward either.

It is in this contrived alienation of philosophy, this Gnostic base camp, that all consolations of death are cultivated, whether they are given explicit expression or not. To question, and so admit the possibility of there being questions, is to automatically initiate an exit strategy, as to look back on ourselves and the world we must first leave them behind – first enter the mental illness of reflection. Thus the surfeit of the world's reality, its comprehensive answer, brings about a paradox: we believe the world by ceasing to believe in it. There is, moreover, yet another reversal that occurs as a result of the waning of our distancing belief, and once again it is the profusion 'of reality that makes us stop believing in it. [...] Deprivation of dreams, deprivation of desire. And we know what mental disorder sleep deprivation induces.'[66] In this eventuality the distance remains but the belief that engenders it is gone. There are no answers, there are no questions, there are only questions about questions. And it is this second reversal that leaves death even further divorced from anything the world is able to reveal to us. We cannot sleep. We cannot sleep even in death. We are dreamless and awake, and without sleep to countervail against it, this state of wakeful reality is itself nothing but a kind of sleep, a Pessoan sleepwalker's life, a life so deadened there is no longer any need for death. 'This is no longer the age of metaphor':[67] the interchangeability of life and death has already arrived and all that's left is the imaginative burden of either re-establishing the lost distinction or else moving beyond it altogether.

Notes

1   Baudrillard, *The Intelligence of Evil*, 166.
2   When barbaric experiments are conducted on animals with a repetitive fervour disconsonant to any conclusions they might yield, the question asked no longer seems to imply the expectation of a resolution, only that suffering reveal answers about itself. This is not torture and suffering for the sake of torture and suffering, but torture and suffering for the sake of the very possibility of these states – some substructure of imagined meaning.
3   Baudrillard, *Intelligence of Evil*, 168.
4   Ibid., 151.
5   Ibid., 28.
6   Ibid., 22.
7   Merwin, *The Miner's Pale Children*, 66.
8   Zamyatin, *We*, 206.
9   Baudrillard, *Simulacra and Simulation*, 137.
10 Georges Bataille, 'Friendship', *Parallax*, 7:1 (2001): 9.
11 Baudrillard, *Symbolic Exchange and Death*, 183.
12 Georges Bataille, *The Accursed Share: An Essay on General Economy, Vols. II and III, Vol III: Sovereignty* (New York: Zone Books, 1991), 216–17.
13 And pain does not place us anywhere for long, for its duration and its intensity qualify only for putting us outside its reach.
14 As if wanting in essence isn't the 'poster boy' of futility.
15 Baudrillard, *Simulacra and Simulation*, 4.
16 Ibid., 5.
17 See Baudrillard, *The Intelligence of Evil*, 161.
18 Baudrillard, *Simulacra and Simulation*, 6.
19 Ibid.
20 Céline, *Journey to the End of the Night*, 156.
21 Baudrillard, *The Perfect Crime*, 7.
22 Ibid., 9.
23 Ibid., 8–9.
24 Ibid., 10.
25 Baudrillard, *Seduction*, 44.
26 Baudrillard, *The Perfect Crime*, 68.
27 Ibid., 65–66.
28 Ibid., 11.
29 Bruno Jarrosson in Ibid., 14.
30 Ibid., 12.
31 Ibid., 17.
32 Ibid., 18.
33 Ibid., 22.
34 Ibid., 23–24.
35 Ibid., 26.

36   Ibid., 32–33.
37   'We arrive then at this paradox, at this conjuncture where the position of the subject
     has become untenable, and where the only possible position is that of the object.
     The only strategy possible is that of the object. We should understand, by this, not
     the 'alienated' object in the process of de-alienation, the enslaved object claiming its
     autonomy as a subject, but the object such as it challenges the subject, and pushes it
     back upon its own impossible position.' (Baudrillard, *Fatal Strategies*, 143–44).
38   Baudrillard, *Fatal Strategies*, 117.
39   Baudrillard, *The Perfect Crime*, 37.
40   Baudrillard, *Cool Memories*, 20.
41   Baudrillard, *The Perfect Crime*, 38.
42   Ibid.
43   Ibid., 39.
44   Ibid., 40.
45   Ibid., 41.
46   Hence Baudrillard's illustrative phrasing of this perpetual open-endedness in: 'Death
     itself is under threat of death' (Baudrillard, *The Perfect Crime*, 49).
47   Baudrillard, *The Perfect Crime*, 46.
48   Baudrillard, *Seduction*, 69.
49   Jean Baudrillard, 'The Vanishing Point of Communication', in *Fatal Theories*,
     ed. David B. Clarke, Marcus A. Doel, William Merrin and Richard G. Smith
     (London: Routledge, 2009), 17.
50   Baudrillard, 'The Vanishing Point of Communication,' 17.
51   Baudrillard, *Seduction*, 56.
52   See Baudrillard, *Cool Memories*, 222.
53   Baudrillard, *Seduction*, 84.
54   Baudrillard, *Seduction*, 79.
55   Baudrillard, *Fatal Strategies*, 79.
56   Baudrillard, *Seduction*, 62.
57   Baudrillard, *Cool Memories II*, 4.
58   Baudrillard, 'The Vanishing Point of Communication', 20.
59   Ibid, 22–23.
60   Baudrillard, *Cool Memories II*, 7.
61   Ibid., 11.
62   Ibid., 20.
63   Ibid., 47.
64   Fernando Pessoa, *The Book of Disquiet* (London: Penguin Books, 2002), 83.
65   Baudrillard, *The Intelligence of Evil*, 14.
66   Ibid., 15.
67   Baudrillard, *Cool Memories II*, 60.

Chapter 12

BLACK LIGHT: NIGREDO AND CATASTROPHE

The secrets we uncover will be more than secrets, and we will uncover only their secretness, because the 'more hidden than hidden' is not, as Baudrillard claims, 'the secret',[1] but is instead an integrated secretness that reveals only its form and never its content; for secrets can be discovered and their secretness thereby removed, whereas an integrality of secretness is discovered only as far as it exists, its content remaining unknown. This secretness is the last shred of human meaning, and its very redundancy is its power, as 'something redundant always establishes itself where there is nothing left'.[2] Here lies the state of catastrophe, that dead end of proliferating potentialities, that turning with no place to turn, that end that cannot end, for history is finished, and 'once this point of inertia has been passed, every event becomes catastrophe, becomes an event pure and without consequence (but that is its power)'.[3]

This secretness, of ostensibly contentless form, and human death are one. Their darkness is a mutual darkness, a compacted and contained light, a light that illuminates only the decomposing promise of itself, with the corpse a sculpture of this light forever tending to inertia. As Baudrillard puts it:

> We must grasp the catastrophe lying in wait for us in the slowing of light – the slower light is, the less it escapes its source. Things and events have a tendency to no longer allow their meaning to escape, to slow down its emanation, to capture what they formerly refracted and absorb it into a black body.[4]

Black Light *is* human secretness, is our death, is meaning pulled continually forward into the blackened, necrotized corpse, the putrescent body of our perceived emancipation from the body – a freedom we do not understand, a dead light survived by its death.

The Black Light of human death and secretness is never quite at the speed of the living; it is never a light that discloses what it means in terms that meaning can grasp, and then strangulate. It's as if time and distance were different for each of them. Baudrillard writes: 'If light drops to relative speeds, there is no more transcendence, no more God to recognize his own, and the universe lapses into indeterminacy.'[5] But this consequence is not enacted, and no such relativity is achieved, for the Black Light is the body of God: it is transcendence made corporeal so that its promise can be seen but not accessed, it is the 'Lament Configuration'[6] found, even held, but never opened. Any contact with the Black Light would make the speeds of life and death/secretness commensurate, thus throwing us into the chaos of some ultimate reality, a materialized cosmic pessimism the kind of which would see human thought immolate itself at the altars of all previous hells – and who's to say that this Black Light is not already leaking through some imperceptible fissure in its otherwise airtight corpse.

There will be no warning. Even with the world slowed down we would not see it coming. Yet we are waiting for it, preparing for the shock, which is fatuous: as we pre-empt to suffer sooner only in order to avoid the heavier suffering of waiting. We do not wait, as we did, 'for the stars or the heavens, but for the subterranean gods who threaten us with a collapse into emptiness';[7] and we know our idea of emptiness is not adequate to the emptiness that is coming, and so we try to imagine the destruction, but all our earthly simulations fail us: our nuclear explosions, our spaceships the size of countries hovering above us in the sky, our screaming into caskets of inexplicable light … for this, as Baudrillard warned us, is how catastrophe works:

> This is the mental effect of catastrophe: stopping things before they end, thus maintaining them indefinitely in the suspense of their apparition. […] Catastrophe jealously makes sure to destroy the illusion of eternity, bur it plays with it too, fixing things into a second eternity.[8]

It is this second and increasingly precarious eternity, in which the Black Light is acknowledged to exist but left unexamined, that feeds us the sustenance of a brink, of a potential alteration in circumstance, that while couched in doom is nevertheless a lacuna and so a source of salvational exclusion, a possibility for something (anything) else besides our current state. This Black Light of human death and secretness is the last anomaly, the only anomaly left because it must be left, never to be less than anomalous, never to be reduced to normalcy in anything but its surfacing, and its surfacing only to then sink, and to sink without trace, for it is always without trace – excluding the trace of its repeated surfacings, which are themselves (potential) traceless traces, the recurrent arrival of an alteritic absence:

Anomaly no longer has the tragic side of abnormality, nor even the dangerous and deviant side of *anomie*. It is somehow harmless, harmless and inexplicable. It is on the order of a pure and simple apparition, the rising to the surface of a system (ours) something come from elsewhere. From another system? / Anomaly has no critical incidence in the system. Its figure is rather that of a mutant.[9]

Death in this Black Light is a mutant form. Its work on the corpse while barely changing its structure nonetheless manifests the very vertex of mutation. It is *the* mutant form of life, the realizer of the latent deadness of genes. However, this is neither abnormal nor tragic, as Baudrillard makes clear; but it is replete with otherness, albeit a familiarized otherness, as something routine and yet irresolvably impenetrable and bewildering. It is for these reasons that the Black Light convinces us it is not of this world, that its origins lie elsewhere, that death and secretness have entered a system they were not designed to enter – our system, a system in which they remain unknowable and undisclosed in mankind's wan and sickly luminescence.

We are held hostage by this Black Light, this light we cannot see. Sequestered within it, death becomes virtualized by its own incalculability. Death no longer waits but is, and we are hostage to its externality to life, to its reconfiguration of the game, to the arrival of its own interminable suspension. The life is now gone that could await its death, and so too the death that had once assumed its life. There is no waiting and nothing to wait. There is only chance and its contemporaneity, only chance's precipice, the treacherous extremity of which is duplicated over and over to form a bridge high over a swell of chaos occluded by cloud: 'Neither life nor death: this is security – this, paradoxically, is also the status of the hostage.'[10]

The corpse too is a hostage, its power non-transferable. All the hopes we had for our living selves are there in our corpses, unpolluted by consciousness, an irremovable and exquisite waste. The corpse though hostage cannot be released – for its own sake, and so for ours, because there is nowhere for it to go, and nowhere for us to go but where it is. And so the corpse's death comes back to haunt us, because the corpse is dead but can die again and, as Baudrillard intimates, this second death is its reprisal:

It is something very precious that we don't quite know how to get rid of. It burns, and isn't negotiable. It can be killed, but it takes revenge. The corpse always plays this role. Beauty, too, and the fetish as well. It has no value, but is priceless. It is an object of no interest, and at the same time absolutely singular, without equivalent, and almost sacred.[11]

It is this pricelessness of the corpse that allows its state of death to live enough
to once again be killed, for the corpse to be correctly surmised as being not
yet dead. Hence the corpse is the waste of what is left, so that our disinterest
in it, our dismissal of its existence, which must be repeated over and over,
like some form of quailing worship, is just so many more acts of killing it, of
being rid of what there is no being rid of, of keeping it hostage to the ineptitude of our attempts to process it, to reconstitute its withered mass into the
dream of an escape. After all, the sacred only becomes sacred 'by subtraction,
by the state of radical exception in which [it] is put', and like this 'the hostage becomes the fantastic equivalent of everything else'.[12] This hostage that
refuses to take flight, or to be set free, and that will not conclusively die is the
hallowed object, the concentrated spectacle of endurance, the saint at the
end of her journey, filled with stars of Black Light. And remember this: 'If all
enigmas are resolved, the stars go out.'[13]

Death is a sickness, but a made-up sickness. Death is psychosomatic: it gets
you nowhere faster, and not only in lieu of its being 'more poorly defined',[14]
but because it is tailored to an inexplicability we understand. The moment
death ceases to revolt or seduce us there is no more death.[15] There is then
no such thing as a meaningless death. Such a death would be inhuman, and
a death that is not made human can make no claim to death: it is instead a
modification, albeit a kind one. Nonetheless, we also need to avoid death's
seduction of us becoming normalized and too generic; in other words, we
must avoid the commodification of death, for this too is less death and more
the industrialized inclusiveness of living.

12.1 For the Love of Death: A Necrophilic Seduction

What is the acceptance of death but a wish? What is it but the deepest wish,
'the wish to hand one's desire over to another',[16] even if there is no other there
to receive it? But then what better object of love than that which isn't there,
that which is dead, or that which is the imagined focal point of death itself. If
'the only ideal object is a dead one',[17] then better it should never have lived at
all. For while love deadens, and a love of death fatally resolves, a love of that
which is found dead without ever having lived in the first place is the equal to
the limit of our imaginings, and so equal to our wish for it. But this acceptance
is resigned to a promise without promise, an emancipation constructed from
the plans of the old servility – that of problem and solution. Better then, if
one is to live death, to be seduced by it, consumed by its secret. To actively
love death is to passively indulge your own weak grasp of life and to wish to
be free of it, to forfeit it, to pass it onto another. Whereas to be seduced by

death is to engage with its evidential secretion of itself. Baudrillard pulls the two apart as follows:

> Seduction is not mysterious; it is enigmatic. The enigma, like the secret, is not unintelligible. / It is, on the contrary, fully intelligible, but it cannot be said or revealed. Such is seduction: inexplicable evidence. Such is the game. At the heart of any game is a fundamental, secret rule, an enigma; nevertheless, the whole process is no mystery; nothing is more intelligible than a game in progress. / Love itself is charged with all the world's mystery, but it's not enigmatic. It is, on the contrary, heavy with meaning, being of the order, not of the enigmatic but of the solution.[18]

The mystery of death is that it is no mystery, and we all die with incredible ease, even if that ease must be suffered. To be seduced by death is to know what it knows, to know the secret intact in its secrecy, to know that the secret can only retain its intelligibility through remaining a secret, to know that solutions are the death of death, and that reality was never a threat because it never existed. All there was and is just death's beguiling Black Light and its never being seen, a light that while it enchants excites not the merest desire – for death knows that what desires is just another misstep in the irreality of the real, in the apparition of appearance – and it is like this that death inveigles and replaces the desiring subject. As Foucault put it: 'Death left its old tragic heaven and became the lyrical core of man: his invisible truth, his visible secret.'[19]

Death is never a cause, only ever an effect – albeit an enigmatic, or paradoxical effect – never looking back to identify with whatever contingency supposedly brought it about. Only this way can death be sublime. Only this way can death become the fetish it needs to be in order to seduce us, 'erasing the accidentality of the world and substituting for it an absolute necessity'[20] – a necessity brought about by death's removal from its causes. Death in its monstrous foreignness functions like a work of art, the glow of its Black Light seducing 'from elsewhere, from having exceeded its own form and become pure object, pure event'.[21] Nor can death be desired, because to be desired it would either have to thwart our desires for it, which would result in the tired and commonplace frustration with death, the sickness unto death that only strengthens our unhealthy attachment to the corpse waiting to become itself, or else would fulfil our desires for it, which would be more catastrophic still: 'For really nothing is worse than to utter a wish and to have it literally fulfilled; nothing is worse than to be rewarded on the exact level of one's demand.'[22] Such a literalization of death amounts to a resolution of flattening, of razing, of death's own reversed and cannibalistic *nigredo*. This is the gratification of the lost, of those misplaced in the cul-de-sac of their own want, an homogenizing and voided glut, when the one true and 'supreme orgasm is metamorphosis'.[23] And to clarify one further point of possible contention: death is not your other, but rather your own otherness.

Death's meaning, which has no meaning, is also your meaning, and so your double death. The secret of death must become your secret, and its content an irrelevance. It must replace who you are without your ever having contact with it. Death must be allowed to mean nothing, to exude a futility of purpose and insignificance unmatched by anything found in life that is not the living of this death. Hence 'why pride oneself on difference, when indifference is sure to prevail? Why avail oneself of meaning when silence is sure to win?'[24] Say nothing of death, and say it in as many words as you can. Be verbose in your silence on the subject, on the subject that is not a subject, but the absolution of the absoluteness of the object. Remember too that reason cannot get you there, that only irrational schemata can assist in this assimilation, for 'there is no rational form of the absorption of death'.[25]

Baudrillard claims that it is only ever the other that knows 'you are going nowhere, that your life is senseless';[26] a scenario played out exquisitely by Quinn and Stillman in Paul Auster's *City of Glass*, and by Blue and Black in his *Ghosts*.[27] Quinn is Stillman's other and Blue is Black's other, and the reader is both Quinn's and Blue's other; and for each of them, and going ever backwards, it is 'as if someone, behind him, knew that he was going nowhere'.[28] But this disposition of otherness is not the same as that found in death: death does not follow and mirror your life and actions in order to establish that life's integral futility, but instead demands that you follow and mirror it, that you integrate it into you not as an other but as your own immanent otherness, and not then as a realization of senselessness, but as an internal distance from that senselessness.

Death always happens 'in advance of the unfolding of [its] causes', and this 'is the secret of [its] seduction'.[29] Its happening has always already happened. Its reasons which arrive, as they must, post facto, are never comparable to its secret. Just as in those hideous cases of premature burial, in which death has been wrongly ascribed, and the incomplete corpse, consumed by the acutest horror, wakes in its coffin, death pre-empts its own occurrence, occurring before it has had time to occur. And it was not infrequently documented[30] how these too hastily interred bodies resorted to auto-cannibalism, how they ate their fingers, their hands, and the flesh off their arms (and in fact any part of themselves accessible to their teeth) in panicked reflex to a death imposed without its secret, to the promise of a secret with insufficient cause. These unfortunate victims do not find themselves dead, or even left the possibility of death, but are instead exterminated:

> They no longer have the potential themselves for their own death, [...] and that was the actual story of historical extermination in the concentration camps. The people who arrived there were not able to control their own deaths, they weren't even given the opportunity to die, they were already dead – that's extermination.[31]

What recourse is there, when finding yourself dead and yet denied death, but to ingest the very material of your extermination, as if your being trapped there were some abreaction? And what is this but the frenzied mastication of the wrong kind of otherness that is your body? What it is it but that self-same slavish mastery over death thought above ground to separate us from the indentured? (Keeping in mind how 'it's worse to be a slave of oneself than a slave of another'.)[32] How else is there to die of a singularity, but via the removal of your own body? How else to ingratiate yourself with 'that ultimate form of singularity that is death itself'?[33] And as we saw with Diaz's Fabian, death on its own is not enough, for only a self-eradication, earned through a painful and suffered process of appearing, can deliver this indispensable end:

> Dying is nothing. You have to know how to disappear. / Dying comes down to biological chance and that is of no consequence. Disappearing is of a far higher order of necessity. You must not leave it to biology to decide when you will disappear. To disappear is to pass into an enigmatic state which is neither life nor death.[34]

Who alive in his grave could bring himself to voice the following Baudrillardian sentiment: 'The capacity to pass from one life to another, and not to die in only one life – that beats everything'?[35] Who having not only died once but died and disappeared, could want for more than the middle for which he was inexplicably born and for a lifetime denied sufficient access to?

Notes

1 Baudrillard, *Fatal Strategies*, 25.
2 Ibid., 30.
3 Ibid., 36.
4 Ibid., 37.
5 Ibid.
6 See Clive Barker's *Hellraiser* (Film Futures, 1987) and the subsequent franchise.

7   Baudrillard, *Fatal Strategies*, 40.
8   Ibid., 43.
9   Ibid., 47.
10   Ibid., 57.
11   Ibid., 70.
12   Ibid., 71.
13   Ibid., 79.
14   Ibid., 82.
15   See ibid., 90.
16   Ibid., 126.
17   Ibid., 135.
18   Ibid., 137.
19   Michel Foucault, *The Birth of the Clinic: An Archaeology of Medical Perception* (London: Routledge, 1989), 211.
20   Baudrillard, *Fatal Strategies*, 145.
21   Ibid., 149.
22   Ibid., 152.
23   Ibid., 160.
24   Baudrillard, *Fatal Strategies*, 155.
25   Baudrillard, *Cool Memories*, 169.
26   Baudrillard, *Fatal Strategies*, 165.
27   See Paul Auster, *The New York Trilogy* (London: Faber and Faber, 1987).
28   Baudrillard, *Fatal Strategies*, 161.
29   Ibid., 198.
30   See Jan Bondeson, *Buried Alive: The Terrifying History of Our Most Primal Fear* (New York: W. W. Norton, 2002).
31   Sutton, 'Endangered Species? An Interview with Jean Baudrillard', 217–24, 220.
32   Baudrillard, *The Conspiracy of Art*, 227.
33   Baudrillard, *The Spirit of Terrorism*, 94.
34   Baudrillard, *Cool Memories*, 24.
35   Ibid., 63.

APPENDIX 1

WHITEOUT: SPATIOTEMPORAL INTERSTICES, NECROPRESENCE AND THE IMMORTALITY OF NOW

Any endurable immortality would have to be one in which we did not figure (at least not as we are, or in some diluted form), or else would need to be experienced outside the passage of tense, or at the very least within a tensed series reduced from its triplicity to a self-replicating present, and through this latter the former, the depressive weight of the past and the anxiety of the future in absentia, with only the spatiotemporally boundless present left behind, its nothing becoming our nothing, its deathlessness becoming our site of uncreatured potentiality, our necropresence – or that state in which possibilities expand away from us like some infinite beauty we cannot see, reliant on not being seen, and we lose ourselves to be born like this,[1] gazing translucent as if dead men wakeful in the forever of time's material decomposition. What brings us here is the thought and the enactment of stopping, so that once immobilized we view the swell via the very enervation that propelled us to inertia, for this 'sensation of expansion toward nothingness present in melancholy has its roots in a weariness characteristic of all negative states', a weariness that 'separates man from the world'.[2] And it is in such weariness that necropresence strays from life and the world without finding death, a compromised presence in which man finds a peace[3] that kills him without killing him, a state achieved by first relinquishing the past we were in and the future we were moving towards, expanding the falsely contracted blip of the now, as time becomes space expanding outwards without end. 'If we were here, we would be full of wonder',[4] but necropresence is the only here and it is now and everywhere and through its growth becoming nowhere (invisible) once again – and we can only be lost and only replete with wonder when at last we find 'the still centre of the world that came to claim'[5] us, necrotizing those extraneous appendages we'd used to keep the world so close.

Ballard's 'The Enormous Space' opens with its central character, Geoffrey Ballantyne,[6] making an extempore decision, a decision to stop,[7] to cease from everything but his house and his existing in it – to close his front door on his still-idling car, to forget his obligations to a job, an ex-wife, the entire edifice of his London suburb and the rest of the world around it – but '[t]here is no stopping place in this life',[8] so while his retreat is enacted on the spot, he experiences continuance in greater measure than he does hiatus, and his decision thereby seems to him immediately ineffectual as a result: 'given that this is the most important decision of my life, it seems strange that nothing has changed'.[9] Ballantyne is well aware that it is the context of his resolution (the relative luxury of his life and his locality's innocuity) that makes it momentous, instilling in him the feeling of having stepped outside something that before had consumed him. (Which is not to say the nothing itself has not changed, the nothing that he now finds himself dreaming of,[10] for that nothing is already, at this inceptive stage, making itself known as a replacement for the 'overworked hologram'[11] that had formerly deprived him of the empty space in his head and in the world outside it.) What it is that remains unaltered is the recognition of change itself, of time as 'affection of motion'[12] that his desistance has not yet purged. Nothing has changed because he's still in the presence of change and all that change has come to represent: tense, finitude, strategies, the possibility of success, of failure, of catastrophe, of time itself. But change, as it transpires, remains only so as to perpetuate its own absence, to rectify these aberrations, have them recede into the artificially enclosed zone that his decision has irrevocably corrupted. He had 'expected the walls to tremble, at the very least a subtle shift in the perspectives of these familiar rooms',[13] but none of this happens at the start, and that these things do not happen is a signal to us, whether he notices it or not, that the house's interior has already begun to mimic the evacuative quintessence of his pledge. Nothing appears different because the decision is still there, keeping everything in place, for it is only once the decision has been forgotten, or rather made irrelevant, that spatial anomalies become visible. If the walls had begun to wane and warp at this early stage, the house would be revealing its secrets with the world still present: the calmness he experiences, the house yet refusing to show itself, is the lure to keep him there until decisions (and the purpose they carry) have lost all meaning. And after all, 'walls are the basis of everything human'.[14]

The onset of Ballantyne's necropresence mirrors his diminishing food reserves, and he auspicates this from the start: 'I would eat only whatever food I could find within the house. After that I would rely on time and space to sustain me.'[15] The deteriorating sway of food – as he works his way through the contents of his kitchen, the birds and local pets that fall prey to his traps, and the dour TV repairman who 'sadly yielded to the terrors of light and space'[16] – is facilitated by the house's continued expansion, making its procurement increasingly treacherous: 'What is the scale of now? It isn't a matter of informing the mind, but of deprogramming the body.'[17] The more the house shows itself the thinner he becomes, the house consuming him as it stretches away into a distance for which he has no point of reference, a distance that he could neither approach nor hope to return from. The accelerating emptiness of the house is symbiotic with his own, as they increasingly become one thing, a no-thing, reconstituted with time and space as incongruously essentialist constructs, as theoretical (the house itself resembling 'an advanced mathematical surface'),[18] as philosophical problems in which it is only possible to get lost.

By the end, all Ballantyne has left to exist in is the 'visual room' (the kitchen, then the pantry), the house having receded so far from him as to become equivalent to the room he remembers entering but whose dimensions, already being those of a 'universe', have dilated beyond his grasp, making his acute disorientation and consequent inability to negotiate his surroundings inevitable, for this ' "visual room" is the one that has no owner. I can as little own it as I can walk about it, or look at it, or point to it'.[19] However, unlike the standard difficulties encountered when describing our visual perceptions in terms primarily applicable to that perceived, there is no longer the distinction between the visual room and the material room, the two having become conflated in a single 'visual continuum around [him], and the play of air and light'.[20] And so we 'might also say: Surely the owner of the visual room would have to be the same kind of thing as it is; but he is not to be found in it, and there is no outside'.[21] This is not, however, just a modification of speech, but a spatiotemporal occupation of both presence and presentiment, a collaborative emptying and engulfing of not only subject and object but subjective and objective as viably distinct categories of thought – the man and the house accelerating ever outwards, growing into more enhanced states of invisibility, disowning the space and time that themselves became disowned of content when they rushed in to fill the void of a decision with their conjoined unreality, their hidden realm of the nothingness in everything.

Movement that is both accelerated and contained[22] gives the appearance of growth at the expense of movement. Ballantyne's rooms turn into universes, into completenesses that nevertheless keep expanding, spaces that he becomes unable to navigate, because their cosmological immensity is such that he cannot grow into it, the 'planetary vastness of the house'[23] eluding him more and more, leaving him acutely adrift and progressively inert, until he can no longer even contemplate movement. The house overtakes him, and finding himself stilled and placeless he is denied further growth. That the house is always seen to change means it never stops expanding: 'I have a sense that there are more rooms than there appear to be at first sight. There is a richness of interior space of which I was totally unaware.'[24] Having occupied this alternative realm, it is this realm's increased richness that constitutes all further movement, in the form of expansion, at the price of his own, for having moved there he finds his growth confined by the inertia obtruded on him by expansion from without. It is the house that moves and so grows and in which he cannot move, having no stable and recognizable locations in which to discern his own conveyance. Denied a similar expansion, he contracts instead into 'the irreducible core where reality lies',[25] into 'the still centre'[26] where he will eventually disappear. While still caught up in the *overworked hologram* of the world, 'a person may love their own sickness insofar as it serves as a way of keeping the world 'about' them'[27] and the world about them in turn gives their nothingness a shape; but once free of the sickened states of his existence – his employment, his ex-wife, his societal responsibilities – the world reveals itself and so recedes from view, leaving the artifice of the outline of the person to finally fold in on itself.

What opens the world for Ballantyne are the gaps he observes in it, the spaces that had been there before but which he'd skipped over, those intervals between objects that he'd failed to notice, but which he can now imagine himself interacting with, inhabiting even. He talks of these negative presences as comprising a 'reversed spatial universe',[28] one which yields previously unexplored entrances, and corridors emitting oddly resonant radiographic light, an invading light that will eventually expose the house's true dimensions. Ballantyne becomes convinced that he is encroaching ever deeper into some ultimate reality, occupying the light that in turn has occupied the house; and that with the house as its medium a more fundamental level of reality, that was before his experiment invisible, is gradually revealing itself. The more the house shows itself, the more vertiginous he becomes, because the more the house shows itself, his 'senses tuned to all the wavelengths of the invisible',[29] the more it is seen to grow outwards into obscurity, into a seemingly infinite expansion with which he cannot hope to keep pace until he too has receded from view, for '[i]nfinity is inseparable from nothingness'[30] and can be grasped only through contiguity with it, which in turn precludes grasping. Within this realm of previously indiscernible requisites, his giddiness marks his own inability to become likewise comprised only of essentials: 'the physics of the gyroscope, the flux of photons, the architecture of very large structures'.[31] The freedom he experiences is that of slowly relinquishing the need to circumscribe oblivion, his own and the world's, of acknowledging but ultimately overriding the fact that '[o]ur last abyss wants to be bounded … by us'.[32] And this failing boundedness appears to establish a distinctly Leibnizian metaphysic, only to have it unravel. His initial sense of oneness with the house, as he finds himself no longer an animated something within a body but as a larger substance, with his body reduced to phenomenon within it, as if within the monad of his soul (i.e. the house, which has revealed itself as animated, a conscious reservoir of distinctness and memory), is disrupted when the space and the house withdraw from him (and 'Matter goes insane'),[33] its substance becoming unstable, the faltering mechanics of the world opening up the subterfuge of the extended (and extending) material world, within what should have remained the unextended substance of the monad/house, and the perfections of his retreat come apart (the house in becoming animated revealing not its perfection but its imperfection), the pre-established harmony abraded to powder, all former synchronicity extirpated, as he realizes that the supposedly objective order of things is 'not necessarily on [his] side'.[34] His hubris, then, is to attempt to uncover everything the house contains, '[b]ut a soul can read within itself only what is represented there distinctly; it could never bring out all at once everything that is folded into it, because its folds go on to infinity'.[35] Ballantyne has uncovered a glitch in God's faultless arrangement, and finds himself demoted[36] to the condition of a bare monad, a fact made plain by, among other things, his increased passivity: 'We can see from this that if none of our perceptions stood out, if none were (so to speak) highly seasoned and more strongly flavoured than the rest, we would be in a permanent daze. And that is the state that bare monads – what I am here calling "mere monads" – are in all the time.'[37]

'Nothing matters'[38] for Ballantyne once his retreat is finalized. Becoming fluent in purposelessness has itself become the purpose. That no external meaning will redeem him becomes his meaning; and likewise existence its own measure, for only when its measurements can no longer be computed is he free of it, dead in an aliveness that is not life – a shrunken embodiment inside the daze of himself. Encapsulated in his original decision was something akin to the view that 'life is a secret mission',[39] but through his actualizing that mission, the mission is found only to be lost again, the secret uncovered as immanently other and receding, its life always now and always unending and never anything but death as its own impossibility. If we are to glean anything from Ballantyne's investigation, it is that the endgame is contraction, uniformity, the debasement of a living death, the frozen growth of space that is its own forever, witness to nothing and its own near nothingness, prevented from disappearing completely by the irresolvable daze of whiteout. 'The phenomena of inertia accelerate, frozen forms proliferate, and growth is immobilized in excrescence',[40] and so Ballantyne's waning consumption effectuates the 'ice palace', the glacial universe that takes his own existence out of his reach, removing the illusion that it was ever within reach. 'If you want to find ICE, try thinking about what is blocking you out of the past. It certainly isn't a law of nature. Temporalization decompresses intensity, installing constraint.'[41]

Necropresence, or the immortality of now, is an endstate. (As Augustine back from the dead will tell you: 'I have no tomorrow. I am. I have only nowness.')[42] But why this presence is thought to have undergone necrosis, and how it is this presence may be connected to immortality in an ever-expanding present, is not yet clear. We need to consider more closely the temporal aspects of this disintegration we've viewed as growth. Just how Ballantyne's necropresence plays out with regard to well-trodden philosophies of time, while often not exactly transparent, is nevertheless a valuable source for further speculation. If the future is unease and the past desolate, then the present is what never gets decided, what never truly arrives or goes,[43] the reality of a perpetual doing/ undoing and us wiggling inside it like translucent worms. Given the earlier Leibnizian connections, we might be automatically led into thinking that Ballantyne's predicament must represent some reductionist account of time, that any substantivalist notion of time would prove somehow ill-fitting with a scenario in which time itself appears to have become materialized: the relent-lessly self-replicating present attending only as the swell of space,[44] in which *now*, though 'delimited as a moment', is pluralized not 'as linear succession',[45] but non-linear distension. However, the increasing emptiness of this spatial realm could instead suggest that the possibility for empty time (for empty-time-as-space) has been accommodated, something the reductionist cannot entertain. For while growth does not abate, it becomes progressively content-less, just the continued expansion of nowhere and nothingness; and though not independent of that which fills it, being allied as it is to space, the merger itself behaves such that the groundwork for substantivalism's defence of time without change is laid out in front of us as the meaningless expansion of the two as one, so that while a relationist affiliation seems immediately apposite, the whiteout of time mirroring the whiteout of events, the emptiness itself continually pulls us back towards what looks like an aberrant perspective on time as it is in itself, an absolutist's conception of time as pure state made observable by reductionist principles.

If this is muddy, there is still the question of where Ballantyne's experi-ence might situate itself when it comes to each of the two definitions of four-dimensionalism – both as a stance against presentism and as a claim for perdurance over endurance. Taking non-presentism first, out of the two major strands (*eternalism* and the *growing universe theory*, or *growing block theory*) it is the latter which seems directly applicable here, and the extent to which it wins out over Ballantyne's obvious presentism will ultimately determine the extent of his voracious unmasking of territory. Presentism tells us that only what exists now exists, that there is no room for expansion, only existents passing through their tensed passage, and yet it is through his submitting to this present that Ballantyne unearths a formerly invisible realm itself defined by growth, which would lead us to surmise that he has become witness to a fundamental ontological shift. And yet despite this awareness of growth there is no mention of content, only a disorientating empty dilation – his '[c]ollapse into now. Time-zero',[46] ('or time-in-itself')[47] transformed into a collapse into always or, more specifically, a perpetually distending always. It has been frequently argued that one kind of four-dimensionalism leads to the other, and Ballantyne is an example of there being just such a connection, for at no one time is he wholly present and enduring, but rather a series of temporal parts of some four-dimensionally extended thing, a perduring object forever closing in on wholeness via extension. After all, faced with this horrific expansion, it 'is impossible to endure. You either die or go somewhere else. Or both.'[48] And yet only as incongruities could space and time combine to swallow him up in such a way that he can feel it happening, a state without motion or growth that establishes belonging in the same.

Inexhaustible time is equivalent to no time at all: 'I paint the unattainable "forever." Or "for never," it amounts to the same.'[49] Or as Baudrillard puts it:

We no longer have the means to end processes. They unfold without us now, beyond reality, so to speak, in an endless speculation, an exponential acceleration. But, as a result, they do so in an indifference that is also exponential. What is endless is also desire-less, tension-less, passionless; it is bereft of events.[50]

For to be truly present in time that does not end is to be outside time, to be so inescapably in the perpetual dilation of the when that 'present in time' becomes a mere euphemism for the impossibility of an outside, of a distance from, which thereby necessitates a conscious segregation from temporality in general, as when trapped in an Escher staircase where the eternal climbing of one is cancelled out by the eternal descent of the other. An eternal ascent that is also an eternal descent equates to an impossible performance of the negation of motion and event and so (on the reductionist account) a negation of time itself. Outside all extrapolations of within, this presence in time exists as something swallowed by an inverted mouth that has already consumed its own history, already expanded beyond itself to become itself, the 'never' preventing becoming just as the 'forever' did when we thought it without feeling it, when we were still skittish things circling inside an eternity of deathless presents from which we could see no way out. Like this, Ballantyne 'no longer needs to think and now finds himself close to the grandeur of the nothing', and skirting that obliterative immensity in which all things disintegrate into being, into the undoing of our misfortune at being anything, he sees 'true incommensurability is the nothing, which has no barriers and where a person can scatter their thinking-feeling'.[51] He is not ultimately defined in terms of either space or time, nor a conflation of the two; nor is he defined by the expansion around him, nor some reactionary contraction, but instead as something that seeks difference in order to exist at all. And the ultimate stillness, the stillness that has come for him, is the interstitial, that which has remained invisible when all else was revealed, that being-between which is the only nothing, and to which he can belong only by not belonging.

Peace is nowhere and nowhen. The endstate is in no state. Stillness is penumbra. Necropresence is the abstraction of nothing in the midst of everything and always. Distinct = indistinct. Ballantyne clings onto this till the end, makes it his end. Nobody is there to see it achieved. WHITEOUT.

CODA

Speed is the triumph of effect over cause, the triumph of instantaneity over time as depth, the triumph of the arid surface of pure objectality over the profundity of desire. Speed creates a space of initiation, which may be lethal; its only rule is to leave no trace behind. Triumph of forgetting over memory, an uncultivated, amnesic intoxication. The superficiality and reversibility of a pure object in the pure geometry of the desert. Driving like this produces a kind of invisibility, transparency, or transversality in things, simply by emptying them out. It is a sort of slow-motion suicide, death by an extenuation of forms – the delectable form of their disappearance. Speed is not a vegetal thing. It is nearer to the mineral, to refraction through a crystal, and it is already the site of a catastrophe, of a squandering of time. Perhaps, though, its fascination is simply that of the void. Speed is simply the rite that initiates us into emptiness: a nostalgic desire for forms to revert to immobility concealed beneath the very intensification of their mobility. Something akin to the nostalgia for living forms that haunts geometry.[52]

Notes

1   'I'm losing myself to become alive' (Pessoa, *The Book of Disquiet*, 358).
2   Cioran, *On the Heights of Despair*, 29.
3   When Rumi asks, 'What is this giving up?' he concludes that it is 'a peace that saves us' (*The Essential Rumi* (New York: HarperCollins, 2004), 79). Supplant 'saves' for 'kills' and we are closer to delineating this necropresence.
4   Brad Liening, 'Radioactive Skull', in *O Gory Baby* (London: Schism² Press, 2016), 31.
5   J. G. Ballard, 'The Enormous Space', in *J. G. Ballard: The Complete Short Stories* (London: Fourth Estate, 2011), 709.
6   Unlike the protagonists in many of Ballard's other fictions (*Concrete Island*, *High-Rise*, *Crash*, etc.) Ballantyne is forced to confront not the real beneath the surface, but the

surface of the real, and it is this that makes 'The Enormous Space' his most revelatory work, his most Baudrillardian work, and the work in which the future must look for itself.

7   This (on the neurological model) is itself a reenactment of a future that has already stopped, and with which he is merely falling in line.

8   Meister Eckhart, *Meister Eckhart: A Modern Translation*, trans. Raymond B. Blakney (New York: HarperCollins, 1942), 32.

9   Ballard, 'The Enormous Space', 697.

10 See ibid., 698.

11 Ibid., 702.

12 Aristotle, 'Physics', in *The Complete Works of Aristotle*, Vol. 2 (New Jersey: Princeton University Press, 1991), IV, ch. 11, 218b.

13 Ballard, 'The Enormous Space', 697.

14 Zamyatin, *We*, 40.

15 Ballard, 'The Enormous Space', 698.

16 Ibid., 707.

17 Nick Land, 'No Future', in *Fanged Noumena* (Falmouth/New York: Urbanomic/Sequence, 2011), 398.

18 Ballard, 'The Enormous Space', 701.

19 Ludwig Wittgenstein, *Philosophical Investigations* (Oxford: Blackwell, 1994), 121.

20 Ballard, 'The Enormous Space', 701.

21 Wittgenstein, *Philosophical Investigations*, 121.

22 Containment allows something's full size to be observed and growth to be attributed – to 'see everything as it is' (Ballard, 'The Enormous Space', 705) – for without containment, partial instances of growth can themselves be interpreted as movement.

23 Ballard, 'The Enormous Space', 708.

24 Ibid., 702.

25 Ibid., 708–9.

26 Ibid., 709.

27 Nicola Masciandaro, *Sufficient unto the Day: Sermones Contra Solicitudinem* (London: Schism Press, 2014), 35.

28 Ballard, 'The Enormous Space', 704.

29 Ibid.

30 E. M. Cioran, *The Book of Delusions*, trans. Camelia Elias, in *Hyperion*, 5: 1 (2010): 70.

31 Ballard, 'The Enormous Space', 699.

32 Róbert Gál, *Signs and Symptoms* (Prague: Twisted Spoon Press, 2003), 33.

33 Land, 'No Future', in *Fanged Noumena*, 397.

34 Ballard, 'The Enormous Space', 705.

35 G. W. Leibniz, *Monadology*, section 61.

36 Whether this is temporary or permanent remains equivocal.

37 Ibid., section 24.

38 Ballard, 'The Enormous Space', 699.

39 Clarice Lispector, *The Passion According to G.H.* (London: Penguin Books, 2014), 184.

40 Baudrillard, *Fatal Strategies*, 31.

41 Nick Land, 'Meltdown', in *Fanged Noumena*, 451–52.

42 Flann O'Brien, *The Dalkey Archive* (London: Macgibbon & Kee, 1964), 45.

43 As Lispector explains: 'For the first time in my life it was fully about now. This was the greatest brutality I had ever received. / For the present has no hope, and the present

has no future: the future will be exactly once again present' (Lispector, *The Passion According to G.H.*, 78). And again: 'You've shown up for an instant and it is forever' (Lispector, 'Another Couple of Drunks', in *Complete Stories*, 101).

44   And there should be no surprise here, given that this collapsing of tenses into the present realizes something approaching a tenseless theory of time in which, given its reliance on the static time series, it is notoriously difficult to satisfactorily distinguish between space and time.

45   Land, 'No Future', 394.

46   Land, 'No Future', 391.

47   Ibid., 398.

48   Ibid., 391.

49   Clarice Lispector, *Água Viva* (London: Penguin Books, 2014), 6.

50   Baudrillard, *The Vital Illusion*, 43.

51   Lispector, *Água Viva*, 82.

52   Baudrillard, *America*, 6–7.

APPENDIX 2

PURE DREAMING: RADICALIZED AND VERMICULATED THOUGHT, OR DEATH AS AN EARWORM

The recurring prospect of death is silent music, soundless sound, an intrusive tune not heard but thought, its infinite capacity for return rendering us deaf and indifferent to all but the thinking of death's lost musicality. We are not making our way towards death, death is making its way towards us, for the umpteenth encounter, a series of events awaiting the event. We are not returned from the dead, but are instead the conduit through which death makes its perpetual return: not zombies but hosts for a vermicular hoard of zombified reprisals. Our task is to feel these earworms bite, to become sensible to their gnawing presence in our ears and in the soft tissue of our brains, to reverse the process of digestion, to feed on them as they feed on us. Death's haunting fugue is no longer haunting, and it's no longer a fugue: it is instead an advertising jingle selling us back our dreams made full and productive, selling us the death of death.

While a question remains as to its susceptibility to use (whether its uselessness can be put to work), like death, or as death, the earworm is recursive, negative, unpurposive, spontaneous, valueless, dysfunctional, abstract, uncommunicative, non-narrative, directionless, autistic, mute, and therefore potentially unrestricted, potentially free. Having ascertained such a comprehensive list of negative freedoms, there remains the question as to whether they might equate to any kind of positive freedom: with so much removed it is at best unclear whether there is enough left to exact anything but that negativity. Are these worms of the dead free to do anything but feed on the dead? That there may be some radical use for the earworm's uselessness (and so for death's uselessness) is central to any consideration of worms and the vermicularity of death that does not pass over how the worm is not only a tunnelling organism but is itself the embodiment of a tunnel, a routeless route, a conveyance to extremity and in extremis: 'Freed of curiosity, of forecasting tomorrow and contemplating yesterday, unburdened by knowing or caring, the thought that an earworm is becomes free to be useless, free to deploy itself as radical thought, to be more of what thinking is.'[1]

The onus here is to give voice to this voiceless channel, to invoke Baudrillard's conception of what it means for thought to be radicalized, when 'radical thought is in no way different from radical usage of language'.[2] We must speak in the language of death, in the language of earworms, in the language they don't yet have. We must verbalize this tunnel that leads nowhere, this useless self-repeating hole, while at the same time being restricted to a medium that self-identifies as usage, that is couched in narrativity, that cannot communicate without communicating. And maybe we cannot hope for much, for while 'earworms may escape the destiny of daydreams to become a properly non-functional form of thinking, it may be that in the end that begins over and over again begins over again, again, begins again and over again, all they have to show is what the fate of human thinking that is free to lead nowhere thinks like'.[3] But then this is most likely enough, and already seems too much.

If we think of the earworm, and the earworm-as-death, as a tunnel, it makes good sense to think of organisms in general as displaying similarly tunnel-like characteristics, and indeed their destinations as being of equal vacuity, being either shit or vomit: 'It is easy, starting with the worm, to consider ironically an animal, a fish, a monkey, a man, as a tube with two orifices, anal and buccal: the nostrils, the eyes, the ears, the brain represent the complications of the buccal orifice; the penis, the testicles, or the female organs that correspond to them, are the complication of the anal.'[4] The entirety of humanness itself is the complication of the directionless tunnel, the negative something of the hole, the hole in us that is us.[5] And while we may consume shorter (in both size and duration) tunnels, like pinworms, in order to rub ourselves up against the world, all this is arse itch, and the dissemination of life's foul eggs. And yet the direction of transit is all one way, and so a purpose is imagined. For whatever enters the anus dies there, goes to die there. Even male sex organs, oozing AIDS like Derek McCormack's fashion designers, die,[6] and through dying kill, like the candiru, that having swum into the urethra or the anus dies there, its spines hooked into the muscle, where it rots and infects and kills its human host, which in turn rots and infects and kills its own recursive instantiation of death's earwormy burrowing through humanness. And the problem with tunnels is that they collapse.

Death in the coma of living, earworms in the anechoic chamber: both transits too brief and too slippery to facilitate digestion. There is time and use only for the going in and the route to exit, for the entertainment of the prospect of repetition, the repetitive promise immanent in each return. There need only be these happy conduits of death, of death's earworms in one ear and out the other, with no pause in which to be digested, or suffered, only the steady flow of the thought that refuses to be thought, of the sustenance that in of itself cannot sustain, but which approximates some perpetuity of nourishment via the illusive promise of such excesses of intake for which room must be made, and the time taken to savour and metabolize hailed as some nefarious extravagance. Human peristalsis is in overdrive. But the tunnel is also a place to get stuck, and as Vilém Flusser notes, the worms digest what enters them.[7] However, although what enters the worm lingers, the worms themselves pass through, are perfectly adapted for such accelerated passage. Their contents are not divulged. Their Black Noise (a purely functional corollary of Black Light) is not given time or the environment in which to escape. The earworm slips through the mind, as if propelled by some cerebral laxative, to make way for its next incarnation:

> Where there is simply input and output – sensation as information – there is only swallowing and shitting: no memory, no digestion, no gathering up of awareness in a difference that makes a difference. [...] Our diversions, which have no bureaucracy apart from their vying for increasingly refined forms of immediacy, render sensation nothing but a direct, concrete, and fleeting fluctuation of being that feeds into nothing but the next immediacy.[8]

But just as our bodies are wormlike, so too are we ('we': just illusory structures that imagine they *have* bodies), and like worms this interiority retains some slim aptitude for digestive indulgence – or indigestive extrapolation. However, pace Flusser, this vermicular cognisance, this thought-feeling of internalized awareness, is not essentially optimistic but pessimistic. For if earworms constitute some form of 'psychic coprophilia', it is not because there's any pleasure to be gleaned from the taste of shit, but because the very act of tasting consolidates our presence, and that presence is always, when happened upon, a nervy bolus of sickening that in finding itself wants rid of itself: the fleeting reassurance that tasting can still occur does not equate to a love of what is thereby tasted. If the earworm can momentarily bring us to ourselves, then this positive sensation of some internal source of experiential content being evidenced to itself is quickly displaced not only by the foul and formless faux materiality it arrives at, but also by this reawakened internality's imminently (and immanently) recursive disappearance. The selves themselves are earwormy, are not only reflexive but in a state of refluxing reflexivity, are at the choking point of being anything, and so 'expressive of a sheer fluctuation, a lived abstraction, or a pure sign of variation that epitomizes entertainment's principle of indigestion. But at the same time earworms mark the limits and fate of indigestion.'[9]

How then to put earworms to work without exploiting them? How to hear-think the recurring tune of death without having our purchase on it make it, as a consequence, purchasable? How to have death mean something without it being obscured by, and swallowed up in, that meaning? How to forget the taste of shit and remember only the tasting? If we could imagine ourselves inside the earworm. If we could imagine what it's like to be the earworm, sensate and brainless. To be and to live our own periodic deaths, to embody the theme tune to our infinitely repeated passing away. And by doing so once again follow the advice of Baudrillard:

> Ciphering, not deciphering. Operating illusions. Being illusion to be event. Turning into an enigma what is clear. Making unintelligible what is far too intelligible. Rendering unreadable the event itself. Working all the events to make them unintelligible. Accentuating the fake transparency of the world to spread a terroristic confusion, to spread the germs or viruses of a radical illusion, that is to say operating a radical disillusion of the real. A viral and deleterious thought, which corrupts meaning, and is the accomplice of an erotic perception of reality's trouble.[10]

Maybe if we could get the feedback of the worm's Black Noise to become indistinguishable from the feedback of our own Black Noise, to occupy that feedback for longer than a momentary spell of dizziness, and without dread, at the expense of the reality of the real, then Baudrillard's disruptive rule might just be put into effect: the 'absolute rule of thought' whose task it is 'to return the world as we received it: unintelligible. And if it is possible, to return it a little bit more unintelligible. A little bit more enigmatic.'[11] And to remember that the medium of this mutilating and distorting act, this radicalizing event, is an underlying nothing in what is written, an offloading of the mechanisms of order and control, an outsourcing of inspiration to chance, to the randomness of the world-without-us, the earworm empty with Black Noise, coming through us and back out the other side.[12] Maybe to deposit some digestive acids on it before it exits. Maybe to have our concentration push and pull the worm further outside of its already formless shape. Or better still, to have a state of concentration squash the worm's diameter to an implausibly slight dimension in order that its repetition become a continuance, a narrowed and persistently strangulated worm constricted to a mere albugineous thread, a pinworm, feeding through our heads like the sheerest gossamer and without end and without purpose and with no hint at noise but the imagined implication of a noise that cannot sound. And what's here is written (impossibly). And what's here is intensity. And what's here is emptiness:

what gives intensity to writing, be it the writing of a fiction or the writing of a theoretical fiction, is emptiness, an underlying nothingness, an illusion of meaning, an ironic dimension of language, which is corollary to an ironic dimension of the facts themselves, which are never what they are – in all meanings: they are never more than what they are, and they are always only what they are – a perfect amphiboly.[13]

This is the technology of sound internalized, the need for playback devices made moribund, the mind having assimilated their processes. This is 'a way of listening that's [...] not listening',[14] a way of writing that's not writing,[15] a way of making use of uselessness for the cause of uselessness. This distraction from ourselves is the purest concentration, an alertness focused on nothing but the pressure of its own concentrated state, and so of the distortions such pressure manifests.

Death like music cannot be localized: their 'local signs are incorporeal'.[16] No corpse or dying entity contains death. As with music, death is hosted, and its effect is everywhere at once: peculiar to no one organism, it is 'a lived abstraction'[17] of death. For death is always lived, and it is this living that has tainted it with a humanness it does not otherwise contain, and this living that we hope to forfeit for the possibility (which is not even that) of someday hearing (as non-hearing) death's Black Noise. Hence the idea is to imagine death's earworm inverted, its interior, its empty hiddenness, exhumed in that which it passes through, and the worm, as it is, a concentrated, solid and unending and loopy impossibility of concretion (a noose?), and having imagined it, imagine further that the secret was not revealed to us but us to the secret. In other words, we come to see the point in pointlessness by having already managed to absorb the vacuity of the secret, having already seen the conduit as an endless sprawling present going no place: a tunnel now a guide rope with no purposeful direction or mindful destination, and to regard this not as a finality but a place from which to depart. At the death of death's secret, what is left but death's return, 'the messy imminence of [its] perpetual conclusion'?[18] And what is left of that return but a noiseless viral echo in which we find ourselves digested, and indigested, as some placeless locus of corrosive unease?[19] The digestion (and indigestion) we envisage here is not therefore merely symbiotic, but symbiotic to the point of indistinctness. We eat Black Noise and Black Noise eats us, and what's left over is neither us nor Black Noise, but instead an aperture from which some new worm might surface, some new blackness for some new sense. And because that sense cannot be written it must be written. This thought-music cries out for the implausibility of being written, for 'relieved of listening by the thought of listening itself, music, ironically, makes room for radical thought in the form of a hopeless but happy audition', a written audition. And yet between music and text there is a gulf, a chasm of despondent potentiality, an arroyo of inexplicable and intangible slime, and it is here we must squirm in our final excavation. This putting mindlessness to work, in the form of uselessness, in the form of death, is to mark (literally) this dysfunctionality not with its opposite, but with an automated transcendence of function and productivity. The work is the non-work of drowning to be born as that offending liquid.

This dilemma removed of the reasons for its being so is reminiscent of the old man in Urs Allemann's *The Old Man and the Bench*, his twaddling, and the twaddling state of the book itself. Twaddling is the compulsive emptiness of possibility and the possibilities of an empty compulsion, which goes on at the human limits of limitlessness, and is the result of a conscription into a freedom in which the world and the requirement that something, anything, be documented are still present, but from which all health and purpose (beyond the purposeless purpose of recounting its own purposelessness) have been removed. Whether or not twaddling is an active pursuit or a passive response is not clear – 'twaddling abandons ends and means, origins and goals, compulsion and liberation. Or it may be the result of having been abandoned by them'[20] – but insofar as twaddling may be thought of as a sprawling and suffocating and rootless weed, such a classification is in a sense meaningless; or rather, its whole enterprise hangs on this difference, on its not being a difference at all, on the eventual conflation of what we do and what is done to us. It is both a refusal to think and thought's refusing to be thought. Refusals that are themselves thought. But this is just the start, for what is called for here, by Baudrillard's radicalization and by the hidden promise of earworms, is to move beyond twaddling, to consider twaddling as representing a foundational set of circumstances, not the end but the inception of a new end which will not itself end. And of course twaddling does not end either, so this inception must instead be thought of as a continuum, at best a branching off, from an indulged overthinking of one's refusal to think and thought's refusal to be thought. As the old man himself, approaching an end that cannot finish him off (any more than he has already finished himself off through his embracing inconsequentiality to the point of his own vatic eradication, a ghostly forlornness from which he is now inseparable), realizes: 'Think once instead of twaddling too late.'[21] What's missing is a single instance of rigour: a rigour of emptiness, a rigour of death, a rigour of meaninglessness, an eruptive alien rigour that in a single instantiation can churn the barren fields and the dying weed and make fruit from our waste. And while we know that this fruit can only taste of shit, it will at least have grown in the last breath of what it meant to be human.

The incontrovertible master of the daydream, however, is Fernando Pessoa, for whom the world is little more than a corpse from which to siphon dreams. And dreams like earworms cannot be owned, for the trick is to allow the dream to not exactly own you, which would involve an unnecessary and obliterative servitude, but to nevertheless seduce you into submitting to its infinite dead-end, which is also your own infinite dead-end. The dreams valued most highly by Pessoa are *pure dreams*: dreams isolated from reality, those inoculated from associations with a reality that through its decay threatens to take us with it, to have our dreaming it rot inside us. The pure dream has its own logic, its own materials, and is not permeated with those of the world which at any moment might fall away and take us, the invested dreamer, with it. Our dreams then should not imitate the world, rather the world should be seen as dreamt, and these pure dreams internalized universes,[22] realized illusions with their own rules of decay, earworms feeding on their own emancipated stream of Black Noise. To dream our waking life, to have the two cohabit and intertwine, is to risk the disfigurements and dying imposed by the world instead of emulating the distracted concentration unearthed in the earworms of death. Only the pure dream enchants, and only the pure dream of death enchants the life that, if adulterated, it would otherwise menace. The unprocessed vacillations of reality cannot touch us in this state of dreaming; although the real does not disappear altogether, but remains as a point of flight, a futile set of coordinates from and outside of which the purest dream will consciously abscond – consciously, because the phenomenon of dreaming is never left behind, and about this there can be no illusion.

The air is bad in the world; it causes the lungs to bleed: only the dream has air fit for infinity. We should not, however, imagine that the Pessoan dream escapes futility, provides satisfaction, or establishes some end, for the dreamer has no use for completion, is enriched by disappointment, and regards futility as the immanent truth of possibility. His dreaming follows one core edict: 'Since we can't extract beauty from life, let's at least try to extract beauty from not being able to extract beauty from life.'[23] Only if we imagine that some perfection may be found, and found complete, can we find ourselves tortured by its absence. The dream must remain inside us, for outside of us it would be absorbed into the world, and our wakefulness, as ones who dream, thereby lost in the unconscious dreaming of reality. Only through this internalization can possibilities proliferate without end: externalized they rot as the world rots. The dreamer becomes the earworm: 'To reform reality in the intellect, to tell of the images of one's dreams in a voice nobody will hear: this is how to survive the world and its dismal ministry.'[24]

Death, like love, is not fulfilled in the world. And so for death to realize the dream of itself, its threat of materialization must remain a threat, a threat in which the internalization finds promise and impossible potentialities of meticulous extrapolation. And love and death, once internalized, do not come apart: both 'chaste like dead lips, pure like dreamed bodies, and resigned to being this way, like mad nuns'.[25] And so the possibilities for this dream of death should never touch the dead: awareness should be restricted to the anti-thetical reawakening of our senses in the dream so as to, paraphrasing Pessoa, *externalize death on the inside*. And what of this madness of death? For isn't death, like the nun, an absorption and a contextualizing appropriation of madness, an exchange, a justified tergiversation of relative sanities? For if 'the earworm is a reversal and product of madness', and death is just such an earworm, a limit thought enacted as an impossible possibility, then no madness can survive death, any more than madness can survive love. Just as an earthworm aerates and improves the soil, death's earworm allows us to breathe the end.

To write is not to act: if it seems like an act it is because it amounts to the act of not acting, the active refusal to act. ('To write is to forget. Literature is the most agreeable way of ignoring life.')[26] It always occurs as a recoiling from the shit of the world, even when its subject is nothing but that shit. But the writing called for here requires more than this inbuilt disassociation: it requires that a pure dream write itself, that the earworm's thought noise be promiscuous with its own recursive iterations, and that those iterations each become endlessly discursive. And there is no suiciding from the inside. For while our internal landscapes may be dead, they were made dead from the outside, made dead via some active participation with the world, with an alterity that destroys. The vermicular consumption of the self in dreaming is not then a form of suicide, but a kind of maximally protective coating insulating us from death. After all, the human corpse can only plague us if its dreams for us are allowed to overcome our dreams for it.

The Pessoan dreamer dreams with his intelligence (thought and feeling fused), and through this dreaming maintains truth while also reconfiguring it, because to dream is not to falsify, for as that dreamer tells us, 'while dreamed things please me, false things disgust me'.[27] His approach is speculative and creative. His currency is impossibility and all its possibilities. His universes are not impossible universes but universes founded on the impossibility of their creation. His only interest is to dream what cannot be dreamt – and to be dreamt by what cannot dream. The dream and the dreamer are one, each performing the other. The dreamer's only fondness is for that which is absent, for absenteeism itself. The dreamer makes death and is not made by it, for his dream of death is closer to him than any exterior death could ever be. Thus his dream of death protects him from death's dream for him. The dreamer knows to reach into the world is to necrotize that reaching appendage. And yet still the coordinates of the world do not fall away completely, but inform the dream with a verisimilitude of its own richness. And while the source is always external ('everything comes from outside'),[28] it can never remain itself, can never escape dismemberment and deliquescence: the corpus of the world is there only for the dreamer to tear at, to burrow into and through, to rip into a million pieces of gouged abstraction. 'For primitive people the moment of greatest anguish is the phase of decomposition; when the bones are bare and white they are not intolerable as the putrefying flesh is, food for worms.'[29] The world is populated with these, Bataille's *primitive people*, people drawn inescapably to the bare bones of an integral reality. It is the dreamer that grows fat on the rot of the world, and the putrefying earth that feeds the dreamer's dream of death. The world's degenerating mass thus becomes the dreamer's living mass, and it is in this blackened gloop that the power of worms (and earworms) to process what is dead, moving through and around and with it, is witnessed most clearly, for '*nigredo* is an internal but outward process in which the vermicular differentiation of worms and other corpuscles makes itself known in the superficial register of decay as that which undifferentiates'.[30]

Like a legion of such worms, the Pessoan dreamer does not rest. He is always leaching from the world whatever might be dreamable, and the external world he leaves behind him is just so much waste, the useless by-product of his constant dreaming – a tapeworm removing nutrients from the world, growing and fattening as the environment surrounding it starves. And so if neuroscience has a picture of cognition sympathetic to capitalism's perpetual call to work, 'an image of thought in which all cerebration is rendered purposeful, useful – valuable',[31] it is this dreamer that works hardest to invert it, sucking purpose and use from objects only to have them unravel in countless digressions leading ever deeper into purposelessness – the tapeworm outgrowing its host. And yet for Eldritch Priest (our eponymously sacerdotal guide) daydreams and earworms are significantly distinct, each with its own discrete way of arranging content:

> there is something that distinguishes the virtuosity of earworms from that demonstrated by daydreams. My sense is that the former's technical origins and repetitive character makes it less available for recuperation than the divagations of the latter. Although unruly in their general aimlessness, daydreams lend their virtuosity to contemporary capitalism's speculative investment in cognitive activity for their digressive yet narrative-esque form exemplifies the type of "creative" obliquity valued by the successful entrepreneur. [...] The earworm, however, is a little more peculiar. [...] Unlike daydreams, whose affair with counterfactuals and anticipated futures makes its streamy content rife with narrative coordinates and trajectories that can be continually

exchanged for possibilities and alternatives, earworms just twist and turn. The earworm's loopy performance, in which its ending is at the same time its beginning, cannot be exchanged for anything but itself, and as such the change or difference that it is and which it demonstrates is nothing but an exchange – a change beyond change.[32]

According to Priest, the earworm's performance is mnemonic, supplementary and imposed, thought/recalled in conjunction with other happenings as an imposition of thought/recall. But the earworm's arrival as thought is not an object of volition: its visitations are disruptive and obstreperous, for 'the earworm's performance of memory is always suffered', and can even be thought of as 'the psychic equivalent of a phatic utterance'.[33] Ultimately, then, the earworm's power lies in its facility to distract through nothing other than being, to exist regardless of purpose or meaning, to exist only to be thought-felt as nothing but the empty excuse for that thinking-feeling. Its very use-lessness assists in creating an interiority in which thought can happen, in which thought can occur without having already been decided upon, in which thought is in a sense unthought and us there with it, fully realized (and so abstracted) selves in some deep space equivalent to directed thinking. And while this distinction is a valid one, the Pessoan pure dream can be imagined as an exception, imagined as the earworm's written (and yet-to-be-written) form. For it is the dream that cannot be written and so the only one that language should be stretched in order to capture. And this is where Baudrillard's radical thought will be found, and where death will be written, if death is ever written. This is where Black Noise and Black Light meet, where the thought of writing it is its being written, where the about is the thing itself.

CODA

What if there were worms within the worms? What if earworms were hosts for Doom versions of themselves, for multiplicities of these Doom versions? What if earworms were plagued with their computerized versions, and what if this malware infiltrated the earworms to effect some worldly return, some payload designed to cash in on these worms' aptitude for replication? What if the world was looking to become limbless and invertebrate? What if like computer worms these worms were bent on distracting us from distraction, of consuming the bandwidth of that distraction, of making targeted deletions, or of zombifying our purposelessness with some earthly foreign purpose? What if the nonconformist origins[34] and perceived uselessness of these worms were to become their camouflage? What defence could we mount against this malicious vermiculation while maintaining our openness, our vulnerability to undisclosed potentialities? What if the earworms were not hosts for these computerized worms? What if the earworms were these worms? What if by running these worms we patch ourselves to the distraction they offer? What if ILOVEYOU equates to IEATYOU or IBOREYOUTODEATH or IMONETIZEYOURSOUL or IBURYYOUALIVE? What if when we write earworms, when we write the earworms of death, we write instead a precoded emancipation? What if we return to an impossible beginning and precode this precoding? What if ...?

And as always what must be written but cannot be written is instead written about, for what else is there? There is it seems only ever the about, the about of impossibility, that sidles up as close as it can to its subject, so that it might by chance be bitten, just once, by one of its plethora of fleas.

Notes

1   Eldritch Priest, 'Earworms, Daydreams, and the Fate of Useless Thinking in Cognitive Capitalism', *Theory, Culture & Society* (forthcoming).

2   Baudrillard, 'Radical Thought'.

3   Priest, 'Earworms, Daydreams, and the Fate of Useless Thinking in Cognitive Capitalism'.

4   Bataille, 'The Pineal Eye', in *Visions of Excess*, 88–89.

5   For how this relates to the borings of boredom see Eldritch Priest, 'Listening to Nothing in Particular: Boredom and Contemporary Experimental Music', *Postmodern Culture*, 21: 2 (2011).

6   See Derek McCormack, *The Well-Dressed Wound* (Los Angeles: Semiotext(e), 2015).

7   See Priest on Vilém Flusser in Priest, 'Earworms, Daydreams, and the Fate of Useless Thinking in Cognitive Capitalism'.

8   Priest, 'Earworms, Daydreams, and the Fate of Useless Thinking in Cognitive Capitalism'.

9   Ibid.

10 Baudrillard, 'Radical Thought'.

11 Ibid.

12 The project undertaken by William Burroughs and Brion Gysin with their cut-up technique.

13 Baudrillard, 'Radical Thought'.

14 Priest, 'Earworms, Daydreams, and the Fate of Useless Thinking in Cognitive Capitalism'.

15 When William Burroughs explained the cut-up technique to Samuel Beckett, the latter famously replied, 'That's not writing – it's plumbing.'

16 Brian Massumi quoted in Priest, 'Earworms, Daydreams, and the Fate of Useless Thinking in Cognitive Capitalism'.

17 Ibid.

18 Priest, 'Listening to Nothing in Particular: Boredom and Contemporary Experimental Music'.

19 'We are losing that habit. I doubt now whether we really see our whole life flashing before us at the moment of our death. The very possibility of the Eternal Return is

becoming precarious: that marvelous perspective presupposes that things unfold in a necessary, predestined order, the sense of which lies beyond them. There is nothing like that today; things merely follow on in a flabby order that leads nowhere. Today's Eternal Return is that of the infinitely small, the fractal, the obsessive repetition of things on a microscopic and inhuman scale. It is not the exaltation of a will, nor the sovereign affirmation of an event, nor its consecration by an immutable sign, such as Nietzsche sought, but the viral recurrence of microprocesses' (Baudrillard, *America*, 72).

20   Patrick Greaney in Urs Allemann, *The Old Man and the Bench* (Champaign, : Dalkey Archive, 2015), 112.

21   Allemann, *The Old Man and The Bench*, 91.

22   What Priest refers to as 'private performances'.

23   Pessoa, *The Book of Disquiet*, 261.

24   Gary J. Shipley, 'Dreaming Death: The Onanistic and Self-Annihilative Principles of Love in Fernando Pessoa's *Book of Disquiet*', *Glossator*, 5 (2011): 107–38, 127.

25   Pessoa, *The Book of Disquiet*, 289.

26   Ibid., 107.

27   Ibid., 460.

28   Ibid., 58.

29   Georges Bataille, *Death and Sensuality: A Study of Eroticism and the Taboo* (New York: Walker, 1962), 56.

30   Reza Negarestani, 'The Corpse Bride: Thinking with Nigredo', *Collapse*, 4 (2008): 131. Or as Baudrillard puts it: 'death by a loss of difference' (Baudrillard, *The Conspiracy of Art*, 140).

31   Priest, 'Earworms, Daydreams, and the Fate of Useless Thinking in Cognitive Capitalism'.

32   Ibid.

33   Ibid.

34   See John Brunner, *The Shockwave Rider* (New York: Harper & Row, 1975).

APPENDIX 3

THE NON-EXISTENCE OF
THE SCREAM

The one thing left to say, we cannot say. It would have to be screamed and the scream has ceased to exist. God is too far away for us to perform this negative expression of nothing.[1] For while the mystics told us what they could not tell us, communicating the ineffable, describing 'delights impossible of description',[2] in sensory metaphors, with God inside them like a sexless lothario, like joy in dung, we long only to scream and cannot, to have some simulacrum of the scream that hasn't already been contextualized into a whimper. But such an honest ejaculation is ridiculous now. The mystic's intimate union with God has become the raped or necrophilic union of quietly imploding cultures and sub-cultures, and these concurrences for all their differences are the same. And yet the non-existence of the scream is still with us – consecrated with piss and shit and blood, with mutilated bodies and hate-filled fucking, with sacrifice and genocide, with torture and millions of pointless expirations – and this inversion of the scream there before the scream had even gone, its inarticulation of consciousness experienced as both isolation and affiliation, its longings unchanged. Accordingly, we have the added futility of the non-scream, a futility in opposition to the futility of fucking the dead, and so more in line with those same dead fucking us: the former's meaningless fucking of what does not comprehend, as if you could rape the germ/seed of your message into the non-cognizant, becomes a defeated return to action via inaction, an inaction that the former had embodied, not as a reactive spreading of hazardous material, but as pure unencumbered spectacle, which now, freed of its asinine delusions, is mute and cancerous and communicated through signs – signs for the unfeasible made impossible.

We have fucked the senseless sense out of the scream, located an enemy there, an aggressor, a dissenting non-voice to be repeatedly entered and exited, comprehensively owned in one hawkish intrusion after another, a concatenation of poisoned utilitarian unions that leave both parties empty and intact. This is the mystic union turned sour, pumping the inexpressibility of godlessness into the echoes of its noise like a dissolving agent.

We remade Jesus as an invisible wound, a soundless flatulence. We officiated in his murder by never allowing him to exist: 'Let Christ crucified be enough for you, and with him suffer and take your rest, and hence annihilate yourself in all inward and outward things.'[3] Or else let the apocalypse signal a new dawn of life, *imitatio christi*, in the hope that what is erased with yet more simulacra might come again to disappear, and so the bravado of owning death is thereby enacted: to be the instrument of the death of Christ is to embody death's ultimate potency, to kill what cannot be killed, to become the device of dispatch for all resurrections of meaning. This murderous intention represents all contrived manufacturing of purpose, a horror/sci-fi scenario whereby killing what will always return establishes logos for the otherwise stultified.

We are not so much raping the dead as refusing to acknowledge that the dead might rape us. Life is that which rapes the dead that is the mystic. If only we could rape the dead, but the dead are not there for us to rape. I might as well bemoan my inability to rape soil – quite literally the earth without care.[4] Such is the desire for the life of death: 'It will be a thousand deaths, / longing for my true life / *and dying because I do not die*.'[5] Outside of dying, the mystic is hardwired to fail at what it is his being mystic demands.

There is no cause to desecrate the scream, to observe a ritual of debunking, for desecration would assume an object, that there is something of the sacred left, and there is none. It would assume that rest has been gifted to those deaf to it, and that those resting might somehow become sensitive to the resonances of what was never voiced or heard. Deconsecration assumes the legitimacy of the consecrate – only a re-consecration can achieve what's needed here, but where there was suffering there is now only numbness. No need to take by force what is free to all comers: this would be the desire that desires itself more than its object, the libido as worthless as its quarry, there only to be used and used up. Not so much the attempted atrophying of desiring through neglect, as the attritional grinding to dust of the worthless against the worthless: 'Like the cave of the sky / The whole body of woman is a vacuum to be filled.'[6]

The mystic is not a practitioner but a conduit of experiential union with God, one who operates outside the rituals of religion so that it may be embodied. He or she is the scream behind the hymn. Mystics desecrate their own graves, the graves of human form, the death of this world and of its life. The three enemies to be overcome, as listed by St John of the Cross in his 'Precautions,' are all there: 'the world, the devil and the flesh'[7] – and of the three the flesh is the hardest to shake off. Not so much for the dead, as for those who invest them with consequence. And there is nothing fleshier than the scream. And there is nothing disappearing quicker than flesh: 'We must adjust our trials to ourselves, and not ourselves to our trials.'[8]

The end of the scream is never arrived at: there is only the perpetual approaching for those no longer able to recognize its inauguration. 'Into the World of narrow-minded thoughts, man brings the emotion of the Universe.'[9] This scream, this admission of illness, of 'the spirit lost in the body',[10] of mindlessness (or rather its experimented form), the knowing that is also the end of thought, the auditory asemia of the nothingness that finds noise but not speech, the untranslatable emptying out of the mystic: all of it removed before it was ever conceived. 'But the seers, the lucid ones, fall into it – this is what we must understand. / What should language be, then, and first of all the sacred language (but we will see that, according to Scholem, there is no other)? What should the language be such that seeing it and falling into it would be the same event?'[11] But remember we cannot fall, we can only hang, suspended from the eventuality of this unearthed earth, an unearthing far beyond the cognizance of Whitman: 'Come now I will not be tantalized, you conceive too much of / articulation, / Do you not know O speech how the buds beneath you are / folded? / Waiting in gloom, protected by frost, / The dirt receding before my prophetical screams.'[12]

For 'in order to scream I do not need strength, I only need weakness, and the desire will come out of weakness, but will live, and will recharge weakness with all the force of the demand for justice.'[13]

'This scream that I have just uttered *is* a dream / But a dream that eats away the dream.'[14]

The mark of the scream is repetition, repetition without interval, for if it had ever started it would never have stopped, could never stop, and here the observance of ritual is escaped through a denial of beginnings, as it is the commencement that loses us, and the hole and the dying that finds us again – not in life's continuation, but in the concept of the end: 'In the infinity of the desert, a grave is an oasis, a place of comfort. To have a fixed point in space, one digs a hole in the desert. And one dies so that one won't get lost.'[15] In Deleuzean terms, this repetition of repetition is the crazed act of differentiating the sameness that eludes itself, the difference *from* the difference *of* the differently repeated, and so a sameness that has no rightful place anywhere.

Notes

1   See E. M. Cioran, *Tears and Saints* (Chicago, IL: University of Chicago Press, 1995), 61.
2   St John of the Cross, *The Complete Works of St. John of the Cross*, 3 vols (London: Burns, Oates and Washbourne, 1934–35), Vol. 3, 49.
3   St John of the Cross, *The Collected Works of St. John of the Cross* (Washington: ICS Publications, 1991), 92.

4   For 'since "Care" first shaped this creature, she shall possess it as long as it lives. And because there is now a dispute among you as to its name, let it be called "*homo*", for it is made out of *humus* (earth)' (Heidegger, *Being and Time*, 242–43).

5   St John of the Cross, *The Collected Works*, 55.

6   Roger Gilbert-Lecomte, *Black Mirror* (New York: Station Hill Press, 1991), 15.

7   St John of the Cross, *The Collected Works*, 720.

8   Ibid., 92.

9   François Laruelle, 'On the Black Universe in the Human Foundations of Color', in *Dark Nights of the Universe*, ed. Eugene Thacker, Daniel Colucciello Barber, Nicola Masciandaro and Alexander Galloway (Miami: NAME Publications, 2013), 103.

10   Cioran, *Tears and Saints*, 113.

11   Jacques Derrida, *Acts of Religion* (London: Routledge, 2002), 198.

12   Walt Whitman, *Leaves of Grass* (New York: Penguin Putnam, 2005), 57.

13   Antonin Artaud, *Antonin Artaud: Selected Writings* (Berkeley: University of California Press, 1988), 273.

14   Artaud, *Selected Writings*, 274.

15   Cioran, *Tears and Saints*, 110.

INDEX

www.ingramcontent.com/pod-product-compliance
Lightning Source LLC
Chambersburg PA
CBHW022356280326
41935CB00007B/210